Vincent W. Grubbs

Practical prohibition

Vincent W. Grubbs

Practical prohibition

ISBN/EAN: 9783743417526

Manufactured in Europe, USA, Canada, Australia, Japa

Cover: Foto ©Suzi / pixelio.de

Manufactured and distributed by brebook publishing software (www.brebook.com)

Vincent W. Grubbs

Practical prohibition

Yours Truly
V. W. Grubbs

"SALUS POPULI SUPREMA LEX."

PRACTICAL PROHIBITION

By V. W. GRUBBS, Esq.,
OF THE GREENVILLE (TEXAS) BAR,

CONTAINING A PLAIN, PRACTICAL DISCUSSION OF THE CAUSES AND EFFECTS OF INTEMPERANCE AND DRUNKENNESS, AND THE MOST EFFECTUAL REMEDIES THEREFOR, INCLUDING EARLY TRAINING, PROHIBITORY LEGISLATION, BOTH LOCAL AND GENERAL, WITH AN APPENDIX GIVING A SYNOPSIS OF THE PROHIBITORY LEGISLATION AND LICENSE LAWS OF THE SEVERAL STATES OF THE UNION; ALSO, A BRIEF SKETCH OF THE AUTHOR, WRITTEN BY HIMSELF.

"I would not espouse either side of an important question if the reasons prompting my course would not bear a faithful and impartial presentation in any form whatever, and should I find them faulty and unfounded in principle, upon thorough investigation, I would abandon my position at once. I am going to publish a book on 'Practical Prohibitton' and scatter it broadcast over Texas, regardless of anybody's 'doubts as to its wisdom and propriety at this time.' I would publish it though I knew that I would never receive a cent in return for the outlay. Please say to your readers that the work will appear on the 1st day of June next, even though I should be forced to dispose of the entire edition by gratuituous distribution."—[Author's Letter to the Paris Daily News, March 29, 1887.

T. C. JOHNSON & CO., BOOKSELLERS & STATIONERS,
GREENVILLE, TEXAS.

DEDICATION.

To PROF. WILLIAM HUDSON, A. M., of Trinity University, as a token of my high appreciation of his varied and extensive learning, the innate goodness of his simple heart, and of my lasting gratitude for the unselfish and disinterested kindness bestowed during the halcyon days of my college life, this book is respectfully inscribed by   THE AUTHOR.

CONTENTS.

SKETCH OF THE AUTHOR'S LIFE............. 6

CHAPTER I.
INTRODUCTORY.
Popular Errors and Difficulties in the Way of Reform... 27

CHAPTER II.
CAUSES OF DRUNKENNESS.
Hereditary—Defects in Training Children's Appetites and Impulses — Bad Examples— Curiosity— Indiscriminate Social Treating—Fashion's Power—Social Condition of the Country 41

CHAPTER III.
EFFECTS OF RRUNKENNESS.
Physical, Moral and Social......................... 59

CHAPTER IV.
REMEDIER FOR THE EVIL.
Early Training — Parental Influence — Good Example— Woman's Freedom from the Vice — Her Special Work 66

CHAPTERS V & VI.
REMEDIES INDEPENDENT OF LEGISLATION.
The Church and its Ministry—The Sunday School 81
Individual Effort—Organized Effort 88

CHAPTERS VI, VII, VIII & IX.
PROHIBITORY LEGISLATION.
Local Option 100
State Prohibition—General Discussion of the Subject... 121
Open Letter from D. B. Culberson.................. 128

Constitutional View — Prohibition and the Democratic Party — The Loss of Revenue and Destruction of Property—Importation of Liquor—An Open Letter Dissected.................................... 151
Letter from John H. Reagan........................ 150
Letter from B. H. Carroll....,...................... 153
Review of the Anti-Prohibition Platform.............. 164

CHAPTER X.
NATIONAL PROHIBITION.

General Discussion — Senator Blai'rs Speech — General Considerations—Review of Progress during the last Century—Forms which Legislation has Taken— The Situation and Requirements — Recapitulation — Importance of Local Option Movements—Action..... 171

CHAPTER XI.
THE LICENSE SYSTEM.

High License — Low License — Free Trade in Whisky— Dr. Talmage on License........................ 206

CHAPTERS XII & XIII.

Prohibition and the Bible........................ 218
Prohibition and Natural Laws..................... 230

CHAPTER XIV.
RROHIBITION AND THE PRESS.

The Daily and Weekly Papers—Anti-Prohibition Speakers and Leaders — Cheering Words to the Temperance Workers 241

APPENDIX 263
   Maine... 265
   Iowa.. 271
   Kansas 275
   Ohio.. 282
   Indiana ;...................................... 288
   Illinois 302
   Massachusetts................................. 307
   Connecticut................................... 318

CONTENTS.

Rhode Island 320
Vermont 321
New Hampshire. 322–370
New Jersey 322
Pennsylvania 322
New York 323
Maryland 328
Wisconsin 332
Virginia 347
West Virginia 349
Kentucky 352
Tennessee 355
North Carolina 357
South Carolina 358
Louisiana 361
Delaware 363
Georgia 363
Alabama 364
Arkansas 364
Mississippi 365
Florida 365
Michigan 366
California 367
Colorado 369
Oregon 370
Nevada 371
Nebraska 371
Minnesota 372
Missouri 373
   Texas—Letter from Attorney-General J. S. Hogg... 373
CONSTITUTIONAL AMENDMENTS 381
CONCLUSION 382

PREFACE.

Sometime in the fall of 1886 I took up a notion that I would write for some paper that would condescend to publish them, a series of articles on Practical Prohibition. Being a regular subscriber of the *Texas Observer*, a religious weekly published at Mexia, in this State, and knowing well the liberal sentiments of its able editor upon the question of prohibition, I requested him to grant me the use of his columns for the purposes stated. At that time I hoped to be able to exhaust the subject, as far reaching and extensive in its scope as it is, in a half dozen articles. My principal object in writing them has been, to awaken a more calm and unprejudiced investigation of the subject in the minds of our people, than has characterized the arguments going the rounds of the press, and the vindictive discourses of a large number of temperance lecturers, who have long been infesting the country and, in many instances, doing incalulable injury to the cause of prohibition ; also to get our people to be more temperate on the subject in private conversation, and to discuss its merits and demerits with more tolerance and less vindictiveness. I did not dream of writing or publishing a book devoted to the subject of Practical Prohibition, at the time I began with the series, nor for a long time thereafter. Certain friends of mine, however, whose attention had been attracted by the arguments contained in the series, approached me with the flattering request that I cause them to be compiled and printed for general circulation in pamphlet form, and I had about decided to act upon the suggestion. A short time ago Mr. Luther Benson, the well-known lecturer, when on his tour through the northern counties of the State, spent a few days lecturing in Greenville, and while here was the guest of the writer. While at my house his attention was called to the series, and, as I had carefully preserved a file of the papers containing them, he took upon himself the trouble to read them in their order. He at once declared that he thoroughly and unreservedly endorsed every line they contained, and urged me to prepare them for publication without delay, and suggested that it would be more satisfactory to have them published in a more durable form than the one in which I had about decided to give them to the public. Upon his repeated assurance that he would aid me in every way possible in the matter of their distribution and sale so that I might suffer no serious loss by the venture, I decided that I would begin at ance the preparation of the work for the press. The idea of personal gain has never entered my mind in the publication of the work, and if the good people of Texas and other parts of the country should think the effort worthy of their favor, I shall be more than satisfied if I am able to come out even on the enterprise. The great cause of prohibition to which the book is devoted is entirely welcome to the long hours of patient study and labor I have given to its pages, which contain the series of articles contributed to the *Observer*, corrected and enlarged. In the preperation of the work for the press I have received valuable aid from my young friend Earle Edmundson Esq., a student of law in my office. I am also indebted to Mr. Sam. H. Dixon of Austin, Tex., Author of "The Poets and Poetry of Texas" for his kindly supervision of the typographical arrangement and other matters incident to the publication of the work. I have been materially aided by the timely suggestion of others in the revision and correction of the manuscript for the press.

V. W. GRUBBS.

Greenville, Tex., June 1st, 1887.

SKETCH OF THE AUTHOR'S LIFE.

Two reasons prompt me to accompany this volume with a brief history of the life of its author. First, I am a comparative stranger to the reading public, and a natural curiosity on the part of my readers will lead them to an inquiry into my antecedents, if I am supposed to have any; second, I hope thereby to encourage the young men of my State, whose opportunities are meager and whose surroundings inauspicious and unfavorable, to push forward with energy and perseverance in their efforts to succeed in life : to inspire them with renewed hope and self-confidence in their struggles with adversity, to make themselves useful in the world. It may be, too, that the secret wooings of vanity and conceit have contributed their shares in due season to urge me to speak, as I am going to do of my varied life and experience. However that may be, I am quite certain that the great desire of my heart is, to accomplish some good by giving the account, which, in the main, I promise, shall be true. Many things which have happened and many of the errors into which I have fallen, and which it would be of no possible benefit to my readers to know, I shall omit. They are ever too fresh in my own memory, and I would to God, that I could forget them, as they have long since served their purposes.

I am the son of William Grubbs, now deceased, and was born in Calloway county, Kentucky, on the morning of the first day of May, A. D., 1848. My father's ancestors were from Virginia. My paternal grandfather was of Irish descent, and my grandmother was of a Scotch family by the name of Duncan. My mother's name before her marriage with my father was Anne Utley Wade. My maternal grandfather, Hon. Vincent A. Wade, after whom I was named, was a man of some political prominence in his county, having been frequently elected a member of the Kentucky Legislature. He was descended, I think, from the Welsh. My maternal grandmother was an Utley, and was born near Raleigh, N. C.; moved thence to Tennessee and was there married to my grandfather, who, in an early day, moved to Kentucky. She was one of the noblest and greatest women I have known, and to her precepts and courageous example in the great battles of life, I owe perhaps, more of what little success I have attained than to the influence of any other person, my own mother not excepted. My grandfather Wade, having been completely broken up by politics and security debts, emigrated to Texas in the early settlement of the State and located near what is now known as the town of Crandall in the western portion of Kaufman county, where he opened up a small farm, and soon afterwards died, leaving my heroic grandmother, Mrs. Phoebe Wade, to raise a large family of children, nearly all boys, the oldest being not over sixteen years of age at the time of his father's untimely death; the youngest, a daughter, now Mrs. Lafayette Murphy, being an infant. Our family remained in Kentucky, but was preparing to follow at the time of my birth, when a misfortune befell my father which made him a cripple for life.

My mother's father dying about the same time, the removal was prevented. The premature death of my father, in 1855, made it necessary for my mother, with her children, consisting of three boys and two girls, the oldest, my sister Jane being then abont ten years of age, to move to

Texas and seek the aid and protection of her mother and her brothers, one of whom, my Uncle Barksdale, usually called "Baz," Wade coming back to Kentucky to wind up the business of my father's little estate, and move us to Texas. He was, indeed, a noble specimen of intellectual and physical manhood, the oldest and grandest of that pioneer family, a fit person in every respect, to be the couselor of his widowed mother, and the guardian and protector of the younger members of the family. He, with his two younger brothers and my oldest sister died of an epidemic about the same time, two of them dying the same day. My mother was an invalid and had been for years. Her nervous system had been completely shattered, and this awful calamity seemed more than she could bear. It appeared for a long time that her mind would give way, under the weight of the affliction in spite of every effort to console her. But she finally recovered, and the climate of Texas and the absence of trouble almost entirely restored to their normal condition her shattered nervous centres. In 1858 she was married to Mr. R. O. Anthony, and we moved to his home in Ellis county, about twelve miles east of Waxahachie, where we remained until the year 1862, returning to Kaufman county. Of that union there were born two sons and a daughter who have been to me as my own brothers and sisters.

My stepfather has been to me more than an ordinary father. No nobler or kinder-hearted man, with all of his peculiarities, was ever permitted to breathe the breath of life. His generosity and unselfishness, his patience in affliction, which has been constant and severe, often becoming dangerous, serious, and distressing, have been, at all times, remarkable. While he never, at any time, so far as I remember, denied me a favor that he was in the leastwise able to confer, his means were never sufficient to keep the others of the family up and justify him in contributing much, if anything, to my education. Indeed, I had not the heart to ask or to receive it when I saw and realized the accumulated necessities of the family.*

My mother and my two brothers, Thueston and William, and my sister Laura, now Mrs. McSween, all three of whom are now living near the old homestead, and surrrounded by happy and interesting families, were, at all times, ready to do anything in their power to aid me in my struggles for an education, even to the denial of themsélves the ordinary comforts and necessaries of life. My half-brothers and sister, Sam, now deceased, Joseph. and Jennie Anthony, (now Mrs. S. W. Roberts, of Kaufman,) were equally selfsacrificing, and my feelings of gratitude towards them all increase and grow stronger as the years pass away. I cannot take time to narrate the ordinary incidents of my wild life from the days of my removal to Texas, in 1855, until I arrived at the age of seventeen, which was about the close of the civil war. The greater part of the time after I became large enough to ride a Spanish pony was spent on the broad prairies as a cow-driver or herder of horses. My school days had been few; my education had been badly neglected. I could ride the wildest and most dangerous horse that roamed the prairies, if I could keep him still long enough to mount him. I delighted in the sport, although it kept my poor mother dying from uneasiness, and often would she try to dissuade me from going into the danger. But my chief ambition seemed to be to acquire the reputation of the best rider in all that section of the country, and in that I was reasonably successful. All on earth I had or cared to have, was a horse, saddle and bridle. The idea of the accumulation of property, or of obtaining an education, much less qualifying myself for a learned profession, never

---

*Since the above was written my step-father has passed over the dark river. He died at his home near Crandall, in Kaufman county, on the 3d day of April, 1887, and now sleeps in the Kaufman Cemetery beside his oldest son, Samuel R. Anthony, who died at the Agricultural and Mechanical College near Bryan Texas, on the 22nd day of November, 1881.

once flitted across my imagination. I concluded in the fall of 1865 that I would go back to Kentucky on a visit, and to gather up the fragments of the proceeds of our old homestead and bring them to Texas. To those people up there I was a great curiosity, and I rather enjoyed the distinction. I started home in February of the following year with about two hundred dollars in gold in my pocket. the accumulated rents ot the old family homestead. Took a steamboat at Paducah and in due time landed in New Orleans. I was good picking for the sharpers, and, had it not been for a kind and fatherly old gentleman, a Mr. Husbands, who then lived in Hunt county, Texas, with whom I had accidentally become acquainted, I should have been fleeced before I could have possibly gotten away from the city. But I finally made it home, and from that good day until the present, I have been satisfied with Texas.

Nothing could have more effectually calmed every feeling of discontent than that wild goose chase to Kentucky. It gave me a lasting impression of my own ignorance, and also of the fact that my manner of life was anything but conducive to the development of my manhood and the accomplishment of any noble purpose of my life; so I set about at once to obtain a good, practical education; sold my horse, saddle, and bridle, and every hoof of cattle, and all other property that had accidentally fallen into my hands, and entered a high school at Kaufman, where I was able, by the kindness of my friends, to remain for two sessions. At the end of that time I had not a dollars worth of property on earth. While there I was taken notice of by Judge Green J. Clark, and he seemed to feel a deep and abiding interest in my future. He called me into his law office one day and gave me the first idea I ever had of making a lawyer out of myself. His kindly words of encouragement sank deep into my heart. The brief history he gave me of his own life and its struggles made a lasting impression upon my mind, and I remember every word he spoke to me on that occasion as well as if it had been yesterday, though twenty long years have since passed away. I thought over the difficulties in the way, and they arose up before me like mountains in the distance, but while they were rising, my own resolution grew stronger, and at length I started on my long and wearisome journey. I had a good friend in Kaufman, Rev. D. W. Broughton, now a resident of Dallas, who advised me to go to Tehuacana and enter the first session of the Trinity University, which began in September, 1869. The months intervening I had given to teaching and other pursuits, by which I had realized about one hundred and fifty dollars, that being every cent I could command at the time I entered the college, which was in November of the year 1869. It was all gone before the close of the session, although I had been quite economical and saving. During the session I had made many friends among teachers, pupils, and the good people of the town and community. Should I undertake to mention the many acts of kindness and words of encouragement which were bestowed upon me from the time I entered the college till I left it, and to mention the names made so dear to the memory of those happy days, it would require all the space set apart for the material intended for this volume. When I spoke of leaving school for the purpose of replenishing my exchequer, there was a positive dissent by every one of my teachers, who insisted that I could easily work my way through, and that they would all help me to accomplish the undertaking. I went home in June, 1870, full of doubt and uncertainty as to the course I ought to pursue. I had by that time acquired a thirst for knowledge that it seemed impossible for me to satisfy or suppress. I spent the entire vacation in the hardest, heaviest, and hottest work of my life. I took a contract to build a barn for my step-father, and, donning my old threadbare clothes and broad brimmed hat, I repaired to the woods, where I cut down and hewed the timbers with my own aching arms, hauled them out, and completed the work just in time for the opening of the ensuing session of the college.

When I had paid up the old score at home, I had sixteen dollars left with which to finish my collegiate education; but by my own work at odd times during the session, and by teaching during the vacations, coupled with the unselfish kindness of my teachers and the friends by whom I was surrounded, I was enabled to graduate with some credit and honor, on the 12th day of June 1872, after nearly three years of assiduous and unremitting application to my studies. I can not forbear mentioning the fact that I was on that day the recipient of the first gold medal ever bestowed by my litevary society, which a few weeks before, had been awarded to me by a unanimous vote of its members. The society included upon its roll of membership at that time many names which have since become prominent in Texas; a number of them who joined in the bestowal of that honor have far outstripped the writer in the race for worldly honors and distinction. Their triumphs, and they have been many and brilliant, afford me a degree of pleasure and satisfaction that could scarcely be surpassed by my own elevation.

During the latter years of my stay at Tehuacana I was specially befriended by a lady, who now lives in Greenville, Mrs. Anne Terrell, with whom I boarded, and had it not been for her disinterested kindness in not pressing me for my board bill, when I could not have possibly paid it, I should have been forced to abandon my studies long before the time for my graduation. She was ever my friend and my sympathizer in time of trouble and despondency. She is true, generous and forgiving when a friend—equally positive in her dislikes. She is a woman of strong, well defined traits of character, and a heart full of kindness and sympathy for those whom she deems worthy of her esteem. I owe a debt of lasting gratitude to Dr. W. E. Beeson, president of the college at that time; and indeed, I could recall many others to whom I owe much for the kindness they were pleased to bestow. But to none of whatever class do I owe more than to the man to whom this first effort of the author is respectfully dedicated; that gifted though eccentric genius, Prof. William Hudson, the then principal of the commercial and art departments of the University. For patient, untiring industry and for broad and far reaching generosity and philanthropy, I have never known his equal. He was unkind and ungenerous to none but himself. Upon others, often unworthy, he lavished his hard earnings, which were usually small, while his own necessities and those of his family went unsupplied. He still lives to do good and to behold the fruit of his labors, in the triumphs of a host of young men and young ladies, who have been permitted to share the benefits of his untiring efforts in the department over which he so long presided. He is now professor of natural science in the same institution; and may he be long spared to bless it and its glorious work in the education of the young people of Texas. I would like to go on with the whole catalogue of teachers and students whose memory I love as I love my own life. Dr. Beeson has long since passed off the stage of action. Professors Quaite and Lowry preceded him. Professors Hudson and Gillespie are the only survivors of the faculty. They are growing old and infirm, and, in the regular course of nature must soon pass away.

I left college perhaps the most happy and hopeful individual who ever entered upon the responsibilities of actual life. I was about the close of the last session elected assistant professor in the commercial department of the college, at a salary with which I ought to have been satisfied. But before the opening of the session in which I was confidently expected to distinguish myself as a teacher, I fell into a fit of despondency which cast an impenetrable gloom over every prospect that had hitherto loomed up so brightly before me. The very memory of the hopes and aspirations which had lit up my path way through college life, seemed to haunt me in my waking hours, and to chide and disturb me in my slumber. They appeared to me in all the hideous and horrifying aspects of so many ghosts that would not "down at my bidding." I was unfit for business, unfit for pleasure, unfit for even the miserable existence I suffered. Had it not been for the thought of my mother and my brothers and sisters, and that inward dread of the great beyond, it is probable that I would have voluntarily put an end to my joyless, hopeless, miserable life.

"Apart I stalked in joyless misery,"

and determined to give up forever the object for which I had studied and return home to live the balance of my days in nameless obscurity. I did not know then that the depression was caused from a sudden relaxation of the mental faculties after a continued strain of so many years to their utmost tension. I could not foresee the end, which I constantly dreaded a thousand times worse than the summons of death, whose approach I would gladly have welcomed had he made his ghastly appearance. It was indeed fortunate that I had but a short time before entering college, voluntarily made the resolve that I would not drink whisky, otherwise I would have in all probability, sought refuge from myself in the deadly wine cup; but, when I contemplated such relief, I thought of my resolution, which I would rather die than to break; such had been the sacredness with which I had been taught from my youth to regard the force of a resolve voluntarily and deliberately taken upon myself. I verily believe that that timely resolution saved me from the snares and temptations into which so many thousands have fallen under like circumstances. I unceremoniously abandoned my position in the college and returned to the humble roof of my mother. She understood me better than any one else in the broad universe. She had suffered from despondency herself, and it was from her that I had inherited the tendency. She humored my every fancy, agreed with me in all my folly, and left nothing undone that could contribute to the restoration of my wonted mental vigor and cheerfulness. She would have the boys and girls to get up fishing parties, and, in some way, induce me to go along with them, which I never wanted to do. Every day or so I would ride out on the prairie with the boys, and drive up the horses and cattle. In a short time I was once more myself, but not until after I had spent a month or more in Kaufman in business as a bookkeeper and salesman.

As an evidence of my unfitness for such business, I am constrained to relate the following trifling incident, which occurred a few days after accepting the situation. My employer had just bought a large lot of cotton, for a place like Kaufman, forty or fifty bales. He gave me the paint pot and brush, and directed me to go out into the yard and mark and number the bales of cotton, giving me the first number, the memorandum given me on a slip of paper being '7 up,' intending, of course, that I should begin with the number 7 and go on consecutively until I reached the last bale. I had studied the science and art of lettering while in college, and felt that I was specially fitted for this particular work. I worked manfully for more than a half day, and returned feeling like I had earned some distinction as a marker of cotton. Imagine the disappointment and chagrin of my employer when he went out into the yard to ship off his cotton finding every bale marked '7 up' in the most artistic letters and figures. But he was a kind-hearted man and too mindful of my feelings to say what he must have thought of my ignorance and stupidity.

During my schoolboy days I had cultivated a fondness for poetry and drawing, and had no little ambition to acquire the reputation of a poet and artist. I spent many hours in writing spring poetry, such as love ditties and acrostics, with which I supplied my lovesick fellow collegians. I spent many other hours in drawing, under the skillful direction of Prof. Hudson, of the commercial and art department of the college, who ever seemed to take special interest in my advancement. Of all the poetry I ever wrote, which would have made a volume of two or three hundred pages, I never had published but two pieces—one devoted to my sweetheart, who had gone off "with a handsomer man;" the other to "modest ugliness;" the publication of the first of which inflicted a wound upon the pure, unoffending and sensitive heart of one, the recollection of whose kindness, and of whose gentle and forgiving nature rebukes my folly and chides me even to this day for my own inexcusable rashness. A thousand times, the bitter memory of that one error, the outburst of passionate resentment for a wrong that existed only in my own morbid imagination, haunts me with the ghostly vision of countless joys, which died long before their time. More than a thousand times have I regretted it, not so much for the disappointment of my own heart, which was bitter enough, as for the consciousness of having perpetrated an unprovoked and deliberate wrong upon one of the purest, sweetest, and best of her gentle sex. Although I have never realized the joys of the married state, I deem it not improper to state that it has not been caused by any failure on my own part, to appreciate and admire the virtues, goodness, and ennobling characteristics of woman. A strange fate seems to have followed me all the days of my marriageable life. A fate that I cannot account for. I could relate a history of my matrimonial mistakes, that would far outstrip the alleged "mistakes of Moses." They would, with a very small amount of coloring, furnish the groundwork of a half dozen interesting novels; but I cannot record them here in a book whose purpose it is to deal with more important and practical truths. But I cannot dismiss the consideration of this part of my personal history without disposing of my poetry and the products of my devotion to the other fine arts. I had read Byron, Burns, Shakspeare, and others of my favorites until I could recite *verbatim et literatim* many pages in succession of their finest productions. I verily believe that I could at that time have repeated two-thirds of Childe Harold, and I have no idea how many others I had at my very tongue's end. In the line of poetical quotations I was fully equipped for the responsibilities of life, which lured me onward and upward to the contest. I soon found that poetry and painting were not the kind of armor I needed. Having fully realized this fact, I promptly decided to abandon both to their fate; and having ransacked every nook and corner for the manuscripts of poetry I had written, I gathered them up and piling them into a great heap, set fire to the mass. and in less time than it takes me to record the account, the product of my whining, lovesick muse went up, amid flame and smoke, into the regions of nothingness, for which they were by nature peculiarly adapted. I love good poetry yet, in its place. I admire pictures as but few others can; but the stubborn realities of life are to me a study more grand and important, a work more glorious and profitable, than the lifeless, speechless shadows upon the canvas of art. I have ever been a lover of the "harmony of sweet sounds," and have attended a score of singing schools in my life; and, while I can sing tolerably good bass by practicing long enough, I have never been able to tell the difference between a sharp and a flat, or between the key of A and the key of F, or any other letter. In fact, I never could distinguish one note from another on the staff, although I have studied for days and weeks in an effort to learn it. It is, I believe, an impossibility for me to learn music by note. I have no music in my soul except as it is beaten into it by the most untiring and persistent effort, and then it won't stay there.

I began to study law in the spring of 1873, and in the latter part of the summer I unfortunately became involved in a political canvass, for which I was not, in the slightest degree, prepared, especially in the matter of finance. My acquaintance was too limited, my friends were not active and numerous enough; and the result may be easily guessed by my readers. I can not say that I seriously regret my course in that canvass, but it is better, for many reasons not necessary to mention, to pass over in silence that somewhat extraordinary canvass, considering my age. Suffice it to say that nearly all of those who vigorously opposed me in my premature candidacy for State Senator at that time, have, long since, become my steadfast friends and supporters in anything I have since seen proper to undertake.

On the 4th day of March, 1874, I was licensed to practice as an attorney and counselor at law. This event occurred in the town of Canton, VanZandt county, and the late lamented Judge Bonner pronounced the sentence of the Court upon me, which consigned me to the practice of law. His charge to me, as I proudly stood before him to receive the license which I prize so highly, I shall never, I can never, forget. He was ever afterwards my friend, and never lost an opportunity to encourage me in my profession, not only while he presided over the District Court of our district, but while he occupied, with distinction, a seat upon the Supreme Bench of Texas. Before the ink was dry upon my license, I was employed as counsel in two cases of some importance, on the docket of the court which issued it. I made my maiden speech at the bar within two hours after I was admitted to practice, and, of course, made a botch of my client's case, but, so far as I know, he never found it out—at least he did not complain at the payment of my fee.

On the first day of April following I settled at Kaufman and opened an office. At that time I did not have a book, a single article of office furniture, or money enough to purchase a postage stamp; and it pains me to acknowledge that I hadn't credit for two sheets of legal cap paper that I was aware of at the time. I was, at the expiration of the first month, ejected from the hotel, where I was boarding, for nonpayment of my board, and lived for nearly a week thereafter upon cheese and crackers kindly furnished me by my next door neighbor, Mr. W. A. French, who was in the grocery business, and my personal friend from his earliest boyhood. I was, time and again, refused board without the pay in advance; and the " pay in advance " was a commodity which I did not possess. But I did not complain. I did not think hard of the lady who expelled me from her house. She was under no sort of obligation to trust me, and the appearances fully justified her in supposing that I never would pay her, that I would not be able to do so. I never blamed any one else for refusing to credit me. The prospects for getting their money were gloomy, indeed, and I could not conscientiously assure them that I would ever be able to pay them a cent. It was an experiment with me, and my all depended upon the result. I went for days, and weeks, and months, without being able to see my way a week ahead of me. But I would not give up to despondency. I kept my troubles entirely to myself. I sought no friend to "counsel or condole," and at all times pretended that everything was lovely and that the "aquatic fowl was at a respectable altitude."

One day shortly after I was admitted to the bar, I was in the court room taking notes of the proceedings with a view of learning the practical part of my chosen profession. I paid close attention to every speech that was made, and generally accepted everything the older lawyers said as the law, so far as it went. The district attorney was prosecuting a man by the name of Everhart for an aggravated assault upon a friend of mine by the name of Tom Shannon, the defendant having struck him on the head with a billiard cue, inflicting a serious injury, which I learned afterward was the ground of the aggravation, but which I did not know at the time, as will shortly appear. The able, and now distinguished gentleman who was then prosecuting the pleas of the State, used substantially the following language in his speech to the jury: " Gentlemen of the jury, this is a very aggravated case; it is the most aggravated case of assault that I have ever been called upon to prosecute. It is in evidence that the defendant, before he struck Mr. Shannon with the billiard cue, insulted him; that he grossly insulted him;. that he insulted him in a way that no well bred gentleman has ever been known to insult another in this Lone Star State of Texas, the land of the free and home of the brave, where every man is permitted to worship God under his own vine and fig tree according to the dictates of his own conscience. Why, gentlemen of the jury, he refused to drink with him." This speech made an indelible impression upon my mind, and I felt that I had learned something of statutory law that might answer a good purpose.

Not long afterwards I was called upon for a definition of aggravated assault, and in enumerating some other grounds of aggravation, I stated it to be the law that when a man should ask another to take a drink with him, and that other man should refuse to accept the invitation, and decline to drink with him, and thereupon should knock the man so asking him to drink down with a billiard cue, he would be guilty of aggravated assault and battery. I had just got my license, and though I felt my importance—did not know any better. I was quite inexperienced, and my progress was slow, if progress it could be called.

Thus things went on for several years. My failure was

predicted by many, but as I moved along the rough and uneven tenor of my way I gathered friends by the dozen. If the scope of this chapter would permit, I would like to build right here a monument to their memories that would be more durable than brass or Parian marble. But I cannot speak of one without disparagement to others equally dear to my heart and to my memory. I must make one exception, which, I know, will be approved by others who have done so much for me. I can not go further without paying a just and merited tribute to my true and ever steadfast friend of those dark and trying days of my professional life, Mr. Henry Erwin, and with him his estimable wife. He was at that time the county and district clerk of Kaufman county. He was moved by a feeling of my dire necessities to offer me all of the work in his office that he could not do himself with the assistance of his regular deputy, Mr. T. J. Broughton, another good friend. He also took me to his home and fed me for the work I did for him in his office, until I was able to make a living out of my profession. No better man lives than Henry Erwin; no nobler woman ever blessed the home and household of a worthy husband than Mrs. Erwin. I have never been and will never be, able to compensate them for their kindness. May God grant them a long, happy, and prosperous life on earth and a rich reward in the world beyond. During the last six years of my career at Kaufman, I boarded with Mrs. L. J. French, whose many acts of kindness I shall ever remember with gratitude.

In April, 1878, I entered into co-partnership in the practice of law with Nestor Morrow, Esq., a young man with whom I had been intimately associated during the latter years of my college life. We had, during those years, become friends, and it was not long after he obtained his license to practice that we became inseparably connected in our chosen profession. I say inseparably connected because nothing, I think, could have dissolved the relationship as long as we both remained in the country. His name, wherever he is known, is the synonym for honesty and personal integrity; his legal ability is of the first order, and as a safe and reliable counselor he has no superior, and but few equals of his age and experience, His caution is, perhaps, too fully developed to insure for him the reputation for brilliancy as a practitioner.

We were reasonably successful during the seven years we remained together and accumulated some money. He began saving up and investing his part of the net proceeds of the business much earlier than I did, and, as a consequence, was many thousand dollars ahead of me in a financial point of view when we dissolved our co-partnership. I attribute it, to some extent, to the fact that he married soon after we went into business together, and I didn't, for reasons not necessary to mention.

Not long after I began to practice my profession at Kaufman, I was engaged for a nominal consideration to write occasionally for the local columns of the *Star*, a weekly paper published by Messrs. Clark & Walker, who were at that time quite friendly towards me, and in the spring of 1880 I took charge of the editorial management of the *Sun*, succeeding Mr. L. R. Brown, well known throughout Texas as "Hightone" Brown, and who ranks among the most brilliant and accomplished journalists of the State.

My short career as editor of the *Sun* was fraught with many amusing incidents and adventures, but I can only relate one, which is, perhaps, above an average sample in point of interest. About the time I retired from the editorial chair, an article, or rather a communication, appeared in the columns of the *Sun*, which was anything else than complimentary to a certain tonsorial artist of Athens, a little town about forty miles from Kaufman and in our judicial district. A week or so after the article was published I went to Athens to court, and, as was my custom in those days, I never neglected an opportunity to give annoyance to the fair ones, who would give me a chance; and having an engagement to call on a lady friend, and in order to appear to advantage, I went around to the barber shop to get shaved and otherwise "done up" for the occasion. As soon as I seated myself in the chair I noticed something very peculiar in the appearance, tone of voice and general manner of the barber. He appeared very nervous in every movement he made, but I attributed it to a slight touch of "temporary insanity," which at that time was very common among barbers and some other classes of people. As he whetted his razor he set his eyes, glistening with fierceness upon my face, remarked in any other than a pleasing tone of voice: "You are from Kaufman, ain't you?" I assented as politely as I knew how. "Your name is Grubbs, I believe." Thinking perhaps that he might be desirous of paying me a compliment, such as that he had often heard of me before, I promptly replied that that was my name. Said he: "You are the d—d fool editor of the *Sun*, I have been informed." To that question I was instinctively as silent as the tomb. Indeed I was so embarrassed by the nature of his language that I could not reply. Having lathered my jaws sufficiently, he began to draw the razor carelessly about my face. He then halted suddenly, and, standing majestically before me as he waived the cold steel over his head and all around him, he says: "You have published a d—d lie on me, and I am going to have satisfaction." He cursed out the paper, and swore that he could whip any man who would acknowledge that he originated the scandal. He said that he had been wanting to see the editor of the paper, and that he would make it hot for him if he did'nt take it back and set him right on the matter. I never was so completely, "cornered" in all my life; I felt that my earthly pilgrimage was drawing to a close, and that something would have to be done in the way of scientific lying, or I would be a mutilated corpse almost in the twinkling of an eye. I was not guilty, but I was so badly embarrassed that I was not certain whether I was or not. I tried to reason the matter with him, and finally told him upon my honor as a lawyer and a truthful man that I had never written a solitary line for the paper. That, while it was true that my name appeared as editor and proprietor, it was only done for the benefit of the true editor and proprietor who was a very ordinary man; and that the reason he wanted my name as editor was, to give tone to and increase the circulation of the paper. I finally reconciled the irate barber, but I did not tarry very long when I escaped from the horrors of the awful situation. I filled my engagement with my lady friend, but my mind was so completely distracted by the recollections of my desperate adventure that I could not enjoy myself. The thought of having lied to the barber troubled me sorely, as I was not used to lying, except in the legitimate discharge of my professional duties. Since that day my ambition to swing my euphonious name to the editorial masthead of a paper has not been so strong as it had been before.

In the year 1884 I became a candidate for district judge of the eighth judicial district. My opponent happened to be more popular than I, and the result can be easily conjectured. My own county gave me over fifteen hundred majority, and my vote in the other counties of the district was, I think, creditable, considering the huge jokes that were told during the canvass. It would be folly to go into the details of that good humored canvass, or to attempt to unveil the secret impulses which prompted the actions of some men of my own county in conspiring to defeat me for the office. As soon as the result was ascertained I promptly decided to abandon Kaufman county, the scene of my early professional struggles, forever, and on the first day of January, 1885, I moved to the city of Greenville, where I have since resided. During the first year of my residence in Greenville I was associate editor of the *Herald*, and contributed regularly to its columns. In July, 1885, I formed a co-partnership with T. D. Montrose, Esq., under the firm name and style of Montrose & Grubbs, with whom I am at this time associated in the practice of my profession. On the first day of January, 1886, I voluntarily severed my connection with the editorial department of the *Herald*, and have since devoted the whole of my time and energies to the practice of law, the results of which have been reasonably profitable and satisfactory to myself and partner. In politics I have ever been a democrat of the Jackson type, although at times I have broken over the traces and gone into business on my own hook, politically apeaking. Perhaps this accounts for the fact that I have to this good day been permitted to enjoy the quietude and *otium cum dignitate* of private life, so to speak. I have always voted for any and all sorts of prohibition, whenever an opportunity presented itself. In doing so I have not burdened my conscience with the slightest doubt of the constitutionality of the measure, nor have I stopped to consider seriously whether it was democratic or undemocratic. I have long since satisfied myself on the only question that could possibly unsettle my mind upon the subject. I have decided that it is right.

CHAPTER I.

INTRODUCTORY.

POPULAR ERRORS AND DIFFICULTIES IN THE WAY OF REFORM.

When a physician is called to the bedside of a patient, the first thing he will do, provided he understands his business, will be to make a proper diagnosis of the case. Before he can safely administer a dose of medicine he must not only know what disease his patient is suffering from, but he must understand the nature of such disease, and of the causes which operate to produce it. When he has fully satisfied himself of these by the use of the means afforded by the symptoms and such other information as he may be able to obtain relative to the temperament, habits, etc., of the patient, he is prepared to begin the course of treatment adopted, and can anticipate with reasonable certainty the effects of such treatment and the progress of the disease, and its cure. This is equally true of every character of remedial effort. Any other course necessarily results in failure, and the wonder is that such failure is not oftener foreseen by those engaged in finding out and applying the remedies for the multiform evils in every department of our political, moral, and social fabric. In no other cause, perhaps, have there been more mistakes made by the moulders and leaders of public sentiment than in the methods adopted for the prevention of drunkenness and its concomitant vices and the ultimate suppression of the liquor traffic. While there are some engaged in the work who have taken the trouble to investigate thoroughly the nature and causes of this fearful disease which has destroyed more of the lives and happiness of our people than any other known in the catalogue of human ailments—physical, moral, and social combined—there are many who work entirely upon the surface, and instead of accomplishing anything in the direction of temperance reform or practical prohibition, they rather aggravate ánd encourage the evil by their misdirected efforts to destroy it. They are of the class who are unfortunately lacking in common sense generally. They do not understand the first principles which enter into the constitution of the human mind and heart. They never see but one side of a question, and fail to see that in its true light. They can cherish at the same time but one thought and desire—can entertain but one idea, and are never satisfied without a hobby, with which they bore the very life out of those with whom they daily come in contact. Many of them are called "cranks" because of this one-sided and impractical way of thinking and acting upon matters of the greatest concern. They generally mean well, and if they could succeed in carrying into execution the visionary conceptions of their brain, the millennium would be certain to come. There would be no necessity for further delay.

An error quite common to temperance workers is that they try to accomplish too much by a single effort, and are too easily discouraged by the apparent failure of their too sanguine expectations. They are too often sadly deficient in patience and perseverance, and if they are unable to bring about a great revolution in public sentiment on the subject of prohibition and temperance, in a day, a month, or a year, they become despondent; and it is not unfrequently the case that they go over to the enemy and become as enthusiastic in their opposition to the cause as they were before in its favor.

I have often seen them work faithfully and efficiently for

weeks and for months in an effort to secure the adoption of local prohibition in their precincts and counties, not only spending their time, but their means with the greatest liberality in the promotion of the cause. In such efforts they have been deluded with the fervent expectation that the adoption of this salutary measure would absolutely put an end to the use of intoxicating liquors for purposes prohibited by the law within the boundaries of the territory for which it is enacted, and for several miles beyond the limits of its legal operation. I have afterwards seen these same individuals among the first to declare local option a failure, and heard them express grave and serious doubts as to the efficiency of any form of prohibitory enactments. To see one or two men staggering from intoxication upon the streets or in the alleys of a local option town is, usually, entirely sufficient to convince them of the utter impracticability of the enforcement of the law, and to make them ashamed to acknowledge that they ever voted for local option. They are equally as uncertain, unstable, and unreliable in other important undertakings which require the exercise of unswerving resolution, patience, and perseverance. John Bunyan's Mr. Pliable aptly represents the true characteristics of this class of temperance workers. Many of them are good people, and with a sufficient amount of will power, stability and determination, would do much in the great work of bringing about the temperance reform which is certainly a "consummation devoutly to be wished." Having said this much by way of introduction, I will endeavor, in the chapters which are to follow, to discover some of the causes of drunkenness, to portray some of its fearful results, and to suggest for the consideration of those whose curiosity may lead them to peruse them, some of the practical remedies for the evil which has produced so much of human despair in the world's history, and which is to-day destroying the lives and happiness of millions of people. It is the purpose of the writer of these chapters to awaken, if possible, a more intelligent enquiry into the nature of the disease which has been so long preying upon the very vitals of society, and, if possible, direct the remedial efforts of our temperance reformers rather to the very seat of the disease than to the temporary suppression of the effects of the social ailment. We have already tried the latter sufficiently, and while it cannot be said that much good has not been the result of the treatment of the symptoms, in the timely use of these remedies which afford temporary relief to the patient, it must be admitted that the patient, the great body of our people, has advanced very slowly, if at all, in the direction of a permanent cure. But before I proceed to the discussion of some of the causes of this blighting evil, I desire to speak of the difficulties in the way of bringing about the much needed reform.

The first obstacle in the way is, that the disease of the body politic has been of such long duration that it has become thoroughly constitutional. This accursed tendency to drunkenness reaches back almost, if not quite, to the cradle of the race. As far back in the dim ages of the past as we have any record, we find men, some of whom important and prominent characters, at times giving way to this thirst for strong drink. While I shall in the further discussion of the subject insist that the origin of this strange appetite for voluntary insanity is to be found in the perverted habits of mankind and not the economy of nature as put into operation by the hand of the Almighty, I must admit that it reaches beyond the beginning of history. I find that shortly after the flood which swept mankind from the face of the earth, with the exception of one family, the head of that family drank wine to a degree of beastly and humiliating drunkenness. I find in the impartial biographies of the patriarchs that this vice is mentioned among their manifold weaknesses. It is useless to attempt to conceal these blemishes in the personal habits of some who, on account of their virtues or wisdom in other respects became great in spite of their frailties. Indeed, the great men of history in all ages of the world have had their faults, their foibles, and their vices. Besides, the personal history of latter day heroes invariably leave out the dark spots of their character. It is doubtful if there has ever lived a man in the world, (not including the Savior of the world), who would give his consent to the publication of a true history of his life, a true portrayal of every phase of his personal character. A great man's history is written either by his friends or his enemies. If by the former, his great actions are extolled to the skies; his bad traits or his personal frailties are studiously suppressed: if by the latter, his greater vices are shown up in all of their enormity; the smaller, such as partake of a private character, are overlooked and left in the dark.

In our day the fact that a great man is given to excessive and inordinate drinking is of so small a matter that not even his enemies will think enough of it to give it a place in his biography. In olden times it was not so. The sacred historians, who were impartial above all historians on earth, thought drunkenness a matter of sufficient importance to demand a place in the history of the lives of their heroes. They certainly did not regard it as an exemplification of true greatness, but they must have regarded it as an illustration of the weaknesses of the flesh, which may dwell in the same house of clay with the elements of true greatness of mind and of soul. But this branch of the subject will be thoroughly reviewed in a subsequent chapter. That mankind are naturally prone to do evil may be assumed. In assuming that fact, fully taught by inspiration, it must follow that mankind are naturally prone to drink whiskey just as they are disposed to do other acts of wickedness. Moreover, it must be evident that it is, perhaps, above all others one that has never lacked for cultivation and development. All history, aside from our own personal observation and experience, teaches this beyond question. The result is, that the world has become filled with constitutional drunkards, leaving out of the estimate all of the moderate drinkers, who are fast drifting into the same unhappy condition. To cure a disease of so long standing as to become chronic or constitutional, sometimes requires many years of unremitting treatment, even by the most skillful physicians. None but the charlatans in this noble and useful profession pretend that they can cure them in a day, a week, or a month. Nature requires time to collect her shattered resources, and through the timely aid of approved remedies, after a long while the system may be restored to its normal condition of vigor and health. While the quack by the use of opiates, sedatives, and his long line of palliative preparations and prescriptions, temporarily relieves the agony of the patient, the skillful physician who understands his calling administers those remedies only which tend to the removal of the causes which operate to produce the disease. I fear that the great body politic, writhing from the effects of this deadly and destructive disease, has been treated by too many professional quacks, and, that the true causes of the great social ailment have not received the consideration from the doctors that their importance has imperatively demanded. Too many quacks; too many King-Cure-alls; too many electric-infallible-instantaneous remedies, which merely destroy the pain which is ever intended as an index of the ravages of the disease, the sign board for the direction of science in the application of effectual remedy. Why is it that the politicians and prominent men of the country persist in their quackery? Why is it that they dare not make a solitary effort to crush out and destroy this deadly disease which is wasting the vitals of the great body politic for which they pretend to have so much concern.

Before taking up the discussion of the main questions involved, I shall now attempt to answer that important and pertinent question. It is because of their insatiate desire for office. They are fully cognizant of the true situation. They are aware of the time honored weaknesses and prejudices of the people. They thoroughly appreciate the political power wielded by the whisky element of the State. They know that whisky is practically invincible at the ballot box, and they know full well that if they incur its displeasure and combined opposition, they will be left "when the roturns are all in" and the votes are all counted. They are mighty in the defense of time-honored principles and the blood-bought rights which have come down from the days of our revolutionary fathers; they can stand up in Senates and other high places of the government and defy the god of War clothed in the thunders of destruction, aspecially when afar off, but they are paltry cowards when it comes to making and prosecuting a war against popular prejudice and error, against popular vices, against whisky, whose ravages are strewing our fair land with the wrecks of humanity, their kindred, their friends, and last, but not least in their estimation, their beloved constituents. They believe it to be unpopular even to be a hero in such a strife. They temporize, they halt, they finally go over to the enemy, while they profess to be friends to humanity. Such statesmen! such demagogues! From such political quacks and inglorious time-servers, "Good Lord deliver us." But I am not going to say hard things about them. If they will only condescent to read and consider the contents of the following chapters, I shall be content, hoping that they may find some thought which may lead them to see this question in its true light, and to realize the error of their way before it is too late. I shall not call it a crime. Let us here compromise on a name for their indifference to the interests of the public which they so much love as they profess, and call it "innocuous desuetude."

Another serious obstacle in the way of expeditious temperance reform is the prevailing opposition on the part of the great masses of the people to any sort of innovation upon long established custom. This persistent adherence to precedent, though based upon popular error and though proved beyond question to be at variance with every principle of reason and of expediency, has stood in the way of every effort of genius in the advancement of intellectual, moral, social, or material progress. So thoroughly are they wedded to the errors and follies of the past that they refuse to believe the truth when practically demonstrated through the medium of every one of their five avenues for the accumulation of experimental wisdom. When the lonely pioneer in science, politics, or religion, has been able by dint of long hours of unremitting study and perseverance to evolve one truth from a great mass of long accepted error, he is regarded with suspicion and disfavor by the unskillful masses who accuse him of conspiring with the devil or some hateful political party to destroy the long cherished institutions of our fathers. They cry out, "Let him be crucified," and if it were not for the protection given by the laws of the country, they would crucify him in the very light of the boasted civilization of to-day. In other times the pioneers of truth suffered martyrdom; they were put to death by the most cruel methods contrived by the barbarous ingenuity of popular vengeance. In those times the science of human government was unknown; statutes for the protection of the innocent—bills of right, *habeas corpus*, and the long catalogue of constitutional barriers which to-day shield and protect from violence the humblest and the weakest of our citizens—did not exist. If they did not at this time stand in the way of popular ignorance and prejudice, the very ground upon which we stand while we boast of our advanced civilization, would be drinking the blood of martyrs who have dared or may dare to doubt or gainsay the wisdom of our ancestors. There may be those who cannot think so at first, but if they will only look abroad and take note of the bigotry and intolerance, which everywhere exist among the ignorant and superstitious, they must realize that the broad agis of our constitution and laws is all that protects us from the fires of persecution, not only for religious, but for scientific and political heresy. Why, the altars of popular ignorance, bigotry and intolerance would be everywhere smoking with the blood of their victims condemned, immolated and sacrificed for no other crime than an assault and battery upon popular error. Moreover, we may say that the devotees of science in all its departments are even now suffering a martyrdom little less severe. Social ostracism, personal villification, and every humiliating insult and injury are constantly being inflicted upon them with impunity.

Let a man advance a new idea about any thing whatever, and a lot of aping boobies, by whom he is surrounded will swear that he is crazy. They will not only accuse him of being hopelessly insane, but they will absolutely prove him to be guilty. There may be no writ *de lunatico inquirendo* issued against him, but he will be crazy all the same, and, like the lepers of old, he will be forced to remain outside of the camps of the multitude. His life must ever be one of hopeless solitude. If he should ever be restored to soundness of mind and discretion, it will be long years after he is dead. It will be after the truths of his transcendent genius has evolved, have undergone the test of experience and have received the stamp of popular approval. The very boys around him despise him and refuse to be caught in his company. They mock him, as he walks the streets alone wrapt in the serious contemplation of his own social banishment. If he has unfortunately lost his profusion of "capillary substance," they tell him as they did one of old, "Go up, old Baldhead." He is equally despised by the girls. The children whom he loves so much to caress ever mindful of the unkindly words of their parents towards him, turn away from him as they would from a viper. He is, indeed, "a stranger in a strange land with no friendly tear to be shed for his suffering." Is it strange that he should grow weary of life? that he should grow despondent? that he should long for a summons to "join the innumerable caravan?" that he should grow impatient, and tiring of life rush unbidden into the presence of his Maker, who, alone is able to give him the rest he so much desires? Is it a wonder that he seeks refuge from the terrors of a persecution, scarcely less rigorous to his sensitive nature than the great inquisition? The sneers of the heartless masses, who have neither the capacity nor the disposition to understand and appreciate the truths he has wrought out and promulgated, have driven more men of acknowledged brilliancy to self-destruction than any other agency, and yet the world keeps on sneering and will continue to keep it up until the requiem of time shall be sounded by Gabriel. I may have occasion to recur to the perils to which genius is exposed in its contests with ignorance, prejudice and error, in a future chapter of this work. I return to the consideration of the difficulties in the way of reform as applied to the subject of prohibition and temperance.

The world is full of doubting Thomases; those who doubt the wisdom, propriety, and practicability of every conceivable measure; of every character of effort that may be undertaken to check the spread of the evil, or to ultimately suppress it. They doubt the wisdom and propriety of preaching temperance from the pulpits; of proclaiming it before the people from the forum and upon the highways and hedges; of teaching it in any form or manner whatever. They doubt if it is a moral question; they doubt if it is a religious question; they doubt if it is a political question; and, finally, they doubt whether it is a question at all. They particularly doubt the efficiency of legislation, however stringent and severe, and however great the facilities for its execution, to accomplish anything whatever in the way of checking or suppressing the infamous liquor traffic. It is truly a wonder why they do not doubt the wisdom and propriety of a law to punish a man for theft of horses, knowing as they do that it does not absolutely prohibit some men from tampering with forbidden horse flesh. These systematic doubters, and the world is full of them, doubt if such law is right and they doubt if it will prohibit. They doubt the right of a majority of the people to interfere with the drinking proclivities of others, and then doubt that they would drink less upon the passage of such laws than they do under the license or any other ssytem. The latter doubt is quite easily removed by a featherweight sophism of an anti-prohibitionist orator. They soon become convinced that prohibition is bad, because it prohibits, and worse, because it does not prohibit. Beautiful sophistry! My dear, doubting friends, what are you going to do? Do you realize that drunkenness is an evil? Do you observe that the evil is abroad in the land? Do you know of any better remedy than local option? Do you know of a more efficient one than State prohibition? If you do, then lay aside your doubts and come to the front. Let us hear from you at once. There is no time for delay. Moral suasion, preaching and weeping have done all they can; they have done wonders. If it had not been for their efforts in checking the spread of this evil, the Lord only knows what would have become of his people. These potent influences have done much to keep men from committing the ordinary crimes and misdemeanors of the country—perhaps about as much as the penal laws of our State—but they have never been supposed to possess sufficient power and efficiency to take the place of the criminal code. The influence of the church and the Sunday school has, doubtless, kept many a man from meddling with things which did not belong to him: yet, we find it necessary to have laws against theft. And so on through the whole catalogue of crime. Suppose that the constitutional doubters should be permited to have the full benefit of their doubts, and that the Legislature should by one omnibus bill repeal the entire criminal code of Texas, and leave the material interests of the people to the protection of moral suasion, religious training, the "blatant preachers," and crying women. Then set afloat the idea contended for, that personal liberty is supreme. Do you see the absurdity? Do you comprehend the legitimate conclusion of the false logic?

But there is another class of people—the antipodes of the doubters, who demand passing notice. They are the over credulous. They take everything for granted, skim around upon the surface of every popular movement or question, and that they are prohibitionists to-day is no sign whatever that they will be prohibitionists to-morrow. All of this class who have sense enough to discern the current of popular sentiment are professional politicians. They shout at every camp-meeting, and are loud-mouthed advocates of Christianity when camp-meetings and Christianity are in season. When the sporting season comes around, they are good sport for the devil. In doubtful seasons they assume the "livery of the court of Heaven," and go about hurraing for the cause of the captain of the infernal regions. They cry "Good Lord" out of one side of their mouths, and "Most excellent devil" out of the other, alternating between the two sides to suit the changing positions of the popular ear. The weaker members of this numerically great class are the dupes of every designing, unscrupulous villian that comes tramping through the country.

They love to be humbugged, and they are never left without ample resources for the gratification of their passion. They work hard the year round for a small surplus above the cost of a miserable living, and about Christmas some sharper comes along with a patent and "scoops" it all up. Instead of thinking before acting, they do exactly the reverse. They act the fool, and then afterwards sorrowfully think over what they have done, and spend valuable time in useless regrets, wondering why they did not think of it sooner. Before they get through sorrowing over their folly, another sharper comes along and "scoops" them again.

And so they go on through life. Of all people on earth, they deserve the most of our sympathy. They are not responsible for their weakness. God made them to be, or permitted them to remain foolish, perhaps for no other purpose than to confound those who are wise in their own conceit. It is unjust and irreverent to suppose that God has done wrong or made a mistake in the make up of their mental and moral constitutions. They are here for a purpose. We have no right to condemn them. I shall not do it, but, as they are here, we can not ignore their existence. They are wholly unreliable, although they do not mean to be so. When they promise that they will stay with you "through evil, as well as good report," they do not intend to be false; they do not calculate to deceive you. If you are a candidate for an office, every one of them will pledge himself to vote for you, and if the voting were to be simultaneous with the promise, no candidate would ever be defeated—they would all be elected—a dozen or more to the same office. But as the time for action is usually at a distance, in the intervening time another victim for the sacrifice comes around. They all promise to vote for him, and mean every word of it. When the day of the election comes on, such a man will go to his voting place without the least idea whom he will finally decide to vote for.

A "good worker" is on the corner watching his approach. He goes to him and oftener than otherwise makes out his entire ticket, marches him to the ballot box and votes him just as he would use a machine manufactured to order for the purposes of voting with dispatch.

Such is a brief outline of human character as applied to public affairs. In the matter of popular elections I have had some opportunities to observe, and, as the short sketch of my life has already shown, I am not without some little experience. Having said this much by way of introduction, I will proceed in the next chapter with a discussion of some of the causes of drunkenness and the milder forms of intemperance.

CHAPTER II.

CAUSES OF DRUNKENNESS.

HEREDITARY—DEFECT IN TRAINING CHILDREN'S APPETITES AND IMPULSES— BAD EXAMPLES— CURIOSITY — INDISCRIMINATE SOCIAL TREATING—FASHION'S POWER — SOCIAL CONDITION OF THE COUNTRY.

It is not proposed in this chapter, nor is it necessary to the purposes in view in the present discussion, to go into a lengthy dissertation upon the hereditary laws, nor to speak at length upon those constitutional tendencies to inebriety, found to exist in perhaps no inconsiderable class of our people. That the thirst for intoxicating drinks is often transmitted from father to son through successive generations is, I believe, a generally conceded physiological fact. It is, to some extent, demonstrated by our own individual observation, but it is not without its numerous exceptions. It is by no means an uncommon occurrence that while the father is from his youth up a sot and a drunkard, not one of his offspring may ever manifest the least disposition to intemperance. It is doubtless sometimes the case that the very example of the parent has a tendency to neutralize such hereditary inclination, and to cause the mind to revolt at the degradation to which a protracted indulgence in the use of intoxicants ultimately leads. Such considerations would necessarily have great influence upon the mind of an individual possessing a reasonable degree of self respect, coupled with strong will power and self control. Without the latter, the parental example will most naturally be followed by the son, and a long line of drunkards will ordinarily be the result. This hereditary tendency towards intemperance and drunkenness could not have been originally planted in the human constitution, but must have had its origin in the perverted habits of some of our ancestors, and has, in many instances, become more and more rampant and incorrigible through the indulgence of succeeding generations. Those who unfortunately belong to a line of constitutional drunkards are greatly to be pitied, and in every instance where it may appear that no remedy is adequate to the removal or correction of the evil, the victim should be taken specially in charge by the government, and treated and cared for as other classes of unfortunates who are provided with asylums and other available means for their comfort and protection. But this branch of the subject will be more fully considered in a future chapter.

Leaving this class of confirmed and constitutional inebriates in the hands of a higher power, we will next consider specially some of those causes of drunkenness which are directly attributable to human agency, through the medium of patent defects in our social system, and which it is certainly possible in some degree to remedy by human agency, both through the instrumentality of individual effort and the exercise of legislative authority. In the first place, our educational system is defective. In childhood and youth the appetite, the desire for good things to eat and good things to drink is the controlling passion and most powerful incentive, and its demands are at all times the most imperative and apparently insatiable. The average child is not happy except when it is eating and drinking, and its most miserable moments are those it endures while waiting for the older persons of the household to get through eating, so that it can have full sway at the table. This is all right—it is the voice of nature, and the child is not to be chastised or even scolded for the want of a biscuit and a cup of milk between meals. If it did not cry for its "hourly bread," that fact would be unmistakable evidence that something was wrong with its physical system. The constant desire of parents to satisfy this appetite and to please their children leads them, especially those who are able to afford it, to give them highly seasoned victuals and stimulating drinks, which, though not relished at first, become practically indispensable as they grow older, and until they pass beyond the pale of parental control and correction. While whisky, brandy, rum, etc., are usually enumerated as intoxicants, there are many other things regarded as entirely harmless as articles of ordinary diet, which are quite stimulating in their nature, and while they might not be hurtful in that way to an adult person, are peculiarly so to children and young persons. In a normal state the human system does not require or demand a stimulant, but rather revolts at its effects as it would at a poison. When a young man who has never taken a drink of whisky finds himself thirsting for intoxicants, he may know that the thirst has been produced by something which preceded it. He has probably been raised in luxury; from his youth up he has indulged in "riotous living;" he feels a singular depression of his spirits; his sensibilities become benumbed; he wants something to brace himself up, goes to a saloon, and with his first drink begins the downward road to drunkenness and depravity. He may have first begun with coffee, then advanced to tobacco, and on and on, from one step to another, until the ill-spent life is ended.

Sallust, the Roman author, says that humanity is twofold in its nature. One part mankind possesses in common with the gods; the other in common with the brute creation. The mental characteristics of human nature, and perhaps the emotional, in part, at least, are supposed to partake of the attributes of divinity, and to link the human race to its creator and to its immortal destiny; the appetites and passions, on the other hand, have a tendency to degrade man to a position even below the level of the ordinary beasts of the field. The life of the average of mankind is a constant struggle for the mastery between the opposing forces of his nature—the one endeavoring to lift him upwards in the scale of existence: the other to pull him down to the gratification of those desires which are common to the lower orders of animated creatures. The latter force is naturally the stronger, and requires no peculiar system of cultivation in order to aid its development. Like the weeds and grass which spring up in spontaneous profusion and grow to maturity, sapping the substance and destroying the valuable products of the farm and giving so much annoyance to the husbandman, so the baser appetites and passions, if unchecked by the influence of a liberal education and of the necessary moral restraint, continue to grow stronger and stronger, while the mental and moral forces become proportionately weaker and weaker. Take a boy of ordinary intelligence, or even of more than ordinary mental power and activity, coupled with an average moral and physical constitution; permit him to grow up in the unrestrained indulgence of his appetites and passions; let his motto be from the beginning of his life: "Eat, drink, and be merry;" let no special pains be taken in cultivation and development of his mental and moral faculties: and the result will be a mere brute in the form of a human being. His very appearance will betray his character. Beastliness and depravity will stamp themselves unmistakably upon his face and upon his entire being, and it would require no special skill in the science of physiognomy to enable even a casual observer to determine his true character. That such a man will in nine cases out of ten drink to excess and to drunkenness need not be doubted for a moment, and why should he not? He has no well defined object or purpose in life, no aspirations to urge him to the attainment of honors, no ambition to become famous, no desire to be useful, and no hope of ever acquiring a reasonable degree of respectability among the higher classes of society. His only happiness is in the satisfaction of the demands of the depraved passions and perverted appetites of his nature.

There are all around us hundreds and thousands of just such characters—men who have grown up to maturity and become old without the restraining influence of education, without the privileges of refinement, strangers to good breeding. Many of them are drunkards, no small number are tramps, vagabonds, and outcasts, and but few of that unfortunate element are within the reach of the effects of temperance or moral reformers. It is practically useless and futile to consume time with an effort to redeem them; although the ultimate salvation of some may not be entirely beyond the range of human possibility. But there are those who will say that education, coupled with wholesome moral restraint, is not always effective in the prevention of the contraction of intemperate habits, and doubtless, a few who will say that education rather increases than diminishes the tendency in that direction. Some of them will say "there is the son of a preacher, or of an upright and consistent elder, or deacon, who is a great drunkard," and by taking a few such examples they jump at the conclusion that ignorance is more conducive to sobriety and temperance than a high degree of mental culture and intellectual development. In the very nature of things, it can not be true. By education is not only meant the correct training of the mental faculties, but the moral powers as well, which are closely allied and connected with those of an intellectual character. The cultivation of these necessarily strengthens them and adds force to the will. Give to the mind the true conception of the difference between right and wrong, and to the moral forces the strength and courage to enforce the mental conviction, and they together will subjugate the opposing forces of human nature which would otherwise triumph in the struggle. That drunkenness is an evil, that it is wrong, that it is detrimental to the individual and to society, will be denied by none, not even the greatest drunkard that can be found in the gutters. The young man as he finds the habit fast taking possession of his being, must know that it is not only wrong, but ruinous in its effects, and the reason why he persists in its indulgence, is, because he is lacking in moral courage and personal resolution. The principal causes of the great amount of drunkenness among the well educated classes will be more fully treated hereafter—causes which do not operate so forcibly upon the ignorant and uneducated classes of our people. But before passing from this branch of the subject I desire to speak briefly of the causes which often lead the sons of preachers, and others of the truly pious classes of people, into dissipation and drunkenness.

There is such a thing as being too strict. In childhood and youth, curiosity is one of the predominating traits of the mind. This disposition to pry into every mystery and find out every thing that is going on is implanted in the youthful mind for a wise purpose. It urges on to the rapid acquisition of knowledge and experimental wisdom. Young people are always experimenting, and in following this natural impulse or desire they necessarily fall into many pitfalls of error. But they will experiment in spite of every effort to prevent them from it, and in spite of all the pains they are made to suffer by their daring. Over pious people are inclined to restrain this natural tendency of their children while they are able to keep them under their immediate control and supervision. When they get out from under such control, they usually make up for lost time, and in doing so, get the reputation of being worse than those who have been suffered to grow up without the usual restraints. A child should be allowed to learn by experience while he is getting the benefit of the experience of others. The idea of raising a boy to be twenty-one years old without permitting him to experience the taste of whisky, or to know its peculiar effects, is more absurd than otherwise. It is better that he learn all that his curiosity may lead him to find out before he passes beyond the pale of parental control.

Next to what may appear to some a morbid curiosity, which serves to lead the young into all sorts of mischief, may be ranked as a leading trait or characteristic of the youthful mind, is imitation. It is this inclination of the mind which causes the boy to take so much delight in building play houses, hitching up his little wagon, riding stick horses and yearlings, and doing a thousand things often extremely hazardous, which go to make up the miniature world that he lives in. It is this natural disposition to imitate the actions of grown up men which causes the boy to smoke cigarettes, chew tobacco, swear, and indulge in all kinds of profanity of which he has so many pernicious examples before him. He is permitted to go upon the street at all times of the day, and often of nights, where he comes in contact with men who engage in these things. His first impulse is to imitate the example. The desire is greatly increased by the fact that he sees and hears other boys smoking, chewing and swearing. He thinks they look manly, because men engage in these habits, and when we see the inability of the boy to contemplate results, we must not attach so much blame to him for the contraction of bad habits as we may be often inclined. This inate disposition to imitate grown people is implanted within him for a noble purpose. Without it his life would be out of harmony with society and with his surroundings. By the proper exercise of this imitative faculty he gathers many, if not all, of the graceful and ennobling traits of his character from the best models of human excellence, which are presented to his mind as worthy of imitation. By constant association with moral, refined, and intelligent people, he will naturally imitate their virtues. On the other hand, by prolonged exposure to the companionship of the low, vulgar, and vicious of society, he will intuitively and gradually assume their characteristic mental, moral, and social deformities. It is impossible for a pure stream to flow from a corrupt fountain. It is equally so for a pure character to be formed and maintained amid corrupt and villainous associations. That the individual will partake of the general character of his associates, is a rule with few, if any, exceptions. Otherwise, the discord would be intolerable, and the companionship could not long exist. To return more closely to the subject before us, it is through this leading faculty of imitation in the youthful mind that the boy, if permitten to choose the objects of its exercise from the low, vicious and immoral, is led into habits of intemperance. His father, his uncle, or his fullgrown brother is a habitual smoker, and thinks nothing of setting the example before him. He is frequently thrown in the company of men and boys who indulge in this habit, which is, for the average boy, the first step to dissipation. He imitates the example, he smokes his cigarettes, and feels as large as his father who puffs his flavored Havana. The habit becomes fixed, and by the time he is of sufficient age and discretion to contemplate results, or to fully realize the difference between a moral and an immoral action, between decency and indecency, he has entirely lost the power to overcome the pernicious habit. The same is true of the habit of chewing tobacco. The nervous centers become shattered and paralyzed. The system is fully prepared for the next step on the broad road to drunkenness and ruin.

That chewing tobacco and smoking cigarettes invariably lead to the use of intoxicating liquros, is, by no means, true, as the experience and observation of us all must necessarily establish; but that they are a species of intemperance will be generally admitted by fair minded and unprejudiced persons, even among those who are themselves addicted to such unseemly habits. The use of tobacco has a pernicious and demoralizing effect upon the nervous system. It is a passion, although milder and much les destructive in its nature than alcohol. It stimulates nervous action, and its protracted use so affects the nervous centers that they become thoroughly upset and deranged, when the use of the stimulant is temporarily suspended. So severe is the effect upon the nervous system of the withdrawal of the stimulant that few are able to support it for a sufficient length of time for the system to return to its normal condition.

Not long since the writer was a member of the General Assembly of the Cumberland Presbyterian Church, in session at Sedalia, Missouri, when a resolution was introduced and discussed, the object and purport of which was to discourage the use of tobacco in any of its forms by the ministry. Just before the resolution was put to a vote, an aged brother, palsied by the weight of years, arose to his feet and implored the Assembly, for his sake, not to pass the resolution. The tears rolled in great drops down his sunken cheeks as he related his experience in his repeated efforts to break off the habit. He spoke feelingly of the trouble it had caused him, and of the many hours of earnest prayer he had spent in a fruitless effort to break the fearful spell that had enchained him for years. He said that he would be forced to abandon the church, in whose service he had spent the best years of his life, if it were intended by the resolution to force him to quit the use of tobacco, which he could not possibly do. The resolution did not go so far as the good old brother thought at the time, as it was not intended to be of binding force as a law of the church, but only an unequivocal expression of the Assembly upon that subject which has been so long overlooked in the effort to suppress King Alcohol.

I come now to consider a branch of the subject in hand

from which I am inclined to shrink by reason of a realization of my inability to do justice to its importance as the prime and immediate cause of so much drunkenness and the milder forms of intemperance prevalent in our country. I come now to speak of the objection that education does not always have the effect to destroy or diminish the desire for intoxicating liquors, and to consider the reason why so many belonging to the intelligent and highly educated classes of our people become addicted to their intemperate use—to make plain, if possible, the mystery which puzzles the understanding of many who have never endeavored to unfold it by probing into the interior structure of our social system. We take the example of a young man who has had all the advantages of correct moral training at home, has received his intellectual culture from the highest and best colleges, has perfected himself in the knowledge and practice of a learned and lucrative profession. Socially, he stands upon the highest pinacle of respectability. Wealth, honor, position, and all that human avarice, cupidity, and ambition could desire, are his in abundance. Perhaps he may have a lovely young wife and growing family to gladden his heart and make home happy and attractive. He is pointed to as a model of human excellence, is the pride of his family, and the central figure of a host of admiring friends. Ought he to drink? Will he do so?, and if so, why? What is it that can entice him away from the contemplation of his happy surroundings and finally drag him down to the level of the lowest outcast and drunkard—the low estate of the tramp and the vagabond? His strange life, his rapid descent from the highest degree of human respectability to the lowest depths of disgrace, is the common remark and wonder of his former associates. Those who at one time courted his favors, who thought themselves honored by his recognition, pass him unheeded and unnoticed upon the streets. They may ask themselves what can be the cause of the wreck of so grand a specimen of physical and intellectual manhood. They pursue the inquiry no further, and often go on heedlessly, regardless of the example before them, finally themselves reaching the same depths of human depravity. If you were to suggest to them the true cause of their friend's hopeless ruin, and intimate that they were traveling the same dismal road, and would themselves become drunkards and vagabonds like him, they would not hesitate to insult you, if they did not use personal violence to avenge the indignity offered to their honor and their standing.

And right here I am going to attempt to solve this great mystery and explain this strange freak of human nature and character. It comes from the accursed, demoralizing and dangerous custom of social drinking and promiscuous treating. How long it has been customary to treat every body to strong drink as a token of friendship, liberality, or general good will, I have not the least idea. I do not know that its origin marks any distinct era in the history of moral depravity. It is more than probable that it has gradually grown into universal custom along with other vices which have done so much to corrupt the morals and destroy the happiness of the people among whom they have become prevalent. But we are not so much interested in the question of when and how this prolific progenitor of drunkenness and wretchedness made its advent into our social system, as we are in the contemplation of its offspring of evil and human despair, beyond all possibility of description. Still more ought we to be interested in its ultimate destruction and banishment from society; and when that is done there will be but little left for the exercise of local or general prohibitory legislation. Ask the palsied inebriate how it came to pass, and he will tell you that he never thought he would be a drunkard until he had gone so far on the downward road that he conld not turn back. He will tell you that he began by taking an occasional glass with his friends for the sake of sociability and that he unthoughtedly kept it up until the habit became fixed and his system demanded its continuance. He finally lost the power of controlling his thirst for liquor, and as a consequence is a hopeless wreck of his former self. Fashion absolutely controls the half, if not more, of human action. There is no one who is entirely free from its influence or independent of its imperative commands. The dictates of fashion are far more arbitrary than statutory enactments of ecclesiastical proscriptions. The great mass of mankind will follow the fashions, if they know them, regardless of the laws of health or the reasonable restraints of morality and religion. So long as social dram-drinking and mutual treating have the impress of fashion or general custom, they will go on, to a large extent, in spite of law, in spite of moral persuasion, in spite of religion and of every possible restraint that can be used to prevent them. To be out of the fashion, with no small class of people, is to be out of the world. I have no doubt that there are many who would not hesitate to follow the dictates of fashion in preference to the dictates of conscience, at all times, when called upon publicly to make the decision in a practical manner. Rather than be laughed at as old fogyish and unfashionable they would willingly crush out every secret suggestion of the silent monitor within. If fashion says drink it, conscience need not object. Down goes the deadly potion; down goes the victim to ruin and disgrace.

See the young man when he first launches out in the gay and giddy world of fashion. The first years of his life have been spent, perhaps, upon the parental farm. His week days have been passed amid the familiar scenes of plow-boy life, his Sundays hallowed by the sacred teachings of the country Sabbath-school and the practical and unsophisticated sermons of the village parson. His hours of recreation have been passed in the enjoyment of the inoocent pleasures and amusements incident to country life. The allurements of the town or city draw him thither. He is at once taken into full fellowship by one of the soft handed gentry whose whole ambition has been to play a successful game at billiards and to pose himself as the champion dude of the city. The unsuspecting youth is invited to walk into a saloon near by and imbibe. He hesitates, but is told that he can not be "one of the boys" unless he yield to the pressing invitation to enter the den of vice, though with many doubts and misgivings as to the propriety of the step. He thinks of his mother's parting words of warning which call him back, but the pressure is too strong for his feeble resolution. His seducers point to the screen which will shut out his action from the cheerful light of day, and the hackneyed criticisms of the "old fogies" who may perchance take notice of his entrance. He is asked to take something, and when called upon to decide upon the strength of his first drink, of all the evils before him he endeavors to choose the least. He calls for lemonade, but is at once told that he must drink something stronger; nothing weaker than beer will suffice, and more frequently than otherwise he will be prevailed on to take "whisky straight." He is informed that social drinking is fashionable, and it is every word the truth. In that he is no wise deceived. He is furthermore reminded that it is not polite to accept a treat without setting them up himself. The first impulse of his manly nature responds to the suggestion; and—will it be necessary to pursue the illustration further? It does not require the exercise of prophetic inspiration or the mysterious gift of an astrologist to cast the horoscope of his future career. The history of his life is no new history. It is one of those histories which are continually repeating themselves. It is one that will apply to thousands and hundreds of thousands of our unfortunate race.

Not many years ago the social condition of Texas was peculiarly conducive to the promotion of drunkenness and all sorts of dissipation and rowdyism. Its population, though brave, generous, patriotic and hospitable, was made up of the bold, enterprising and venturesome classes of the older States. Many of them came to the wild prairies of Texas to seek refuge from the social restraints which an advanced civilization had drawn around them. They had grown tired of these restraints and of the cold formalities incident to refined society, and having learned that in Texas they could find the longed-for relief, they bade adieu to the hallowed associations of their youth, and came, buoyant with hope and the spirit of liberty, to a country in all things adapted to their restless and enterprising natures. Arriving in Texas, they at once laid aside the Procrustean system of ethics and good breeding under which they had grown up to manhood, and adopted the prevailing manners and customs of the early pioneers, which had been formed without reference to approved examples. Coming as they did from all States and from all countries, and bringing along with them their customs, their virtues, and their vices, a new social system partaking in its general features of the systems of all of the civilized countries whose population was represented in the organic structure of Texas society. That there were among these early settlers of Texas many refugees from justice, many who had dyed their hands in the blood of their fellow-men, many who had committed crimes of the most henious character, many who were dissipated and immoral in their personal habits, is too well known to the history of the early settlement of our State to be seriously doubted. That the general features of Texas society were quite angular and unseemly at that time and for many years after the first settlement of the country, is well known, and especially was this fact appreciated by the people of the other States, who were satisfied to stay where they were, and desirous that everyone else should do likewise. So thoroughly and indelibly was this fact impressed upon their minds that they have not till this day been made to realize and understand that the social condition of Texas at this time is not in the same condition that it was forty years ago, At that period the laws of the State were quite meager and defective, and even such as existed were poorly executed, because of the inability of the moral element to enforce their penalties upon the law-breakers who were decidedly in the majority. Such a thing as a legal conviction in the courts of the country was a thing rarely heard of, and the idea of sending a man to the penitentiary for stealing a yearling never entered into the mind of the most able and vigorous prosecuting attorney. It was regarded as no crime to wilfully and knowingly mark another man's yearling; that is, if you did not get more of his than he did of yours on a final account. In the latter event compensation was made, and the matter was fully adjusted without resort to the civil or penal laws of the State. All other transgressions were looked upon with charity and forbearance, and especially in homicides and all grades of assaults upon the person of another. For such offenses, the commission of which apparently indicated courage and bravery, there was always found a sufficient excuse to justify an acquittal. Only the premeditated, cold-blooded, and cowardly murders were punished, and not then unless the proof was overwhelmingly conclusive of guilt. A prosecution for assault with intent to murder usually resulted either in an acquittal or in a conviction of an aggravated or simple assault, most generally the latter when there was a conviction for any offense. To kill a man while under the influence of whisky was looked upon with feelings of pity and regret, and generally treated as a case of negligent homicide of the lowest degree. The reason for this condition of public sentiment is not difficult to understand.

First, the perils of frontier life demanded that personal courage should be cultivated; and in order to its development deeds of personal daring and individual bravery must be rewarded and esteemed as the highest virtues and great skill and expertness in their despatch reckoned the highest accomplishment. Second, a people bound together by the constant realization of a common danger are more generous and charitable to the faults of each other than they are in a state of comparative independence. They have great sympathy for the weak and unfortunate; they are inclined to "bear the infirmities of their friends" and in no way disposed "to make them worse than they really are." And third, the standard of morality under such circumstances is much lower than it is in a high state of civilization and refinement. The word virtue was in Cæsar's time synonymous with personal bravery and daring. Indeed, the word itself in the language from which it is derived meant nothing more than individual courage. In such condition of society as above described as prevailing during the early settlement of Texas, when the terrible results of drunkenness, the legitimate offspring of the liquor traffic practically unrestrained by legislative enactments, were lightly esteemed, and, in some degree, encouraged, it would necessarily be the case that the parent of these manifold vices would be regarded as no extraordinary evil, deserving legislative interference or social criticism. Before social order had been fully established in Texas, the great Civil War came on and brought along with it those disturbing social elements which for a time put an end to the rapid progress of our civilization, and the country relapsed into a condition no better, if not worse, than it was in the years of its first settlement; in the days of the Regulators and the Moderators whose bloody career is well known to every intelligent reader of our history. I can not stop to portray the moral, social, and material desolation which followed in the wake of that unfortunate struggle. Not the least of the vices which prevailed throughout the length and breadth of the State and the south was that of intemperance. It sprang up, and for years flourished I can not say, "like a green bay-tree," but like a moral incubus, which deadened every ennobling impulse of our social system.

This dread destroyer of human happiness and prosperity stalked abroad in every conceivable disguise, leading his bloody cohorts of crime and social disorder and destruction; making widows and orphans by the hundreds and the thousands; applying the torch to the homes and dearest interests of our downtrodden people, consuming not only their dilapidated fortunes, but every lingering hope of happiness that had been left them by the cruel fate of a war which, as they believed, had already deprived them of every guaranty of their liberties that was worth fighting to maintain.

I can not stop here to speak at length of the rapid progress that has been made since these sorrowful days; that history is known to the reader. I could not make it more plain than it must seem to every reasonable mind which will only take time to contrast the past with the present. I can not take time to speak at length of the common schools and the colleges, the railroads and the telegraphs, the vast institutions which have sprung up as if by the wave of the magician's wand; the millions of people and the countless millions of material wealth; all the grand and glorious work which has been done, and its results having in view the development of our resources and the elevation of our moral and social condition. It is unnecessary to do more than to invite the reader to walk upon the elevated platform of his own personal observation and experience, and make a survey of the passing glories of the situation. Look around you and behold what a change has taken place during the last quarter of the century. Behold with a thankful heart what great things have been wrought around and about us! Then turn to the contemplation of the indescribable wretchedness of the inebriate's home. Then wonder why it is that so many noble specimens of our race are dying and weeping, starving and shivering from the dreadful ravages of a demon fostered and encouraged by the protecting care of a government claiming to be civilized and civilizing in its purposes and objects. The reader will then behold, and he can not escape from the picture, the strangest, most glaring inconsistency ever tolerated in an enlightened government. Was this government made for the protection of all, or was it only intended for a few? Was the constitution framed with a view of conferring upon the whisky dealers of Texas the inalienable right to make paupers and lunatics out of a large class of our people? If the proposition be established that the constitution can not rightfully be changed so as to protect the best interests of society at large, then must society forever remain at the mercy of the cormorants who are feasting upon its vitals and spreading desolation and ruin throughout the length and breadth of the land. It would be better to have no constitution at all, and that the dearest rights and interests of the people be committed to the caprice of every partisan legislature.

CHAPTER III.

EFFECTS OF DRUNKENNESS.

PHYSICAL, MORAL AND SOCIAL.

In the preceding chapters I have endeavored to discuss briefly such of the causes of drunkenness as may be termed general in their character. To call attention to the many anomalous cases which may seem to be exceptions to the general rules regulating human conduct with relation to the subject, or to proceed from causes which appear rather accidental than otherwise, would require more space than is contemplated by the scope of the discussion before us. Among these may be classed circumstances of domestic infelicity, sudden and repeated misfortunes, such as operate to destroy hope, and plunge the victim into the depths of despondency and unutterable despair. There are doubtless many who from such causes have resorted to the fatal cup and gone down to the lowest depths of drunkenness, who, under other circumstances, would have lived sober and useful lives.

I come now to speak briefly of some of the effects of the intemperate use of alcoholic stimulants upon the human system and upon society at large. I might, very properly, I think, leave out the word *"intemperate,"* and let the discussion apply to the use of the article in any other way than as other poisonous substances are administered in the treatment of physical disease. That it has its proper place in *materia medica*, and that the alcoholic principle is necessary in the promotion of many of the useful arts, may, and perhaps must, be fully conceded. The elimination of that one element in the composition of the universe of material things would doubtless result in a general dissolution of organic matter, and the final extinction of animal life. The writer does not intend by the foregoing to even speculate upon the result of the utter destruction of that element in nature, which, through the medium of the distilling process, becomes the arch enemy of human happiness—the fierce and ruthless destroyer of so much of human life and of human character. Nor would I pretend to say that the use of alcohol in medicine and in the arts may not be practically dispensed with by the substitution of some harmless preparation which can be used without danger to the race. But, be this as it may, I take the position that the human system in its normal state never demands or requires the use of alcohol as a beverage to any extent whatever. From the very best of medical authority I submit the following propositions:

1. Alcoholic liquors are never necessary in health.
2. They are always injurious to health.
3. They are never necessary as a food for man any more than they are for the lower animals.
4. They do not warm and give strength to the body, but diminish both.
5. They do dot increase the power of resistance and the endurance of mental and physical fatigue.
6. They do not increase mental vigor.
7. They do not give tone to the heart, but the accelerated action, which is always temporary, is followed by a reduction of tenacity.
8. They may for a short time increase nervous tension, but are followed by relaxation and debility, and the nervous system is more quickly worn out under their influence.
9. They build up no tissues of the body, but in severe cases they cause a deposition of adipose tissue, which is a

source of weakness and destruction to the heart and to all other muscles.

10. They are specially harmful to brainworkers, who take but little exercise.

11. They produce a tendency to appoplexy and paralysis.

12. They are never necessary in a physiological condition of the system in any quantity, either large or small, but are often beneficial in disease, in which they should be prescribed by an expert.

It will be seen from the above propositions, if correct, that the use of alcoholic stimulants is in no way beneficial to the system which is free from disease.

It is also stated that it tends to produce a certain class of physical diseases. Nature is the greatest physician of them all, and if it were possible for the human mind to understand the language of her directions in the application of universal cure, and if it were possible for human resolution to curb the unnatural and perverted appetites and passions, and strictly to follow the directions of that great physician in the treatment of all human ailments, but a few generations would pass away before disease would be banished from the land, and the whole race of mankind would rejoice in perfect health and happiness. The warnings of nature to those who habitually violate her immutable laws are understood by few and practically heeded by none. As the result of this, the worst of ignorance and heedlessness, we have become a race of invalids, and a perfect man or woman is rarely, if ever, to be found. The use of alcoholic stimulants is contrary to nature. The pains the inebriate would thus allay are inflicted upon him for the purpose of informing and constantly reminding him that he has either wilfully or ignorantly transgressed some law of his nature, and if he is wise he will not cease to inquire of every available source of information until he has learned the cause of the timely warning, if it is discoverable. Instead of benumbing his sensibilities and shutting his eyes to the fatal consequences, if he is wise, he will seek an effective remedy for his ailment. If mentally depressed and cast down, he will do likewise rather than resort to the use of stimulants, which only serve temporarily to excite the brain and nervous system, which unnatural excitement and exhilaration is soon followed by greater prostration and depression. It is unnatural; it is injurious.

Passing to the moral effects of intemperance, it is scarcely necessary to do anything more than refer the reader to his own experience and observation. It is not necessary to speak at length of the dreadful results of intemperance which are everywhere seen by the casual observer. Can any one doubt the evil results of drunkenness in a moral point of view, when he contemplates for a moment the great catalogue of murders, crimes, and misdemeanors it produces? Will he be heard to say that it is harmless when he counts over the once happy homes it has destroyed? Will he dare to assert that it is not the giant evil of the land, when he beholds the all but countless hosts of women and children who are each year cast friendless upon the cold charities of a pitiless world? Will he so degrade and prostitute his own intelligence, which God has given him for a better purpose, as to espouse the cause of this ruthless enemy of mankind, when he considers the great work of devastation and ruin it is carrying on all over the world?

Figures and statistics are altogether inadequate to express or describe the great work of material, moral, and social destruction produced by this monster evil of our land and country. And yet there are those all around and about us who say that the liquor traffic must go on. There are those who say that it ought not to be stopped. Many who say that it can not be checked and that there is no use to try to suppress the great evil of evils. There are always many who take for their motto in life "I can't," and they go through life content to do nothing whatever to benefit mankind, because of that insuperable obstacle "I can't," which forever stares them in the face. A better motto is, "I'll try," and if it can not be accomplished in one way, it may be in some other. To find out the best way to accomplish the purpose is the duty of every one who desires to be useful in his day, and when he discovers the true plan he should bend his energies to put it into successful operation.

CHAPTER IV.

REMEDIES FOR THE EVIL INDEPENDENT OF LEGISLATION.

EARLY TRAINING—PARENTAL INFLUENCE—GOOD EXAMPLE—WOMAN'S FREEDOM FROM THE VICE—HER SPECIAL WORK.

In the preceding chapters I have attempted to discuss first, the erroneous methods so commonly adopted and pursued by the advocates of prohibition in the suppression and prevention of drunkenness; second, some of the causes which operate to bring about and encourage the intemperate use of intoxicants; and, third, a few of the pernicious effects of intemperance upon the physical, intellectual and moral constitution of man, with a bare suggestion of some of its terrible consequences to the social interests of mankind in general. In that discussion I have not attempted to exhaust the subject. I hope, however, that enough has been said upon those branches of the great subject under consideration to form a sufficient basis for the proper understanding and appreciation of the practicability of the methods to be proposed in this and the future chapters of this work, for the suppression of drunkenness, the monster evil of the age.

The complete suppression of this great evil can perhaps never be accomplished. Many generations will pass away before total prohibition can be effected by every possible agency that could be put in operation by the people, either in their legislative or individual capacities. Those who expect to see so great a moral and social revolution in their day are certainly doomed to disappointment. Nothing, save the intervention of divine power, wisdom and goodness in the regeneration of a besotted race, can accomplish such a revolution in a century, if in all time to come. What other agency can reclaim the fallen and lost manhood of the confirmed drunkard who was ushered into this "breathing world" with a natural thirst for strong drink inherited from his ancestors, and whose whole life has been given to the indulgence of the all but insatiable desire for whisky? That such men are going to have their daily and even hourly portion of the vile stuff may be put down as a certainty, that is, if its manufacture for any purpose whatever is permitted. The absolute and complete prohibition of the manufacture of intoxicating liquors need not be expected; it matters not how stringent the laws may be for its prevention or suppression, and when it is made, the topers are going to get it in some way, and they will not be long about devising the ways and means of procuring it.

The first question, then, is, what should be done with this truly unfortunate and pitiable class of our people, whose name to-day is legion? They are rather deserving of sympathy than of censure, and since they are beyond all hope of redemption—beyond the reach of all human effort to reclaim them from their awful condition and avert the terrible destiny which most certainly awaits them—ought we not to do what we can to relieve their necessities, to provide for their protection, and in every way possible endeavor to comfort them in their misery and despair? Why does the State build and maintain at vast expense asylums for the care and treatment of almost all other classes of unfortunates, while no special provision is made for the confirmed and hopeless inebriate, who wallows insensible and oblivious in the mud and filth of the streets and alleys? It would seem, too, that, although no cure could be hoped for in such cases, their removal from their customary haunts and the influence of their demoralizing examples would doubtless have salutary effect upon society at large. But, be this as it may, no method for their redemption will be proposed by the writer, and I desire it understood that whatever plans may be proposed and discussed in this work shall have no reference to the confirmed and constitutional drunkard. Neither local, State, nor national prohibition, high license, or free whisky can operate as even a temporary check upon his downward career to a drunkard's grave, and perhaps to a drunkard's hell, the contemplation of which has not the slightest effect upon his appetite or his actions.

It was said of old by one who ranks in history as the wisest of mankind in all ages of the world, "Train up a child in the way he should go, and when he is old he will not depart from it." To this rule, as well as to all others of a general character applicable to human conduct, there are, of course, exceptions. There are some incorrigible individuals who are so prone to do wrong, whose vicious passions and proclivities so far predominate over their moral resolution, that no training, however strict and conducive to the development of the higher moral sensibilities, is practically of any avail. But while this is true, it is, I think, safe to assume that the great majority of young persons are susceptible of the good influences of correct moral training. Alas, how great the number of our race who have grown up to manhood without such training, but whose lives and characters have been molded and fashioned by chance, and that, too, after the most vicious and depraved models of society! How many have been permitted to grow up in utter and profound ignorance of their own capacities and of their own immortal destinies. How many have grown up in the unrestrained indulgence of every beastly appetite and propensity, while the mind and soul have sunk down to a level with the beasts of the field. How great the number whose intellectual faculties have been cultivated to their utmost tension, while the moral powers have smouldered amid the rubbish of vicious actions and ungodly purposes.

The first question which arises, is, who is to begin this work of reformation? Is it to be the legislator, in an effort to enact and promulgate rigid laws for the punisment of those poor fallen victims to evil training, evil influences, and evil associations? He has his duty to perform, which will be discussed in due time, but he is by no means the only one who should bear the responsibility of the work to be done. Napoleon once said that the one great need of France was mothers. The great men of all ages have conceded to the mothers of the land an influence in the promotion of a nation's welfare and prosperity above all others. It would take too long to attempt to enumerate the great characters in modern and ancient history which were the handiwork of a mother's influence and devotion. From her the tender mind of the helpless infant receives its first impressions. The first touch in the formation of its character is by her loving hand. Its first sensibilities are awakened by the beams of her countenance as she keeps faithful watch over every motion of its tender features. By her are planted in childhood the first principles from which in after life are to spring so many of the noble or ignoble actions which are to mark the distinguishing features of character and determine the extent of its usefulness and respectability. I shall not further attempt to speak of the mother's influence. It is beyond my comprehension, beyond the power of my language to define or to attempt to describe. I only refer to it briefly for the purpose of impressing upon the mothers of our country the importance of the duties which God and nature have committed to them, and to arouse them to the necessity of training their children with a view of making of them examples of sobriety and usefulness. What thinking mother is there in the land who would not rather see her child laid low in the icy embrace of death than to know that it would live to be a drunkard, a vagabond, and an outcast? How many would sink into despair and death if they could unhappily foresee the future career and tragic end of the sweet little one whose childish prattle is now the pride and joy of their homes and hearts. To avert such a calamity should be the constant desire and thought of every mother, as she watches with so much solicitude the mental, moral, and physical growth of her darling boy. But the first thing for her to do is, to study and qualify herself thoroughly for the discharge of the important duty which devolves upon her in the formation of human character. To do this, she must study closely the nature of children. She must know something of the physical, mental, and moral constitutions of the young, and must be able at all times to apply such knowledge in the practical training and development of the character of her offspring. While the influence of the mother in the formation of the habits and in the development of the inherent traits of character of the young can not be overestimated, there are others whose influence in the word of molding and shaping human character deserve some attention in connection with this branch of the subject.

At an early age of life the boys pass from under the direct and immediate control and personal supervision of the mother, and from that time, which marks the beginning of the downward career of many, the father's example becomes a more important factor in shaping the course of their lives, and in the formation of their traits of character which are to insure their destinies for good or for evil. Good precepts are beneficial, indeed, quite indispensable, but they amount to practically nothing unless accompanied by correspondingly good examples. I have often heard intelligent fathers reprove their boys, and not only reprove them harshly, but chastise them severely for chewing tobacco, swearing, and other even more flagrant improprieties, while at the same time they were themselves guilty of the same things, and that too in the very presence of their "young hopefuls," whom they would vainly attempt to reason, coax, and whip into obedience to precepts diametrically opposed to the logic of their own personal examples. I have already mentioned the characteristic tendency of the youthful mind to imitate. The reader's own personal observation must have long since taught him that imitative faculty in childhood and youth is among the very strongest incentives or impulses of nature. It is wise that it should be so, for reasons more fully alluded to in a former chapter which it is not necessary to review in this. And that is the special reason for the necessity for every one who may stand in so responsible a relationship as father, to look well to his own example. He should be careful to allow no action of his own in the presence of his son, or anywhere else, to belie the good precepts, the ennobling principles and rules of moral conduct which he may think proper to give in the discharge of his duty as a parent. These bad examples, which need not be here enumerated, are among the most prolific sources of intemperance and vice of every character, and the only prevention of the fearful results is to reform your own example, and make not only every word, but every action, correspond with the wholesome precepts you may give. If you are a father, you may reason with your boys about chewing tobacco, smoking, and drinking whisky, and may spend half your time in demonstrating to them by scientific methods the evil results that follow such habits, and the other half in trying to persuade them to spurn them or to break them off, and yet the effort will be in vain so long as you indulge in these filthy and demoralizing habits yourself. Of course there are occasional exceptions to the rule, but I claim that it is true as a general proposition. Fathers, do you really want your boys to be sober and useful citizens? If you do, and are in earnest about the matter, I entreat you to become sober and useful yourselves. If you would keep your boy from defiling his lips with profanity, be chaste in your own language, and circumspect in your own conversation. If you would keep your boy from polluting his breath with the sickening fumes of the cigarette, which has become so common among the youth of the country, throw away your own sweet-scented Havana, and by that one act of yours, a sacrifice though it may seem, you will do more in the way of bringing about a much-needed reformation than you can do in a whole lifetime of preaching what you do not practice yourself. Quit swearing, quit smoking, quit chewing tobacco, quit drinking, keep out of the saloons, keep out of the local-option drug stores. By this means you will do more for the glorious cause of temperance than you can possibly do by a continual discussion of the relative merits and efficacy of proposed laws for the suppression of drunkenness and the reform of other drunkards than yourselves. It is only to be wondered at and regretted that these truths are not more generally understood and practiced by those who have so much to do with the formation of the characters and the ultimate determination of the immortal destinies of the youth of the country.

How many disappointed hopes, how many broken hearts and blasted aspirations would have been spared had it not been for the damning and demoralizing influence of bad examples upon shaping the conduct of the youth. A boy naturally believes, and perhaps ought to believe, that what his father does is right. The father's example ought to be, and ordinarily will be, the criterion by which he judges of the conduct of other people. Nature, ever faithful and true to herself, has decreed it to be so. It comes to us with the sanction of holy writ in the form of the fifth commandment, "Honor thy father and thy mother that thy days may be long in the land which the Lord thy God giveth thee"; and this too, without the qualification that the father and mother shall be worthy of honor in the esteem of the party for whose guidance the injunction is given. It is nowhere found in that good book that the child may consider the parents' vices and moral deformities in determining the binding force of the obligation embraced in the commandment, or in the consideration of the question whether or not he ought to be absolved from its observance. The ordinary demands of society require that the son shall respect and care for his father, however much he may fall below the respect of all other people who make pretensions to decency. A story is told with which many of my readers are, doubtless, familiar, but which I am constrained to relate by way of illustration of the truth attempted to be enforced : A young man, engaged in keeping a saloon in one of the larger cities, was in the act of dragging an infirm and besotted old man out of his house by the hair, which was silvered by the impress of near four score years, when a stranger possessing the characteristic impulses of a gentleman, interfered and protested against the outrage being committed upon the helpless old man. The poor old man asked him to go away. Said he in faltering accents : "Forty years ago, when this man who seems to you so reckless, was a little boy, he saw me drag my old decrepit father out of this same door just as he is now doing with me. He is my son; I set the example before him; I am much more to blame for this act, humiliating as it may be, than he who is only following in the footsteps of his father, who ought to have set before him a better example."

This picture may seem to be somewhat overdrawn in the estimation of those who have never thought seriously upon the force of example in the formation of character. Indeed it is a factor whose influence in shaping human conduct can not be over estimated.

I now proceed to the consideration of the question why is it that drunkenness is a vice belonging almost exclusively to the masculine portion of the human family while in a state of civilization? Is there a natural constitutional tendency in man towards the intemperate use of intoxicating liquors, which is not common to woman? If there is any such difference in the constitutions of the two sexes, I am not at this time aware of it. Assuming that there is no such constitutional difference, then why is it that sobriety in man is the exception, while the reverse of the proposition is equally true with the opposite sex? It is stated on good authority that 60,000 men go down into drunkard's graves annually, while statistics take no account of the number of women who go the same way. While there are, perhaps, a few (enough to make the necessary exception to the general rule) who have died from the effects of alcohol, and who may have been included in the 60,000 annual deaths from that cause, it will be readily conceded that drunkenness and even the milder forms of intemperance is not one of the "frailties of woman." The question naturally suggests itself to the enquiring mind, what is the cause of this? And how is it that the female portion of the human race has been able to resist the fearful inroads of this insidious monster into the very heart of our social system? We speak of her frailties and of her weaknesses often without a feeling of charity or of pity, and yet she has ever been a giant in the contest with the demon intemperance, where men, strong in their own conceit, have proved themselves contemptible pigmies. Ah! and to-day if she were vested with the same political privileges that we are allowed by law to exercise, she would crush out the hydra-headed monster in less time than it would take the prohibition party of Texas to decide whether it is a political or a moral question. Whether woman's suffrage is right or wrong in principle, expedient or inexpedient, need not here be discussed;

but one thing will not be disputed, and that is, that if the women were allowed to vote, they would vote whisky clear out of the country by a very large majority. No thinking man will dispute this proposition.

But, coming back to the original question, why is it that the women keep sober, while their husbands, fathers, brothers, and sons are all the time falling into drunkenness and ruin? How often do we see the poor, brokenhearted wife, as she leaves her cheerless fireside in the dead, cold hours of midnight and strolls through the streets and alleys, from saloon to saloon, from grog-shop to grog-shop, in search of her drunken and worthless husband? Does she go there to engage with him in the degrading pleasures of the wine cup? No. She goes for another purpose. She goes as a messenger to bring back and reclaim the lost manhood of him who in times past pledged to her his solemn troth, and promised to defend and protect her, to provide for her wants, to love and cherish her above all others of earth. Would it not seem that if sorrow, if despair, if inexpressible misery and wretchedness should become a perfect excuse for drunkenness, that it ought to avail this poor, pleading, helpless woman, while she drowns the bitter recollections of former days of happiness and joy in the sparkling wine? Then why does she not drink away the sad reflections of her wretched condition, and cease to harbor her brood of corroding cares?

In our social fabric there seem to be two standards of moral excellence; one for gauging the moral rectitude of man's conduct; the other, altogether different, as I shall presently show, is used to determine the moral quality of the same kind of conduct when it pertains to woman. For instance, when a man feels depressed; is uncomfortably cold or unpleasantly warm; has had bad luck or has been unusually lucky, it is not regarded as anything wrong or out of the way for him to take one or two drinks. If he has had a great misfortune, or has "struck something rich;" if he has had a falling out with with his sweetheart, or if he has unwittingly married a termigant, he is quite justifiable; indeed, it is expected of him that he shall get drunk and "paint something red." When Christmas comes, good society demands that he shall "nog" himself up to a few "tones above concert pitch," and even the preacher will take but little notice of the impropriety if he should get "gentlemanly groggy." On the other hand, suppose a woman should, from any cause, voluntarily drink to intoxication, what would be the result? Would she be able to survive the humiliation that would necessarily follow? Would society excuse her for the ungracious act, even though she had been ruthlessly deserted by her lover, in whose life may have centered all of her earthly hopes and aspirations? If a wife, could she plead in justification or extenuation of her effense that her husband had maltreated her, that he had proved false to his marital vows, that his infidelity had plunged her into unspeakable despair? Oh, no. As long as she has one prompting of self-respect, as long as she cherishes a single feeling of self-love, and regards in the least the worth of her good name, she will bear it all; she will suffer death rather than transgress a law of society, even though it operate so unequally upon the two sexes. This state of things, the existence of these two standards by which the moral character of an action is judged of according to the sex of the party who commits it, is the only way I can account for the prevalence of drunkenness in man, while woman is almost entirely free from the vice. While I would not lower the standard erected for the guidance of my fair friends, who have nobly lived up to its full measure, I would have the same standard applied to all alike.

A laudable ambition on the part of woman is, to make herself attractive, not only in her person, but in her mental acquirements and the sweetness of her disposition, that she may become the idol of a brave and manly heart, perhaps some day the brightest ornament of a happy home. To succeed in this, to maintain her high position in society, to be loved and admired by her associates and by her gallant suitors, she must be ever mindful of the spotless purity of her character, which must, at all times, be above the very breath of suspicion. She must be chaste in her language and circumspect in her actions. Suppose it should be said of her, while in the very midst of her victorious career in the conquest of hearts, that she drinks intoxicating liquors; that she keeps it in her closet and drinks it privately, although in great moderation. Suppose the least taint of the vile liquid should polute her virgin breath, though the flowing robes of her splendid apparel shed abroad the rich perfumes of the purest essence of roses? What, O, what would be the result if it should be truthfully said of her, "She is a drunkard?" The instantaneous loss of every claim to respectability, irretrievable ruin and disgrace would certainly follow. No more would her beauty charm or her accomplishments attract the admiration of those who may have been before enchained by her bewitching powers. She would at once be stranded upon a barren rock, lost, hopelessly lost, to every prospect of future usefulness, happiness, or respectability. I cannot think the picture overdrawn. The very idea of a lady becoming a common drunkard is indeed appalling, and it will not be controverted that, should she give way to such a vice, she must at once assume her place among the very lowest of her sex.

But how is it with man? With him who, while he boasts of the superior force of his character, ought rather to be a fit sample for the weaker? And, I regret to say, that for this strange and unfortunate state of society woman is not entirely blameless. It is within her power to fix the standard of morality and respectability which are to regulate the conduct of the other sex. Her influence over the heart of man is transcendent. If she is disposed to do so, she can force the one who demands so much purity in her character to come up to the same high standard of moral excellence himself. The power of love is beyond computation. What a man will not do for the woman he really loves may not be found within the range of human possibilities. If the women of our country would, with one accord, place the seal of their inexorable disapprobation upon the character of the tippler and put the stamp of shame and disgrace upon the habit of drinking in any and all of its forms, it would not be long until drunkenness would only be known to the lowest and most vicious classes of society. If they would say to every young man who aspires to their recognition, "You must be sober. One drink, although it may be but a social glass, will operate to destroy our relationship and blot out our acquaintance"; and not only say it, but mean what they say, the reformation would be wonderful; the revolution would certainly be phenomenal. But instead of this, how often does it occur in this bright era of our civilization that the very fairest and loveliest of the land join themselves in matrimony with confirmed and habitual drunkards? This is no uncommon occurrence. It is truly surprising, too, how lightly such an objection is often treated by those who thus plunge headlong into an unfathomable abyss of despair and regret. But the example is also disastrous. It encourages young men to go on in their dissipation. They see others of their kind so highly esteemed and honored by the fair sex, and they keep on the downward road to a drunkard's lowly estate. Young lady, you need not preach temperance during the week while you spend your Sundays and leisure hours in the society of drunkards and tipplers. You need not deplore the sorrows of your once happy school-girl associates whose lives have since those halcyon days been blighted by the cruelty of their drunken husbands, when you encourage the serious attentions of a drunken suitor.

In addition to what it is certainly within the power of woman to accomplish in the elevation of the standard of respectability among men, she may do much effective work in the way of the training of the young, and in the correction and purification of public sentiment in general. Long experience has proved her special fitness for the discharge of the responsible duties of a teacher. Her tenderly sympathizing nature enables her to exert a most happy and gracious influence over the minds and hearts of young people, and to entwine their childish thoughts and affections around and about such objects and examples as are conducive to their moral growth and development. Her influence in the school-room is ever for good. Her moral teachings are always pure and ennobling in their tendency. She does not fail to implant in the breast of her little darlings a feeling of profound respect and veneration for the teachings of the Bible. She never makes of herself a medium for the spread of infidelity and scepticism. Her whole influence, which is beyond estimate, is thrown toward the side of religion and morality. It is not always thus with others. How much of the seeds of vice and ultimate ruin is sown by a certain class of teachers, it would be impossible to estimate. I have not time to particularize, nor am I disposed to do so, but will here be content to suggest that the deserving women of our State, should ever be encouraged in their desire to become useful as educators of the youth of our country. In the darker ages of the past it was thought that she did possess the necessary mental qualifications for the work, especially as it pertained to the higher branches of learning, but the error is fast being dispelled, and the fetters which so long bound her to menial service, are being broken by the rapid progress of an enlightened and liberal public sentiment. It must be obvious to every thinking, unprejudiced mind that she is rapidly advancing to her proper condition—the unqualified equal of man. Morally, socially, and religiously she is already by far his superior. As the world lays aside its barbarous notions, her sphere of usefulness will become more extensive. Her influence must grow more potential in the advancement of morality and temperance. Who can estimate the results of her efforts in the cause, though hampered as she has been by the opposing forces of prejudice and ignorance?

Look at the great work she has done in the organization and maintenance not only of temperance societies and orders, but in many others, having in view the amelioration of the condition of mankind. Wherever there is suffering, wherever there is distress, wherever there is destitution and despair, there may she be found like a ministering spirit, sacrificing herself upon the altar of her sympathy for the afflicted of her race. There are some who are disposed to speak lightly of her efforts to redeem mankind from the curse of intemperance. Then, there are some who are inclined to scoff and sneer at her for wasting her energies in the promotion of the cause which, above all others, so nearly concerns her own destiny and happiness. There are those who cry out in the language of a distinguished Texas Senator, addressed to the ministry, "Scourge her back" to the narrow sphere of her domestic operations. These are the sentiments of those who talk learnedly of "personal liberty" in everything else, and particularly as it relates to any proposed remedy for the evils of drunkenness and the ultimate suppression of the liquor traffic. To woman's ceaseless and united efforts in this cause may justly be attributed the beginning of the mighty revolution which is most certainly upon up, and which must, in time, sweep drunkenness, with all its concomitant evils and misery, from the face of our country, even as the blight of slavery was lifted from American soil within the last quarter of a century.

CHAPTER V.

REMEDIES INDEPENDENT OF LEGISLATION.

THE CHURCH AND ITS MINISTRY—THE SUNDAY SCHOOL.

Since the days of the apostles there has existed through many vicissitudes of prosperity and adversity, an organization known as the Church of Christ, established by Him as the representative of His visible kingdom on earth. From the cardinal doctrines upon which the great superstructure of the great Christian religion is based a diversity of theories and opinions pertaining to scriptural interpretation and church government have sprung up, giving rise to the many denominations of christians known throughout the religious world. To the broad and liberal mind nearly all of the differences which have so long divided the church into hostile factions and into denominations, often bitterly and uncompromisingly antagonistic to each other, are altogether frivolous, and amount to little more than the distinction between "tweedle dum and tweedle dee." The dissensions that have so long divided and distracted the church, and in so many instances paralyzed its influence for good in the world, are but the outgrowth of human weakness and bigotry. They have no place in the divine economy of the church, and it must be evident to every observing mind that these trifling obstacles in the way of religious progress are fast giving way to a more liberal and enlightened public sentiment. Such a thing as religious persecution; such a thing as the punishment of heresy or any character of interference with the freedom of conscience in the matter of religious belief or opinion so common even within a late period comparatively—is now known and regarded as dark spots upon the pages of ecclesiastical history. That religious bigotry and intolerance are rapidly waning is too evident to require discussion, even though it should be appropriate in this connection. It is quite evident, too, that, while the various denominations of the church are becoming more reconciled to each other, and more nearly agreed upon essentials in religious faith and practice, they are a unit upon the great subject of prohibition, and in their determination to suppress drunkenness and every form of intemperance. They are united in an aggressive warfare against the monster evils of the liquor traffic. In view of this great effort in behalf of religion, morality and humanity, they are laying aside their denominational prejudices, their peculiar notions of baptism, final perseverance and apostasy, and organizing themselves into a solid phalanx to meet the common arch-enemy of the whole catalogue of christian denominations, the fierce destroyer of the very foundations of their religious faith. I am aware that there are a few weak-kneed, "milk-and-cider" members of the church, who align themselves with the devil and the drunkards, and do valiant service in the ranks of the enemy. There are those who go to church on Sundays, officiate in the Sabbath-School, contribute liberally to the preacher, and put themselves up as examples of purity, when occasion seems to justify or demand it, while at other times they may be found lounging about the saloons conspiring with the whisky element to thwart every effort or movement having in view the overthrow of the demon intemperance, and the ultimate suppression of the demoralizing traffic in liquor. There are others who are altogether neutral on the question, as they are upon every other issue which is of sufficient importance to divide public sentiment, and which might in the least affect their personal popularity and standing with the advocates of both sides of the controversy. In other words, they are at all times ready to compromise with the devil on any and all moral questions, provided they can thereby at the same time retain the respect and good will of both the saints and the sinners. They are strictly neutral in all things, and independent in nothing. But, while there are such people in all churches and in all congregations, the great masses of the active membership are in their capacity as citizens of a great State, without reference to church fellowship, reliable and uncompromising prohibitionists. They see that liquor is the great enemy to their cause, the great impediment in the way of religious and moral progress, and they feel it to be their duty to do what they can to destroy and suppress it in every legitimate way possible. They naturally favor every measure proposed, whether local or general in its extent, which has for its object the suppression or mitigation of the evil. And who will have the hardihood to say that they are not right? They can not do otherwise and be true to their profession, consistent followers of Christ and his teachings.

It may seem harsh to some, but I believe that I will be sustained by all admirers of the plain and untarnished truth, that no man can have the right kind of religion in his heart, and at the same time be a sympathizer with whisky and in league with the beastly advocates of the traffic. A member of the church, be he Methodist, Baptist, Presbyterian, or other, who is so depraved in his ideas of a true christian life as to advocate liquor, or become an impediment in the way of prohibition and temperance, ought to be unceremoniously turned out of the church and forced to take his appropriate place along with the "beggarly elements of the world." Such a man has no business in the church. His example is a standing rebuke to the religion he professes. Some people are disposed to reprove the ministers for using their influence to persuade men to become sober and useful, and to take them especially to task for expressing their opinion in the pulpit and elsewhere in favor of prohibitory legislation.

When the able and eloquent Dr. B. H. Carroll, of Waco, Texas, in the exercise of a right and privilege vouchsafed by the constitution and laws to every American citizen, raised his voice in opposition to the terrible evils of intemperance and in favor of local option in his county, the county of McLennan, the great Senator Coke, styled by some, the oracle of Texas democracy, cried out in his stentorian voice, "Scourge them back into their pulpits." These memorable words of this distinguished man have echoed and re-echoed through all of the saloons and grogshops of Texas until this day, and have become the watchword of all the whisky combinations in the State in their disinterested (?) advocacy of personal liberty and death. That Senator Coke should entertain and express such sentiments is not at all strange and unaccountable when we consider the fact that when he was first elected to the high position he occupies with credit to himself, the whisky element in Texas was far in the ascendency, and had been from the first. His prolonged absence from the State while attending to the duties of his office at the National Capital had prevented him from noting carefully the progress of public sentiment in Texas in the direction of temperance and morality. Had the Senator halfway realized the change which was so fast taking place in public sentiment in Texas, and had he ever dreamed of the possibility of so great a revolution on this question as is now at hand, in all probability he would not have made the mistake. But, while the Senator has gone a little wrong on this question he should not be summarily condemned and retired to obscurity because of a single mistake. An opportunity ought to be given him to repent; the door of the church should not be forever closed against the possibility of the voluntary return of this great and distinguished prodigal. The Senator has done too much for Texas to justify any class of our people in dealing harshly with him. When fully convinced of his error, he will, no doubt, "acknowledge the corn." The prohibitionists of Texas can not afford to deal harshly with any, and especially with the great and shining political lights of the country.

But, to return to the preachers and their special work in the cause of prohibition. They have a right, not only to vote, but to talk and work for the cause, and no one however high he may be in authority, has the right to "scourge them back" or dare to "molest and make them afraid." The people of Texas are not particularly interested in the false issue attempted to be raised, that is, whether it is a political, moral, or religious question? It makes no difference whatever, whether it belongs to the one, either of the others or all of them together. Practically, it belongs to them all, and you can not possibly separate it from either. It has much to do with religion, it has much to do with moral progress, it has much to do with the politics of the country, and there is but little difference in degree. It is a question between right and wrong as applied to human conduct. It can be determined to the satisfaction of any unbiased mind by the application of the standard furnished by any or all of the three, religion, morality and politics, and the doctrine of statutory prohibition will be fully sustained. The preachers and the churches are entirely right when they say that it is a religious and moral question, and the statesman is also right when he insists that it is a political question. As a religious or moral question, no one will deny that the church and its ministry have a right to deal with and discuss it; the politicians and the people, including preachers and church members generally, have an equal right to discuss it as a political question affecting the temporal welfare of the people at large. Let the preachers preach temperance and prohibition; let them talk it; let them act it; let them vote for it, and, if possible, induce by persuasion or otherwise their membership and all others to do likewise.

In this connection I can not overlook the influence of the Sabbath-school as an instrumentality for the promotion of the good cause, especially among the young people. The older ones could all profit by becoming constant attendants of the Sunday schools of the country. If all of the children and young people could be brought within their christianizing influence and could be made to understand the importance of a thorough knowledge of the teachings of the Bible, and to feel the necessity of cultivating the moral faculties as well as the development of the intellectual and physical, the progress of society would be wonderful indeed. This would be the result without regard to the special efforts that might be made in those schools of morality and religion, to inculcate in the youthful mind a due appreciation of the evils of intemperance, and of the benefits and blessings arising and flowing from a life of sobriety. Perhaps no other surroundings are more favorable and conducive to the promotion of temperance and those incident to the Sunday schools throughout the land. It is probable, however, that this one important feature has not heretofore received that attention at the hands of the superintendents and teachers as its importance certainly demands. If the boys can be taught and persuaded to detest drunkenness, to despise the saloons and their gaudy attractions, and to live sober through life, they will have learned a lesson which will do them more good than all the philosophy of the age. If they fail to learn this lesson, and to strengthen their resolution to a point which will enable them to profit from their knowledge of its truth, they will with a few exceptions, be worthless to themselves and useless to the world, although they may have the wisdom of all the renowned scientists of the age. What is science, what is wisdom, what is "wealth and fame and all" to him who has become the crouching slave of the wine cup? Did you ever see the brilliant genius prematurely cut down in his career? Did you ever behold lying oblivious in the gutters, a man who seems to be fashioned for greatness; who may have led victorious armies and controlled the destinies of nations, and not be made to feel the wonderful power of this insidious and remorseless enemy of mankind? Could the boys of our land only be made to feel and realize this accursed power of whisky to destroy their every aspiration to become great before they fall into its deadly coils, what an improvement would be the growing generation upon the one which is now passing away.

Let us teach temperance in our Sunday school classes. Let us endeavor to teach and persuade those bright-eyed boys, placed in our charge to beware of the temptation; to be sober, useful and happy. Not only that, but let us who are teaching do what we can to check the use of tobacco, this incipient tendency to dissipation which crops out so early in the boys and is evidenced by the smoking of cigars and cigarettes. I tell you that cigarette smoking in boys is but an index pointing to a weakness which can not and will not brook the temptation to drink when they become older. It indicates a disposition to imitate vicious examples, and a dangerous susceptibility for the contraction of bad habits. Every instrumentality ought to be brought to bear to check this dangerous tendency in youth.

CHAPTER VI.

REMEDIES INDEPENDENT OF LEGISLATION.

INDIVIDUAL EFFORT.—ORGANIZED EFFORT.

Having suggested in the foregoing pages a few thoughts pertaining to the special work of those persons whose peculiar social condition, occupation or calling is such as seems to require at their hands such special work in the cause of temperance and prohibition, I desire now to speak generally of the good influence all persons, irrespective of classes, may exert in the correction of some evils and in the elevation of public sentiment, which is indispensably necessary to the success of any movement in that direction. In a government like ours where the people exercise the powers of sovereignty, public sentiment is practically supreme. It is above legislative enactments, and above constitutional limitations and restrictions. If prohibitory enactments are to be enforced, they must be put into execution by the people through their agents and representatives who are the officers of the law, and by themselves, in their capacity as jurors, a trial by jury being guaranteed by the Constitution itself. It may be humiliating to an American citizen to know it, but it is nevertheless true that laws contravening the strong current of public opinion can not be enforced by any system of jurisprudence which can be devised. Not only will jurors refuse to enforce such a law, but officers and courts, regardless of official oaths and the sacredness of the judicial ermine, will in every way possible, (and the ways are numerous), screen the offender against the penalty of a law which public sentiment pronounces unjust and oppressive. And this is why prohibitory laws are so often practical failures in the suppression of the evils of intemperance.

Every person, however humble he may be, and however insignificant he may feel his influence to be, can do something toward the elevation of public sentiment and the correction of this great popular evil. We are all responsible for the influence which we exert. We are indeed "our brothers' keepers," and it is our duty to so demean ourselves in our intercourse with the world that others, instead of being the worse for our example shall be the better for the good influence we may exert upon the formation of their habits and their characters. Above all, we should do everything in our power, by precept and example, to discourage the evil of drunkenness and intemperance in all of their hideous forms and disguises.

The cause of temperance has, perhaps, suffered more from the intemperance of its advocates than any other movement in the interest of humanity. What I mean by intemperance in this connection is, not the excessive use of intoxicating liquors, to which the term is most usually applied, but to the intemperate use of the tongue. No greater mistake is made than to suppose that bitter words and the application of personal abuse can effect anything in the suppression of the evil. There is implanted in every bosom a spirit of resentment which will ever assert itself when not held in check by cringing fear or some greater opposing force of human nature. The veriest coward on earth feels the impulse of resentment when he is made to realize that an injury has been inflicted upon him, and he is only prevented from acting upon such impulse by the sense of fear, which effectually counteracts his desire of revenge. The brave man, however depraved may be his moral sensibilities, and however low may be his standard of right and respectability, stands ready at all times to resent an insult or indignity intentionally offered to his person or to his own perverted ideas of manhood and personal honor. He might be the keeper of a saloon, a doggery, or any other sink-hole of immeasurable iniquity, and yet be very susceptible of feeling and appreciating an insult. Indeed, a man who has no feeling of resentment in his nature is not apt to do very much good or evil in the world, and it is doubtful if it is worth the trouble of an effort to reclaim or suppress him. We assume that we have to deal with men engaged in this nefarious business who have like passions as others who are engaged in the ordinary avocations of life. Such being the case, they must be influenced, if at all, just like other people are influenced to do right. Take yourself for an example. Suppose that you were engaged in a business, or that you were in the habit of doing certain acts which are not right in the estimation of other people. It may be that you have never been made to see the immorality of the business or of the particular action complained of, and that no compunctions of conscience have ever suggested to your mind the idea of the commission of a wrong not cognizable by the criminal code of the State. Suppose that your neighbors begin to say hard things about you in your absence; suppose that they denounce you as a villain, and abuse you without stint to every body in the community, and to every stranger who may perchance be passing through. Suppose they should publish in the newspapers that you were a criminal and that you ought to be drummed out of the country, and all this without their saying a word to you in kindness in regard to your conduct. Say that all of these epithets had been poured out upon your head before any effort had been made to convince you of the error of your way. The first impulse which would naturally arise in your bosom would be that of resentment. A desire to reform would be among the last. Your determination would then be to show them that you could not be forced into measures or into the adoption of a different line of conduct, and especially if the act complained of is not prohibited by the penal laws of the country. In other words, you would then feel rather inclined to continue your course for spite, although you should have to pay dearly for its gratification. Such is human nature the world over, and there is no use to attempt to ignore it in dealing with those engaged in the liquor traffic.

It is to be regretted that this truth is so often lost sight of, not only by individual temperance workers, but by temperance associations and conventions which are so foolish as to pass resolutions of a character which provoke the very strongest feelings of resentment on the part of the opposition and its sympathizers, without the slightest possibility of accomplishing any good results whatever. All of such foolishness should be stopped. Nothing but kind words should ever escape the lips of the temperance advocate. He need not be afraid to go among the saloon-keepers, nor even into their places of business, if necessary, and reason with them upon the subject. If he will conduct himself as a gentleman, they will listen patiently to his argument. If he will make them know and believe that he feels an abiding interest in them personally, and that he wishes them well in the world, that the only objection he has to them relates to the nature of the business they are following, he will now and then make a convert. Otherwise he can not hope to do so.

No man can be villified into a correct line of conduct. If he is induced to adopt it, it is by the influence of reason and persuasion. And so it is with whisky men, both the seller and the drinker. You can not make a man sober by calling him hard names. You can not stop the whisky seller from making drunkarks by calling him a villian and a devil incarnate. Oh, no! That will never do. "A little word in kindness spoken" will do more in the way of reform than a whole volume of abuse. By dealing kindly with those, not always totally depraved, but certainly deluded people, you need not, in order to be consistent, endorse the moral character of the accursed business they are following. It matters not how severely you may denounce the liquor traffic in general, nor how many uncomplimentary, or even abusive remarks you may use so they are in the bounds of decency and propriety, when called upon to express your individual opinion upon the policy of the government in the license of an acknowledged wrong, the endorsement of iniquity and the encouragement of an evil which is daily and hourly preying upon its own vitality. I can think of no expression whose severity is at all adequate to the proper denunciation of such a wrong, such a palpable inconsistency in legislation; but, while this is true, and while I heartily despise and detest the business of the saloon-keeper, I would not wantonly or intentionally offer him a personal insult, or say anything whatever that might, by exciting his passions and prejudices, destroy or weaken any possible wish or desire to reform and turn from the error of his way that might perchance be slumbering in his bosom, I would rather study to find out, if possible, the better part of his nature, and make an honest effort in the interest of humanity to save him from the thralldom which, most certainly, awaits him along with the hosts whose lives he is blighting and destroying in the pursuit of a legal, though iniquitous and dishonorable calling.

I would not abuse and villify him as a man. It is worse than useless to do so. It only sinks him lower and lower in the depths of his own shame and degradation and impairs his ability and inclination to reform. And the poor, pitiful, and helpless drunkard! what can we do for him? How shall we contribute anything towards his comfort or his cure of the terrible disease which is so fast destroying his intellectual, moral and physical manhood? Should we pass him by as if he were a soulless beast of the field, left on the dreary wayside to die from the remorseless blasts of the winter's wind? I do not think so. I do not believe that these unfortunates of our race ought to be entirely neglected and left to perish alone and unwept as so many of them do in the slimy, sickening gutters and slums of the city, so much of whose boasted wealth and power has been wrought out by the liquor traffic from the decaying fortunes, desolated homes, and the ruined hopes and aspirations of an honest and unsophisticated yeomanry. Ah! How many of the drunken, falling wrecks of humanity we see around us could tell a true story of their descent from affluence and prosperity to the low estate of a tramp and a vagabond that would be indeed stranger than fiction! Many of them, though clothed in villainous garb, though friendless, powerless and penniless, have within their breasts, though smouldering amid a neglected heap of withering and remorseful remains, the noblest principles and instincts of true manhood. While we may not by our kindness be able to redeem them from the lost and miserable condition into which they have been led by the allurements of the relentless demon into whose power they have fallen, we can at least do something to alleviate their sufferings and to comfort them in their despair. Occasionally the confirmed and apparently hopeless drunkard has been restored to his lost manhood, and if I could only feel and realize that through the influence of my kindness and sympathy I had been instrumental in the permanent restoration of one I should feel amply repaid for every kindly action and sympathetic word I may during life be able to bestow upon that truly pitiable and unfortunate class of our people, whose name to-day is "legion of legions."

I have already in a former chapter suggested that the government ought to make special provision for them. But the great opportunity for the exercise of individual as well as combined effort in behalf of the great cause of temperance is in the preservation of the young men of the country, so many of whom are slowly, but surely, marching onward, not upward, but downward, to the valley and shadow of intellectual, moral, and physical death, keeping pace with the oblivious hosts in whose deadly wake they are unconsciously following. Reader, do you drink intoxicating liquors. If so, let your first effort in behalf of temperance and practical prohibition be upon yourself, and if you find that you are unable to gain the mastery over the spell which binds you to the fatal wine-cup, call in all of the assistance within reach, and pray God to aid you and your friends in saving you from drunkenness and disgrace, before it is everlastingly and eternally too late. If you have yourself gone beyond the dead line and you feel and realize that you are hopelessly lost, then do what you can to atone for your sins and disgrace by warning others of the danger and doing what you can to persuade them to return to sobriety, industry, and usefulness.

Whether you are so far advanced or not, have the manhood, goodness of heart and respect and love for common humanity to refuse to be instrumental in leading others who are unsuspecting in their nature, into the awful condition into which you have fallen. If you must drink yourself, do not for God and humanity's sake, persuade others to do likewise. Rather sneak into the saloon and drink by yourself, and have "all the boys" deride you for selfishness and illiberality, than to be in the least instrumental in the encouragement of another, and especially if he is young and hitherto unpolluted by the vile stuff, to cultivate this dangerous appetite for liquor. If you have been so fortunate as to escape the evil, if you have had the nerve and the resolution to resist the manifold temptations which have beset your pathway and to live a sober man, do not go around over the country disgusting other people with boasting of your triumph. Be not like the pompous Pharisee, who stood up in the most public place he could find, and thanked God that he was not like other men with a heart vile, unworthy, deceitful above all things, and desperately wicked, but rather be like the poor Publican, and while you acknowledge your own frailty and weakness, do what you can, however humble the effort to strengthen others by your own example, and in every way endeavor to reason with and persuade them to forsake the error of their way, live sober, and be useful, happy and contented. Let every effort you make in behalf of sobriety be characterized as it should be prompted by a spirit of love and a sincere regard for the true interests of humanity.

"The harvest is ripe and the laborers are few." There is an abundance of work for every one to do in the great warfare which is before us. No one need to fold his hands and say "there is nothing for me to do." The work of overcoming and destroying this monster evil, this, the greatest enemy of mankind, the devil not excepted, is no child's play. Every true man, woman and child, throughout the length and breadth of this besotted land is expected to do their utmost and entire duty in the struggle. If they will only come to the rescue, there may yet be hope for the ultimate salvation of our people from the clanking fetters of a slavery a thousandfold more galling and intolerable than have ever been forged for the vanquished and oppressed by the tyranny of all ages of the world combined. It was Burns, nature's poet, who said:

> "Man's inhumanity to man
> Makes countless thousands mourn."

This is true, but can man's inhumanity at all compare with the numbers of its sorrowing and mourning victims with the demon alcohol, who is each day of the world's existence making countless millions send up the sad, tearful wail of their pent up sorrow and unutterable despair? Is there left in your bosom, my dear reader, one spark of the love of humanity, a single impulse of self-sacrificing charity, one lingering sentiment of true patriotism? If so, then arouse at once from your lethargic repose and indifference, and go to work with all your might and main in an effort to check the onward march of this dread enemy to every human interest, hope and aspiration. Do what you can, however weak and inconsiderable you may conceive yourself to be, however lightly you may esteem your own personal influence, to stay the dreadful ravages and wide-spreading desolation that mark the progress of the damnable career.

Before closing this chapter I desire to speak briefly of the benefit of consolidated effort that leads me to review the work and influence for good accomplished by the organization and maintenance of temperance socities. The fable of the old man and the sticks is familiar to many, if not all, of my readers, and may serve to illustrate the thought intended to be conveyed in the discussion of this important branch of the subject. An old man who had several sons, none of whom had perhaps ever learned the value of domestic harmony and concert of action, gathered up a large bundle of small sticks, which he bound together with twine. He passed the bundle thus bound together to each of the sons, beginning with the youngest and weakest, and bade them break it if they could. Each in turn gave a trial of his strength, and not one of them was able to break the bundle of sticks. He then unbound it and divided them out among his sons; he told them to break them in pieces. This they accomplished almost without an effort. He then impressed upon them the important lesson which he wished to teach by this simple illustration, the great value of union—the maxim that "in union there is strength." This maxim is particularly true when applied to human action and individual resolution. The greatest cowards often become brave and full of courage when cheered by the presence of others engaged in the same hazardous undertaking. How often was this fact demonstrated upon the battlefields of the late war. There were thousands of soldiers on both sides of the conflict who fought bravely and gallantly, distinguishing themselves on many a bloody field, who, at home, engaged in the peaceful pursuits of life, had not sufficient personal courage and manhood to resent the most flagrant insult or injury; who were everywhere known to be arrant cowards who would not fight single-handed and alone under any circumstances whatever. I know many myself whose cowardice at home was such that every one thought when they went off to the war that they would be certain to desert on the first smell of gun-powder, but who returned covered all over with glory on account of their personal bravery and soldierly bearing. The wonder was, how it could be so, but it is not so hard to understand after all. It is, I think, attributable to the fact that individual resolution and personal courage are strengthened and inspired by the association of others exposed to a common danger. Besides, the great mass of the common soldiery are but followers, and while a man may fight valiantly under the leadership of his captain, he may have none of the elements of a commander himself, and would never fight upon his own personal responsibility. And so it is with the great mass of mankind to-day, and in all ages of the world. There are, and in the very nature of things can be, but few leaders in society in any of its phases, or in any of its enterprises, whether political, social, or moral. The majority are content to be followers. They are ready to take their places in the ranks, and while they may be always criticising the conduct or judgment of their leaders, they have no vaulting ambition to become leaders themselves. With all their complaining they constitute the great body of the common soldiery, and are indispensable to the success of every moral, social, or political revolution. Individually, they will do but little, if anything, of value to the great cause, but organize them into bands and societies, and they are a host. They will fight bravely and effectively for the cause in which they may enlist, and get enough of them together and they will come off victorious.

There is no estimating the good which has been accomplished by the many temperance organizations throughout the length and breadth of the country. I can not undertake to enumerate them, or to give even an epitomized history of their labors in the great cause of temperance reform. But I must speak of the work of one council of the The United Friends of Temperance, with the history of which and its results, I was at one time personally familiar. About the year 1873, when the Texas & Pacific railroad was completed through Kaufman county, a little town sprung up in the north-western part of that county, which was named Forney after a high official of the railroad company. Among the first business houses that went up in the new town, was a saloon of the doggery type. The morals of the neighborhood were by no means good previous to that time, but for a while after the town was started it was everywhere regarded as among the hardest places in North Texas for its size and limited opportunities. It so happened that about the time the town started, a few young men settled there who had for years been consistent and active temperance workers, had long been prominent as members of The United Friends of Temperance. They went to work and gathered together a small band of workers, and organized a council at Forney. They kept it up, increasing the membership to a hundred or more, giving periodical celebrations and exhibitions, and in every way using the society in the education of the people. Prominent of these faithful workers I remember the names of the Shands boys, J. W. Walker, now member of the State

Central Prohibition Committee, and Rev. E. B. Thompson, the latter of whom was perhaps the first among this gallant band. There were many others whose names I do not now call to mind. It was many years before they had worked up such a sentiment against whisky that they felt satisfied that they could carry local option. They brought on the election and carried it by a small majority. There were two saloons in full blast at the time. They closed up and the proprietors moved away. They kept up the council; they kept up the enthusiasm. One year afterwards they carried local option again by an increased majority. To the influence of that one society Forney owes her freedom from whisky and much of her material prosperity, which has been truly phenomenal. In the next chapter I will discuss the local option law and its practical results.

CHAPTER VII.

PROHIBITORY LEGISLATION.

LOCAL OPTION.

The constitution of 1875 has an article or section providing a method for the qualified voters of any town, precinct, or county, to decide for themselves whether or not the sale of intoxicating liquors and medicated bitters producing intoxication shall be permitted in such districts, and makes it incumbent upon the legislature to pass such laws as may be necessary for carrying into effect the provisions of said article of the constitution. This is called the local option law, because the law can only be called into effect at the option of a majority of the people of such locality, which can not embrace a larger scope of territory than that of a single county, whatever may be its area or population. In compliance with the constitutional requirement, the State Legislature at its first session after the adoption of the present constitution passed the general law, which has been in force in Texas since the latter part of the year 1876. From the date of its passage there has been a certain school of lawyers, who have assailed the provisions of the general law as in contravention to the spirit, if not the letter, of the organic law of the land, and have time and again attempted to maintain their position before the appellate courts of our State. They have ably presented before our courts of last resort every conceivable objection that can be urged against the law with a view of destroying its force and operation, and of breaking down every barrier it interposes to the death-dealing sway of the liquor traffic. They have as often been disappointed, and having failed to convince the highest courts of the correctness of their position, they have appealed to the "time-honored principles of the Democratic party," and to the prejudices of our people. They go out upon the stump and make long-winded speeches, reminding the dear people who have so long been devoted to the very name of democracy, that their fathers, their grand-fathers, and ancestors reaching back to the days of Christopher Columbus, enjoyed the inalienable, God-given right to sell whisky and scatter abroad the seeds of internal discord and destruction, which have produced in abundance a crop of wars, misfortunes, and miseries beyond the power of human imagination to conceive or to describe. These legal wiseacres and professional demagogues with their *quasi* legal and political sophistry, have done much towards establishing in the minds of our very best citizens the strangest legal paradox known to an enlightened jurisprudence, the unconstitutionality of the constitution. Nor is this the only glaring and flagrant inconsistency in their high-sounding arguments in opposition to the law and in favor of personal liberty, every infringement upon which is an interference with a man's natural right to do as he pleases, regardless of the rights of his fellow-men. The argument leads us at one step to an absurdity. It leads us at once to the abrogation of all law, the instantaneous return to hopeless and inevitable anarchy. The very object of all law is to interfere with personal liberty. What other possible object could it have?

If personal liberty is to be the supreme law of the land, what can be the need of constitutions, what need of statutes? If a man can plant himself upon his natural right to do as he pleases, and measure the constitutionality of a law, though it be a part of the organic structure of that instrument itself, by the standard of his own perverted conscience, and of his own crude notions of absolute personal liberty, then, indeed, we are without law and without government. We are in the very midst of anarchy. and there is no possible escape from it. This may seem to some a desperate conclusion, but I here challenge the whole array of these great constitutional, personal liberty expounders, from the least to the greatest, to show how this conclusion of the argument can be escaped? I dare say that they will treat the challenge with indifference and contempt. They will not condescend to reply to one of so humble a rank in the profession as the author. They will treat him as they have many others, as a foeman altogether unworthy of their steel. They will refuse to "fight down hill," as did once a man of distinction who was invited to settle a dispute by the established code of honor; another one of those rights guaranteed to our fore-fathers by the constitution of personal liberty. But I am not writing this book to bring myself into the contemptous notice of such men. I am writing it for another and an entirely different purpose. I am writing at this time to awaken to an active spirit of investigation the slumbering thought and intellectual vigor of the masses of the people, and especially the young men of the country, who have gone to sleep upon this great question under the soothing odors of the deadly upas tree of personal liberty.

The saloon keepers and their deluded sympathizers are continually saying that prohibition does not prohibit. They also assert that it is ruinous to the prosperity of a town or county which adopts it. They give as a reason for the latter assertion that people who have dry goods and groceries to buy and cotton to sell, always want to go to trade and market their produce to a place where they can get whisky. That the good old farmers of the country who are the very bone and sinews of the prosperity of the towns and the cities are so clamorous for an opportunity to get drunk, that they will withdraw their trade from a market where restrictions are laid upon the glorious privilege of making beasts and madmen out of themselves and their boys. This is a very fine sample of consistency. But I will pursue that part of the argument no further. I propose now to demonstrate to the satisfaction of every fair-minded and unprejudiced reader that even local option will prohibit a little. To what extent state or general prohibition will probably prohibit, will be fully discussed in its order. The idea that either will absolutely prohibit is chimerial, the distorted conception of a disordered imagination. No sound, practical thinker ever entertained such an idea.

That there are a few fanatics who suppose that it will, almost in the twinkling of an eye, dry up the poisonous fountains of double-distilled iniquity, and transform all the constitutional drunkards and confirmed inebriates into temperance lecturers and models of sobriety and purity, is but an instance of the extreme weakness of human understanding, distorted by an irrepressible zeal which mocks at the impossible. That there are a few "sure enough" cranks in the world, we all know too well, but if there is any subject on earth on which a man is altogether justifiable in becoming a crank and fanatic, it is upon the subject of prohibition and temperance. But I must get back to the subject of the efficacy of local option in the prevention of drunkenness. Let us reason upon this subject as persons having some knowledge of human nature, though we may have had no better text book from which to gain such knowledge than our own personal impulses and individual experiences. You are a young man, just entering upon the threshold of your chosen business or profession of life. We will suppose that you have had the benefit of reasonably correct moral training in childhood and youth. You have often been warned by your good father and mother of the evils of drunkenness and dissipation. You have often heard them while on their bended knees, pray God that you may be guided by His fatherly care into the pathways of rectitude and usefulness, that you may be ever strengthened by his power in every effort to resist temptation to vice, and especially that you may be able to shun the deadly enchantment of the poisonous wine cup. You have all had sufficient warning upon the subject to teach you that a drunkard's life is a shame and a disgrace, although he may commit no criminal offense cognizable by the penal laws of the country. You may wonder at times why the law does not interpose to check the drunkard's ungodly and wicked career, and remove his demoralizing example from the association of the young men of the country. You have been taught from the earliest dawn of your intellectual activity to fear and respect the laws of the land. You have learned that it is a terrible thing to be arraigned before the courts of the country on a criminal charge. If you have been reasonably well trained, you can not help shuddering at the very thought of being called to answer a prosecution for a criminal offense, although it may be nothing more than a trifling misdemeanor. You tremble at the possibility of being falsely accused of a crime, and even of being forced to officiate in a criminal case in the capacity of a witness. Assuming this much, we will suppose that the morning on which you attain your majority you bid adieu to your anxious mother and father, and go out into the world alone and unaided by their counsel and constant advice and protection, with many tearful longings and strange misgivings, to enter upon the struggle of actual life. You go to the nearest town or village for the purpose of getting employment or waiting for "something to turn up." You then find on every side gilded saloons with a constant flow of misguided humanity into and out of their gaping doorways, which stand at all times wide open for the admission of the thirsty or the curious.

You meet as you pass by a crowd of rollicking, thoughtless boys with whom you are acquainted. Some one of them will be certain to say: "Let's go in and take something." You remember the words of your father and mother, perhaps the gentle voice of a sweet and loving sister, as she sings "Don't go near the bar-room, Brother," and then you reply, "Please excuse me." But it is of no use; they will not excuse you. If they should, it would be with an insulting remark. They would ask you what grievance you had against them, or any one of their number, that is so serious as to prompt a refusal to unite with them in a social drink. You have much regard for their feelings. You do not wish to provoke them to anger or leave them with the erroneous impression that you are angry with them, or that you feel yourself above them. You have never been taught that it is any great wrong to take just one little drink, especially under such embarrassing circumstances. You finally yield and enter for the first time the doorway of your ultimate ruin. It is needless to go on with the history. It is but the history of a tramp and a vagabond, the history of countless millions of our race. So much for saloons; so much for license.

But, suppose that when you go to that town or village, you find no such dens of iniquity, no such pitfalls of temptation? Suppose there should be a superabundance of drug stores for the population, which seem to thrive and grow rich regardless of the fact that there is no sickness in the country and no apparent demand for medicinal commodities. Suppose, for the sake of the argument, that every one of these drug stores is but a sham, and a device for dealing in whisky in defiance of the law, and suppose that in each one of them there is an abortion, who pretends to be a practicing physician, ready at all times to prostitute the honor which he is supposed to have, but has not, to the base purposes for which he is employed for the paltry consideration of what mean whisky he can drink? Suppose you should, perchance, meet the same crowd of boys that you did under the circumstances above described. Suppose, which would not be at all probable, one of the number would suggest that all hands go to this infamous disciple of Æsculapius just mentioned and get a prescription for the drinks. You would be sure to reply, "I am not sick," and no persuasion would lead you into a participation in the commission of a criminal offense or into taking the risk of being caught up as a witness in the establishment of the guilt of the parties liable to the penalty. The importation of jugs would be almost exclusively confined to that element of society, which has long since passed beyond the hope of redemption. Even among the class known as hopeless and incorrigible drunkards and especially among those who have not lost every feeling of self-respect, you find men who have the very highest regard for their families, and who would not under any circumstances do anything that would mar the feelings or impair in the least the social and domestic happiness of their innocent loved ones.

There are, of course, some exceptions to the rule, but it will be found oftener the case than otherwise that the drunkard loses respect for himself and every other object that binds him to a miserable existence before he gives up all care and anxiety for the well-being of his pleading wife and innocent children. When the thoughts of the feelings and interests of those who are by nature nearest and dearest to his heart, cease to woo him to a better life, he is, indeed, an abandoned wretch, totally unfit for the least of the duties and responsibilities of a husband or a father, or to enjoy the privileges of citizenship. Until he gives up every thought and care for the happiness of his own household, he will never consent that his home shall be made the favorite resort for his drunken associates. When saloons are in full blast, and when every temptation is offered to induce him to join in a beastly carousal, he will often yield to the promptings of his too generous nature and to the importunacy of his friends and go in and engage with them in the degrading pleasures of dissipation and debauchery. But remove these gilded hells of unspeakable iniquity, and leave him with no other facility with which to gratify his perverted taste for strong drink than the importation of jugs from distant markets or sections of the country, and it will be found that he will not drink so much, and that he will be under circumstances which will go a great way to restrain whatever tendencies he may have to drink to excess and to drunkenness. We will suppose that the saloons are closed, and that although local option or other prohibitory law does not prohibit as they say, he is forced by the cravings of his appetite to either patronize one of these professional prostitutes who calls himself a doctor, and to get his bogus prescriptions filled at one of those local option drug stores, or to send off to a neighboring town or county and get his daily portion of liquid hell-fire by the jug or the barrel. He will, if he has any respect for the laws of his country, prefer the latter alternative. He sends off and gets it by the quantity. When it arrives he will generally store it away in his closet rather than rent for himself a house in town for that purpose. It is quite probable that he will take several drinks a day, and it may be expected that he will occasionally drink too much, and, possibly get drunk. How often do you suppose he would go down into town and gather up all the drunkards and professional dead-beats with whom he is in the habit of drinking in the saloons, and take them to his house to insult his good wife, destroy the morals of his son, and pollute the very fountains of his domestic tranquility and happiness? He will not do it; he would not dare to take such an ungodly crew into his parlor, and if he did so, that good wife of his who has borne so long and patiently with his own drunkenness and depravity, would be justified in setting the dogs on them, and if she is not almost an angel in her spirit of forbearance, she would most certainly do it. It may be safely assumed that the jug traffic would be almost entirely confined to the hopeless drunkards who have no power to resist the appetite which urges them onward to the portals of ignominious death. They could not possibly be made worse drunkards than they are, and the check would be placed upon the young men of the country who have not become confirmed in the habit would be very perceptible in a very short space of time.

Another class of imbeciles would thereby be driven from their customary haunts, and society would be to a great extent, relieved of a nuisance which is next to intolerable. This class comprises the countless hosts of dead-beats, tramps and professional "bummers," who hang around saloons waiting for the broad-gauged, generous, well-to-do drunkards to treat them. Not one out of a hundred of them would ever get drunk enough to raise a disturbance, if he had to depend on the jug traffic for his whisky. He would never have enough money to purchase the necessary postage stamp to send off the order, much less to pay for the goods and express charges on their arrival. Every town in the State is to-day full of these shiftless characters, and while they are first-class consumers of the vile stuff, and would be beneficial, perhaps to the public, if the supply of the article were limited to the capacity of their stomachs and they were entitled first to be served. As it is they are worse than the very worst of public nuisances with which society is infested. I have been informed that there are saloon keepers in the land, who actually encourage them to loaf around their places of business for no other purpose than to contribute to the net proceeds of the crowd-treats, the usual and customary penalty imposed upon every block-head who gets the worst of a joke. I do not know this to be the truth, but I do know that those worthless vagabonds are generally to be found hovering around saloons and to see one sober is the exception to the rule, although they are at all times wholly insolvent and impecunions. They never pay a cent, nor miss a drink. They can get drunk and paint the whole side of a town in all colors when they can't get money to purchase a bowl of soup to supply the cravings of hunger. The jug traffic, or any sort of traffic, would certainly improve their self-respect, even though they should, perchance, be able to raise the necessary capital to go into the business on a very small scale. So much for the local option drug-store ; so much for the terrible jug traffic, which is all there is or can be in it, if our judgment of human character and our eyes do not deceive us.

Before closing this chapter as I was about to do, I desire to speak briefly of a class of people who above all others perhaps will usually be benefited by local option or other prohibitory legislation : that is the colored population of our country.

That there should be a natural prejudice in the minds of the ignorant and uncharitable classes of the whites against this truly unfortunate race of people is by no means surprising. When we consider the fact that they had been from time immemorial until the close of the late war, regarded as a class unfit for the blessings of personal freedom and as being but little if any higher in the scale of animated existence than the ordinary beasts of burden; that this view of their mission on earth was strenuously taught in all of the Southern schools of morality and even of theology and religion, we could not reasonably expect anything else than that they should yet be regarded with the greatest indifference, especially by the unthinking and unprogressive masses. This prejudice, however, is dying out by degrees, and while it will never be conceded by the whites (and ought not to be) that the negro race is the equal of the white or the Caucasian. Our fair-minded people are beginning to realize that the colored people are entitled to a place in the great family of mankind—could we ever realize that the poor negro is not in the least responsible for the conditions of his birth, nor for the chains which for so long held his body down to menial servitude while his simple mind was fettered by the worst type of ignorance and superstition, we would feel more like helping him to rise to a higher plane of respectability and usefulness, than throwing obstacles in the way of his intellectual and moral advancement. I believe that the more enlightened our people become upon this subject the more charitable and sympathetic they become in their feelings towards this naturally inferior race. That prohibitory legislation will benefit them there can be no sort of question, although it should be conceded that there are other classes who would be able to evade the operation of the law. There are no colored physicians to prescribe whisky for their sick or "their well stomachs," and there will be found but few "whited sepulchers" in the form of practicing physicians of the white race low enough down to thus pander to the perverted appetites of the negroes. The jug traffic with the negroes would be much less in proportion to their number than with the white race. It is unnecessary here to go over the reasons which must from what has already been said upon that branch of the subject be evident to the mind of the reader. The negro population would do but little drinking away from the low dives which they are accustomed to frequent in the towns and the cities. Break up the dives and you practically destroy drunkenness among the negroes.

A common objection urged against local option, not only by those who favor prohibition, but by those who bitterly oppose it, is, that it does not prohibit, but it is frequently stated that it rather increases than checks the spread of the evil it is intended to suppress. The saloon keepers go down into their phlethoric pockets, and put up thousands of their ill-gotten gain to prevent the adoption of the law in a town, precinct or county, and then proclaim upon the highways and from the hustings that the law, when adopted, is entirely inoperative, and even worse than a dead letter upon the statute books. As before stated, I am bewildered when I attempt to reconcile the action with the statement. If it do not prohibit, but rather encourage the consumption of their hellish commodities, then why do they not favor, rather than oppose, local option? Have they become so much interested in the welfare of the country, and so watchful over the interests of society at large; so tenderly sympathetic in their natures as to sacrifice their own interests and the success of their business, upon the altar of sobriety and temperance? Temperance workers should not allow themselves to be deceived for a moment by the false statements and worse than fallacious arguments of such men, whose very victuals and clothes are dependent upon the insatiate cravings of the torturing appetites they themselves have long fed with liquid fires of damnation. Men, whose business depends upon the spread of an evil, are not to be relied on for advice in the adoption of a plan to suppress it. Much less can they be relied on to devise a remedy for the destruction of a vice which they have given much of their life's labor and thought to develop or create. A man who can so divest himself of the innate selfishness of humanity as to sincerely struggle to break down and destroy his own chosen calling or profession, is too good a man to sell whisky; too good for this world; too good to be contaminated by contact with "this wicked and perverse generation." He ought to be permitted to climb the "golden stairs" and enter the gateways of the new Jerusalem before he has an opportunity to fall under the weight of temptation. No reasonable, thinking man, who has ever studied the first lessons of frail human nature, will believe any such pretensions. Put it down as a fact, beyond dispute, that the man who will voluntarily degrade himself by going into the saloon business, there to deal out liquid damnation by the drink or by the quantity, will do nothing, intentionally, which could possibly contribute to the suppression of drunkenness or any milder form of intemperance. He will sometimes say that he dislikes to see men drink whisky, while at the same time he keeps his sink-hole of iniquity wide open and yawning for victims through all hours of the night.

Nor is that all; if the authorities will let him, he invokes the bewitching power of music to charm by the "harmony of sweet sounds" the unwary and unsuspecting who may happen to pass within range of his deadly portals. In front of the bar he keeps a screen to hide from the idle gaze, of the curious world the forms and features of his misguided, self-accused and guilt-stricken customers; in the rear he keeps free lunches, pool tables, billiards, dominoes and dice boxes, and every other species of gambling devices, the exhibition of which is not positively forbidden by statute. Up stairs he keeps keno, roulette, faro, monte, and all manner of gambling tables and "contraptions," manufactured expressly for the purpose of systematic robbery and theft. Upon every street corner he has a bloated representative whose business it is to ensnare and rope in the unskillful and unsuspecting young men of the country when they come in with their cotton, the well-earned reward of their whole year's arduous labor. These professional swindlers and blacklegs approach a young man who has disposed of his cotton and received his money from the buyer; they pretend that they know him, or offer to do him a kindness; finally work themselves into his confidence, and entice him into their dens of robbery and villainy, where a few drinks must be taken as a prerequisite to admittance up the stairway to the chamber of robbery and all sorts of villainy. Talk about one of the keepers of these dens, which are so common in every city and town of importance, doing anything to stay the murderous hand of the demon to whose ravages he owes all of his wealth and power. It is the very embodiment of absurdity. And yet there are hosts of good, though simple minded people, who believe it all; who suffer themselves to be led to the ballot box and voted in the interest of whisky, because they are told by those foulmouthed saloon keepers that prohibition does not prohibit. Some newspaper whose editor has been "rocked in the cradle of personal liberty," and who knows about as much of constitutions and constitutional limitations as a yoke of oxen, publishes a tirade against local option, or a bogus communication from a bogus correspondent, whose bogus friend claims to have been in Atlanta, Georgia, or in Rockwall or Forney, Texas, and heard some bogus individual say that he heard that it did not prohibit in those places, and that settles the question. I have heard of many of these ubiquitous individuals prowling around over the country hunting up imaginary instances of the failure of such laws to prohibit. One day they are gathering statistics in Maine; next day they are in Georgia, Kansas, or Texas, and it is not unfrequently the case that they are in all of these and a half dozen other places at the same time. But when you undertake to locate them they are nowhere to be found in the land of the living.

A certain class of mercenary papers publish anonymous letters from nobody in particular, together with their unfavorable comments upon the prohibitory legislation in question (for which they get the usual sum of twenty cents a line for first insertion), and these communications and comments are copied extensively by that portion of the country press which is in sympathy with the whisky element, and no further evidence is required to establish the proposition that prohibitory laws are worse than a failure. Why should a wholesale whisky dealer be concerned about the manner of selling liquor in the different States, counties, precincts, or cities so he is able to supply it by the large quantity to those engaged in the traffic either as saloon keepers or druggists? Why is it that he will spend thousands of dollars to buy up congressmen and others who are supposed to have large influence, and to corrupt the ballot-box for the purpose of defeating a measure which not only does not prohibit the sale and use of his merchandise, but actually increases his trade and contributes to his profits? What is the difference to the wholesale dealer whether his moral and social dynamite is retailed by the licensed saloon or by the much cursed and abused local option drug stores? It can not be material to his interest, and if not, why should he organize himself into a stupendous liquor dealers' association and subscribe millions of money to oppose the progress of an enlightened public sentiment in an honest effort to destroy the evil? Above I have mentioned his liberality in the purchase of congressmen and others in high political standing and authority, and in this connection I desire to mention a "rumor" which went the rounds of the papers a year or two ago, and which perhaps some of my readers have forgotten. The liquor or beer dealers' association of the United States of America has for some years kept a paid representative and lobbyist at Washington whose duty, it seems, has been to feel of the representatives of the people upon that question and to use every legitimate means to win them over to the cause of whisky, beer, and the devil. About the time above stated this lobbyist, whose name I now forget, nor is it material, made a report in writing to his constituency, the association aforesaid, in which he positively stated that he had secured the co-operation of a number of congressmen in the Southern States, Texas among the number, in the suppression of every attempt upon the part of the people to check the growth of their business by prohibitory legislation or otherwise. He stated that he had acomplished it by threatening the Democratic party with the power he represented in the next presidential campaign, giving them to understand that if they did not "dance to his music," he would lead all of his inebriate host into the ranks of the Republican party and play havoc with the Democratic party by the election of a republican president in 1888. This alleged report was published in quite a number of papers in Texas, and the only answer I ever saw impeaching or attempting to impeach it was published in the Galveston *News*, not over the signature of any Texas congressman, but as an editorial, and that answer consisted of a general denial and a call for strict proof.

It was substantially that the report of this representative was not in any way binding, that it was not conclusive of the matters it contained, and, admitting that he had made such a report which was not denied, so far as I know, by any one, it was insisted that it was but hearsay evidence and not sufficient to convict. It was expected that certain wise men of our State, who ought to be familiar with every thing that happened in and about Washington city at that time, would at least put in some sort of an answer either denying or justifying the alleged conspiracy against the good people of of Texas. If any judgment was rendered upon the indictment, it was without a plea. At any rate, the whole thing was hushed up and soon forgotten by the great mass of the people. If it were not true, it ought to have been branded as a falsehood by those whose good names were assailed: if it were true, then it necessarily follows that not only the Democratic party, but the government itself is practically in the hands of the Liquor or Beer Dealers' Association of America. If that institution can dictate to the leaders of a great party how they shall demean themselves at home, and what stand they shall take upon so great a question as that of State prohibition, or local option, or any other measure seriously affecting the best interests of their constituents, then indeed is this stupendous combination of immeasurable iniquity supreme in the land, and we had just as well accept the inevitable. No. It can not be so. I can not believe that every drop of true patriotism has gone out of the veins of the descendants of so noble an ancestry. I can not believe that the people of Texas or of the South, as devotedly as they love the name of Democracy and the memory of its heroic struggles for constitutional liberty, will ever even for the sake of that name, or any other empty sound, submit to the sway of a tyrant, whose despotic career out-Herods all of the Herods of antiquity.

There is an old and familiar saying that "the proof of the pudding is in chewing the bag," or words to that effect. When Robert Fulton applied the power of steam to the propulsion of his rude and unshapely water-craft, the great scientific wiseacres of the land said that "it would'nt work." When the great Morse conceived the idea of the transmission of messages by lightning, they said that "it wouldn't work." When the intrepid and tireless Christopher Columbus took up an idea that a new continent might be discovered, the wise men of Europe thought—that "it wouldn't work." They would have willingly taken an oath that none of these visionary schemes would work, and not only these great pioneers in the field of invention, but many others, scarcely less distinguished in science, were in their day pronounced cranks or fanatics. And so it will ever be. The great masses of mankind will cling to the errors and follies of the past, and mock at every effort to correct them, oppose every step in the march of scientific progress or social advancement. The great mass of the people in every age and country are averse to innovation. They are ever disposed to let well enough alone, and they want every one else to do likewise. Demagogues feast upon this weakness. They are to-day trusting to it as they fight valiantly in the motley ranks of the devil and alcohol. Like the world was by Fulton, Morse and others in their day, they say that local option "won't work."

My purpose is to show by actual experience that it will work and that it does work admirably whenever its supporters have the manhood and courage to do their duty in seeing that it is enforced. Notwithstanding the assertion of those who are opposed to prohibition that it has been a total failure in Atlanta, Georgia, I am prepared to say that it has done much in the way of suppressing the evil in that city. Some months ago I took upon myself the trouble to investigate the question for my own personal satisfaction. I wrote a letter to Hon. Geo. B. Hillyer at that time mayor of the city, and in answer, he said substantially, that the measure had been a success; that, while there was a considerable class of the people who would have their accustomed whisky and would send off and import it by the jug; that while others would obtain it in other ways made possible by the law; its effect upon the young men of the city and surrounding country was quite beneficial. He said that, while he much preferred absolute State prohibition as the best, he regarded local option as the next. In addition to the statements made in his letter, he gave such statistics as proved beyond question that the law was a great improvement on the license system. Coming down to our own State, I am able to speak to some extent from my own personal observation. In a former chapter I had occasion to mention the little town of Forney in the northwestern portion of Kaufman county in which I have until quite recently lived since my first immigration to Texas, something over thirty years ago. If there is any people on earth that I do know, it is the people of Kaufman county, and especially those who live in what is known as Forney precinct. I sowed most of my wild oats among them, and it was excellent soil for that kind of produce in those days, beginning with a few years before the civil war, and extending to the years of 1877 or 1878. In 1873 the Texas & Pacific Railroad was completed through the county. A little town sprang up in the midst of as wild a set of people as could have been found in the State of Texas or any where else within the range of civilization. I have a right to speak thus, because I have been one of them myself. But, for all their wildness and dissipation, they were in the main a noble, a generous, and, with some exceptions, an honest people. The first house that was built was devoted to the service of the liquor traffic. It was run by the most prominent man in that section of the country, a man who had accommodated every body, whose friends—and they were numerous—virtually swore by his name and his word. He was looked upon as the chief of the tribe. He was nicknamed "The chief of the Tonkaways," and the name seemed to be very appropriate.* He was soon wrecked and on a cold, wintry night in the latter part of 1875, he started to his home after a protracted carousal, fell down upon the railroad track; soon afterwards a passenger train came along, ran over his body, and launched him into eternity in the twinkling of an eye, leaving the scattered remnants of his once manly form to be gathered up the next morning by his disconsolate friends. He was a man of a kind and generous heart, devoted to his friends, and the author calls to mind the recollection of a thousand personal favors and words of encouragement bestowed upon him in the years of his struggle with adversity.

His influence was wide-spread. He did not intend to injure his fellow man, but, while I cherish his memory for his goodness of heart and for his uniform kindness to me, I must, in justice to the truth, say of him that he and his saloon did much toward sowing the seeds of dissipation among the people of that little town and community. While it lasted, horse-racing,

---

* Bailey Daugherty, an early settler of Kaufman County.

fighting, gambling, shooting, and all manner of disturbances were of every day occurrence. Every Saturday brought on a perfect pandemonium. The justice's court was always in session, and engaged in the trial of those misdemeanors which were the offspring of drunkenness and dissipation. I have already spoken of the organization of a temperance council, and the valiant struggle made by some young men who settled there soon after the town was located. If there ever was a place that needed a large dose of reformation to work off the accumulated iniquity of a few years of demoralization, that place was certainly Forney; and I say it in all kindness for her people and her enterprises. Local option was carried. The saloons "folded their tents like the Arabs, and silently stole away." They went, "and stood not upon the order of their going." Nor has Forney from that day to this good hour had anything resembling a saloon. The temperance element have kept themselves organized, and while there has been an occasional importation of jugs, the moral revolution has been practically complete. The population and wealth of the town and precinct have increased in more than tenfold greater proportion than any other in the county since the adoption of the law. The people have been ever peaceful, prosperous and happy. Local option is a fixture. There has not been an attempt to repeal it for nearly ten years. It has been a success.

Another instance is the county of Rockwall. If you don't believe that the sentiment of Rockwall county is overwhelmingly in favor of its maintainence after a ten years trial, go over there and start a saloon or a local option drug store, and sell whisky in violation of the letter or spirit of the law. You will get the maximum punishment every time a jury of representative men get a whack at you. Not long since a saloon man located in Rockwall, and hung out the sign, "Dealer in Drugs, Medicines, etc." Having purchased a few patent medicines and enough bottles labeled all over with the technical names known to the intricate nomenclature of *materia medica*, the meaning of not one of which he could even give a respectable guess at, he started out to make his long deferred fortune by selling liquor in violation of the law. When it came to paying his license taxes to the State, county and city, he maintained that local option was in force. When indicted for selling whisky in violation of its provisions he stultified himself by insisting that it had never been legally adopted. The author in connection with his partner, Mr. Montrose, was employed by a large number of good citizens of the county to aid in the prosecution. There was no trouble whatever in convicting in every case, and in each one that was tried the highest penalty was assessed by the jury. One of the parties resorted to a trial on *habeas corpus*, and had the privelege of lying in jail for several weeks. He is "at the present writing" languishing in jail awaiting the decision of the Court of Appeals upon the question of the solidity of the law, or rather the alleged irregularity of the proceedings of county commissioner's court in its adoption by the people. Before this book is completed and published, the case* will be decided; but whatever the opinion of the Appellate Court may be upon the question, the people of Rockwall county are firmly established in their determination to suppress whisky, and they will give it another trial besides casting nearly a solid vote for the proposed Constitutional Amendment. Let other counties follow the example.

---

*Ex-Parte Sublett, Austin Term, 1887. Reversed and dismissed because of irregularities in the adoption of the law.

CHAPTER VIII.

PROHIBITORY LEGISLATION.

STATE PROHIBITION—GENERAL DISCUSSION OF THE SUBJECT.

I come now to discuss the living, tangible issue which is now before the people of Texas. It is with much diffidence and distrust that I undertake so weighty and difficult a task. It is heavily fraught with responsibility, because upon the decision of this vital question by our people at the ensuing election perhaps depends the eternal destiny of thousands of immortal souls. On that day ever to be remembered with blessings or curses, we are to cast the horoscope of the lives, and decide the fate of multiplied thousands of our own generation and of the generations to come after us. There are some who treat this momentous question with the utmost indifference. There are those who look upon it as a huge joke gotten up for the gratification of a few cranks, hypochondriacs and hysterical women. There are certain prominent newspapers in the country that indulge in all sorts of ridicule and puerile flippancy, when they take occasion to refer to the undemocratic action of a Democratic Legislature in allowing the people the pitiful privilege of governing themselves long enough to engraft upon the organic law of the State by a popular vote a principle for which they have so long pleaded and petitioned in vain. As often as they have heretofore besought their supposed servants, but real masters, at the State capital to grant them this modest request, they have been rebuked for their impertinence. Petitions almost a mile long, signed by the very best of men of the State, and Democrats at that, have been insultingly thrown in the waste-basket of the solons, or summarily thrown aside in the deference to the clamors of corrupt schemers and unscrupulous political jobbers ; and the wily and insiduous power of ruin has generally found a medium through which to lay its blighting hand and withering clutches upon every embryo movement having in view the relief of the people from the ravages of the red-eyed demon of intemperance. It is well remembered that during the last days of the Nineteenth Legislature, a bill was passed by both houses of that body amending the local option law, making it possible to punish by adequate fine and imprisonment that loathsome class of physicians who so often have been known to issue prescriptions by the wholesale for the benefit of whisky dealers sailing under the colors of an honorable calling. The amendment failed to materialize. The committee whose duty it was to look after the disposition of the bill after passage, charged the clerks with spiriting it away, which is but another name for stealing. The clerks claimed to be innocent of the charge, the matter was hushed up, and what became of the bill is to-day an unsolved mystery, so far as I have ever been informed. That it was suppressed through the criminal agency of the whisky element there can not be the least question. That it was done for the purpose of preventing local option from prohibiting, is not doubted.

But whatever may be the sins of the Nineteenth legislature and its officers, whatever complaints may have been justly made by the people against its predecessors, some of whom were, indeed, "a motley crew," living, breathing masses of political corruption, the Twentieth ought to be held in the highest esteem for the resolution and courage displayed by its members in submitting to the people the proposed constitutional amendment, which is, according to the opinion of the senator from Guadalupe "as innocent of democracy as the devil is of pure and unadulterated religion." In that act they have acknowledged the right of the people to petition their representatives and have construed that right as embracing a corresponding duty on the part of the representatives to respect the petition when presented.

Their predecessors never conceived that there was an inseparable relationship existing between the right of the people and the duty of the representatives. But, to pass on to the merits of the question before us, that of the adoption or rejection of State prohibition.

By the passage of the resolution submitting the amendment, the qualified voters of Texas are given the right to decide whether or not the legislature shall be given the power and that it shall be made its special duty at its next session thereafter to pass a law declaring unlawful the manufacture or sale of intoxicating liquors with some necessary exceptions, and to provide adequate penalties for the violation of such law.

As the constitution now stands, no such law can be passed by the Legislature, and any attempt to do so would be obnoxious to that provision in the Constitution which provides for local prohibition by votes of the people and perhaps other clauses not necessary to discuss.

If a majority voting at the election in August next shall cast their ballots in favor of the amendment, a State prohibitory law will be enacted in the spring of 1889 and possibly earlier, should the Governor call a special session, which is not probable, and the saloons will all have to go hence about the first of July following, perhaps a little earlier, and may be a month or so later. All those who are engaged in the sale of liquors as a beverage and all who have money or property invested or tied up in the business will have fair warning and ample time to drink up or dispose of all of their whisky and kill off the greater number of their best customers and themselves if they conclude that they are unfit for any kind of respectable business, before the law can be put into operation. In that regard State prohibition is a decided improvement on local option. It is preferable in this, that when the State passes a general law upon the subject, there is no chance "to get behind the returns," as is permitted in cases of prosecutions for violation of the local option law.

In a prosecution under the latter the State assumes the burden of proving that the law was properly adopted; that is, that a petition in due form of law was presented; that it was signed by the requisite number of qualified voters; that the prescribed notice was given by publication or by posting; that presiding officers of the election precincts were duly appointed and commissioned; that the election was actually held; that the returns were properly made out and filed; that the Commissioners' Court counted the vote and entered an order declaring the result, and the passage of the law; and if a majority are found to be in favor of the law, and that legal notice was given informing the saloon keepers and all other persons that the law had been passed and that they must desist from the further exercise of their personal liberty to scatter death and damnation in the section of country embraced by the order, unless it is done on the prescription of a practicing physician certifying upon honor that it is necessary as a medicine in cases of actual sickness. In almost every case irregularities are found to exist and in a great many instances they have been held of such a character as to invalidate the law. In that case the prisoner goes free, and by paying up his State and county license, he may like the dog "return to his vomit," if he desires to do so.

The first great question which presents itself to our consideration in the discussion before us is, is it right for a majority of the people of a State to engraft upon the organic law of such State a clause having in view the absolute prohibition of the liquor traffic? The next question in order is that of expediency, that is, admitting that State prohibition is right in principle, will its adoption redound to the best interests of the people at large? Will it tend to promote the welfare and general prosperity of our State morally, socially, or financially? Will it add to or detract from our material progress? Taking every thing together, will it be beneficial or detrimental to the material interests of the State? The opposition interposes the objection that such a law is sumptuary in its character and is an unwarranted interference with personal liberty. I have already discussed at sufficient length, I hope, the personal liberty part of the objection in the chapter devoted to local option and a repetition of the argument is not necessary. Is the objection maintainable on the ground that prohibitory laws are sumptuary in their character, and therefore contrary to the spirit of our American institutions?

A sumptuary law is one that has for its object the regulation and restriction of personal expenses, and may refer to any character of luxury whatever which demands for its support a reckless or unnecessary expenditure of money. A sumptuary law may attempt to prescribe the amount of money you may appropriate to the support of your table and to regulate the costliness, or even texture, of your apparel. It may have for its object the establishment and forcible maintenance of a condition of entire social equality among all sorts and classes of people. It is easily to be seen that a law having such objects in view are not only wrong in principle, but hurtful and injurious in their operation. They are contrary to nature herself. In construing laws, whether they be organic or statutory, the object of the law-making power must be looked to rather than to the peculiar phraseology. They must be liberally, rather than literally or strictly construed, that they may accomplish the purposes for which they are enacted. If the object to be attained is one falling within the purview of legislation, and in no way obnoxious to any constitutional limitation or restriction, the courts will go a long way to uphold it, although it may be defective in its language, and apparently harsh and oppressive in some cases. If the object of a law should satisfactorily appear to the courts to be sumptuary in its character, they would be justifiable in holding it inoperative and void. If the only object of a prohibitory enactment appears to be the regulation of personal expenses, and to reduce mankind to a state of perfect social equality, in spite of themselves, it ought to be ignored by the courts, and no man ought ever to suffer the penalties prescribed for its violation. And right here is the distinction which many of the ablest men of our country have failed or refused to consider. They insist that if the State can legally and justly prohibit the manufacture and sale of intoxicating liquors, it can, upon the same principle, prohibit you from eating bread and drinking coffee or from the enjoyment of any table or other comforts whatever. It appears easily to be seen that the object of prohibitory legislation is not to interfere with individual profligacy, or to restrain in the least the natural desire to live well and dress decently and respectably. Its object is rather found to be precisely the opposite; that is, to aid and encourage all men in this laudable ambition: to remove from our fair State the greatest obstacle in the way of so many of our people in their efforts to attain them and be respectable and happy.

Nor is this the main object of such laws. The experience of mankind fully demonstrates, and no one will for a moment dispute it, that intoxicating liquor is descructive and dangerous to society at large ; that while a man may be a gormandizer and fill himself up with unwholesome victuals ; that while he may go continually dressed in the costliest "purple and fine linen," and yet not become vicious, blood-thirsty and dangerous, he can not fill up his stomach with " busthead," "tangle-foot," or any other kind of liquid malice aforethought, without becoming dangerous to society and oftentimes the terror of his best friends on earth, for whose life-blood he becomes peculiarly thirsty. He becomes a raving madman, and often goes about "like a roaring lion, seeking whom he may devour." When in that fearfully insane condition, he is apt to commit any crime whatever and most frequently satisfied with nothing less than murder. The wife of his bosom is not safe in his presence, his children hide from his terrible aspect, his best friends dare not approach him : he is crazy. He commits murder with apparent deliberation; he is restrained of his liberty and forced to become sober, when the knowledge of his awful deed first dawns upon his mind. He is afterwards put upon his trial for the offense ; he proves by a number of creditable witnesses that he was wholly unconscious of the act ; the law in its humanity says that a criminal intent is an essential ingredient in every offense and indispensable to legal conviction. The case is beyond the reach of penal statutes, no system of laws can be sustained on principles of common justice and humanity that provides for the punishment of an act committed by a person, while in a state of unconsciousness or insanity from whatever cause it may be produced, unless the act was previously contemplated and the insanity voluntarily brought about for the purpose of committing the offense and escaping the penalties through the medium of the plea of insanity. It is, indeed, strange how reasonable men can insist that the State can not legally protect her people from such dangers, that she must not interfere with a man's right to kill and destroy with impunity. How any man can justify the exercise of any force or restraint whatever in the prevention of crime or of injury, and at the same time contend that prohibition is unjust and oppressive and contrary to the spirit of our institutions, I am unable to understand or even surmise.

I can not understand by what right the State summarily puts a check on the importation and spread of infectious and contagious diseases through the means of quarantine orders and proclamations while she is to be handicapped by constitutional limitations which do not exist, and by that undefinable, intangible enemy of all legal restraint called personal liberty, we hear so much about, in her effort to check by law the spread of the deadliest contagion that ever infected human society. I frankly confess that I cannot understand it. Neither do I understand by what right and upon what principle the state can interfere with the sale of intoxicating liquors on the days set apart for popular elections, and how it is that the devotees of personal liberty do not rebel at the law requiring the saloons to be closed and their occupants to suspend business while the sovereigns are casting their ballots, if the right to traffic in whisky is so sacredly guaranteed by the spirit of our free institutions. By what right does the federal government prohibit the sale of intoxicating liquor to the indian? If their is a higher law in this land that overreaches the authority of the State to interfere with this business and that paralyzes her outstretched arm in the protection of her people, I want to know why this power has not been invoked in an effort to resist even the first feeble attempt she has made to lay positive restraints upon the traffic? It is not a question of how much the State may interfere, but as to her right to interfere in any manner or degree whatever, and if permitted at all, no limit can be fixed short of the absolute prohibition of the same, if necessary to the general welfare of the people at large.*

---

*Hon. D. B. Culberson, congressman from Texas, in his open letter to the Anti-Prohibition Committee expresses himself boldly as follows:

"I take great pleasure in making the statement that the democratic party is the devoted friend of the people. In this respect, indeed, it partakes largely of the personal characteristics of its founder, Mr. Jefferson. The party is thoroughly committed to that system of laws which secures to the

There is an ancient and oft quoted legal maxim which declares that the welfare of the people is the highest law: if this is the correct maxim, and we can see no objection to the principle it embraces, then it necessarily follows that there may be a law which is above constitutions. In the very spirit of this established legal proverb the people find the unquestionable right to revolutionize and overturn the government if its longer existence is subversive of the acknowl-

citizen the largest liberty consistent with the welfare of the public. It regards government as a simple repository of right surrendered by the people upon trust, and esteems that government best which governs least. Influenced and inspired by such principles the democratic party has, from time to time, resisted the abridgement of personal liberty and rights when the same could be exercised and enjoyed without inflicting such evils upon the public as endangered good government and the general welfare of the people. You have been pleased to allude to the position of Mr. Jefferson upon sumptuary legislation. His position on that character of legislation is often used by the advocates of the liquor traffic against prohibition notwithstanding the fact that no law writer of his day and time classed prohibition with sumptuary legislation. It has been the labor of a later period to endeavor to extend the scope of sumptuary legislation, in order that the traffic in liquors, regardless of the public welfare, might be shielded from assault by the opinion of Mr. Jefferson. It may be said that had prohibition been submitted to the people of Virginia in his day and time, he would have voted against it, not upon the ground however, that the people did not possess the power and the right to protect themselves from an evil destructive of good order, but rather for the reason that the evils of the traffic had not then assumed such magnitude as to seriously endanger the welfare of the public. The question before the people of Texas involves existing conditions, not conditions which may have existed near a century ago. The evils of the liquor traffic, in Mr. Jefferson's time, pale into utter insignificance beside the monumental horrors that stalk through the land to-day hand-in-hand with this traffic. The feeble and insignificant power for harm exerted by the saloon in the earlier days of the republic has grown to be an overshadowing despotism. It assumes to control the franchise of freemen. It sets at defiance the laws enacted to preserve the good order of society. It enters the high and the low places of authority, and stamps its will over the will of the people. The wrecks of manhood which fill the land; the distress and bankruptcy wrought by its power; the onerous burdens of taxation imposed upon honest industry to defray the expenses of crime, the legitimate offspring of its influence, all show how deeply the public welfare is involved in the evils of the liquor traffic. For one, I believe the time has arrived when this despotism should be broken and overthrown, and the welfare of the people emancipated from its thraldom.

edged rights and best interests of the people at large. It may be a dangerous experiment, but it is nevertheless true that constitutions can and ought to be abrogated and destroyed when demanded by the best interests of the people. Their establishment and maintenance can have no other legitimate object in view than the material and social welfare of the people for whom or by whom they have been adopted. This proposition seems too plain for an elaborate argument. Admitting this premise to be sound in principle, then it must necessarily follow that the people have a national and inalienable right to provide for their own preservation in spite of constitutions, in spite of those time-honored principles of any and all political parties which have nothing but their antiquity to recommend them. If time-honored folly is to control legislation in the very face of experimental wisdom and statesmanship, then why make an effort to improve on the system or systems of government in vogue in the days of our unskillful ancestors. Principle is principle and it gains no force whatever from the fact that it was discovered to be principle in the remotest ages of the past. If it is not correct within itself, it can not grow into perfection though it should antedate the sun. When truth springs forth from whatever source she may come, she is full fledged and remains the identical truth that it was when discovered, through all time and eternity. To talk about time-honored truth or time-honored principle is as meaningless as the phrase, "perfect perfection." And yet you constantly hear demagogues and perhaps others not properly so classed talk learnedly and pompously about the "time-honored principles of Democracy" which have in all the years of the past opposed every character of legislation interfering with the right of the people to get drunk whenever it suited their inclination to do so, regardless of the fearful consequences to society at large. It is not now and never has been the purpose of prohibitory legislation to interfere with any man's personal liberty to do just as he pleases, getting drunk included, provided he does not interfere with the right of other people to be let alone in the peaceful enjoyment of their rights and their privileges. And if all human experience did not demonstrate and prove that drunkenness can not be made to let soberness alone, that drunkards can not be made by any power on earth to keep their murderous hands off of unoffending and innocent people, there would be no clamor or demand for prohibitory legislation. Mankind are generally disposed to attend to their own business, especially while sober themselves.

You will not find one ranting and intolerant prohibitionist out of all the hopeless cranks in the cause who cares three straws how much whisky you drink, or how much of anything else you may eat or drink, however injuriously it may affect you personally if you will only be quiet and peaceable while you are doing it. As mean and illiberal as these prohibitionists are in the estimation of some people, they are willing that you may kill yourself on the very meanest and most poisonous whisky to be found in the most loathsome doggery in the country, if you can furnish adequate security that you will in nowise interfere with sober people in the legitimate pursuit of their business or pleasure. The trouble is, that no sufficient security can be offered. It is ever unsafe for a man to be within pistol-shot of drunkards, and the right of self-preservation, the love of life, and the desire to be let alone themselves, are the motives which prompt them to act vigorously in the matter. If it is mere bigotry and a spirit of meddlesome intolerance which moves them to act, and not a desire to protect themselves and society from the dangers incident to the sale of whisky, then they must surely possess a degree of liberality which genuine bigotry and intolerance do not possess. The very statement is paradoxical and absurd. Such men do not throw away their means and their valuable time in the pursuit of such delusive phantoms. They are too selfish for that. On the other hand, if they prosecute this war against whisky because it is hurtful to themselves and to society, they are unquestionably right, because self-preservation is the first law of our nature. In either event these "crank" prohibitionists must be right. They show themselves to be running over with liberality, notwithstanding the fact that they are the most selfish and illiberal people on earth. More than all others, they show themselves true to the laws of their being. Glorious dilemma! Liberal in their illiberality. Wrong in the very act of doing right.

Before proceeding further with the discussion of the first proposition which I started out in the beginning of this chapter to establish, namely that the doctrine upon which prohibitory laws are based is correct and in strict accord with every principle of human justice and natural right. I desire to examine the constituent elements of right and of its opposite wrong. We sometimes speak in a general way of right in the abstract and may think in a metaphysical sort of way that there is such a thing outside of the visionary and intangible conceptions of the human imagination. I take the position that there is no such thing as right or its counter-part wrong independent of existing realities. We will take for our first example the first person who appeared upon earth whether he came in the glory of his perfection from the plastic hand of the Creator, or was the spontaneous product of evolution. Whether his name was Adam and had for his home the garden of Eden, or Kalakaua I., and enjoyed his personal liberty upon the Sandwich Islands. Suppose, that he was the only living, breathing creature upon the earth, and while that may never have been a fact, we may for the sake of this argument, imagine such to have been his condition. If there were other living beings that could suffer from his acts, then he would find himself bound by the impulses of natural justice to avoid and refrain from acts of cruelty to those animated creatures. These creeping things, however low in the order of living beings, would have a natural right to keep on living until they accomplished the purpose of their existence, and this man Adam or Kalakaua I., however strong his inclination to cruelty and whatever may have been his conception of personal liberty, could not gratify such inclination without a violation of natural law, natural right—eternal and unchangeable justice. His personal liberty would be hampered and restrained in proporton to the degree of his inclination, and the opportunities afforded for its gratification.

I am speaking now of natural rights without reference to any human law for the punishment of the offense of cruelty to animals. But suppose that there were no inferior grades of animated creatures, and to make the isolation of this first man complete, let us suppose that there were no superior being to which he owed any duty or obligation whatever. We now have him, indeed, "monarch of all he surveys," and of a great deal more than he can survey, though he should live a million of years. Now let him contemplate, if he will, the distinction between right and wrong in the abstract. Put yourself in his place, and with all of your powers of abstract reasoning, can you draw the most "vague conception" of such distinction? If you think so, then give it a trial. Let your thoughts take upon themselves the wings of the morning and traverse the dead waste of the universe, and, like Noah's dove, they will return to rest upon the contemplation of your own hopeless solitude, and they will not bring from their wandering a single conception of right in the abstract. The only idea of right of which the mind would be capable under such circumstances would spring from the hot-bed of our own selfishness. We may find out something of the law of self-preservation, but beyond that all is impenetrable intellectual darkness. There can be no possible conception of right in the absence of obligation. The idea of obligation and personal duty presupposes the existence of a plurality of beings to be affected by the terms or restraints of such obligation or duty, whether it points upward to God, outward to humanity, or downward to the very worms of the dust. Obligations and duties do not, and in the very nature of things, cannot exist in the abstract. They are inseparably bound to actual, tangible things. They reach not beyond the well defined limits of reality. The conclusion then follows at once that right does not and can not exist alongside of obligation and duty. It can only exist in a condition of complete isolation. It vanishes "like the baseless fabric of a vision" at the very approach of the conception of a plurality of animated beings, regardless of their relation to each other—regardless of their rank in the various gradations of breathing existence. I can not hope to make this proposition more clear to the understanding of the intelligent reader. The world is full, almost to overflowing, of living beings. The next step leads us naturally to the funeral of personal liberty, whose mocking ghost today stalks aimlessly abroad in the land, frightening the weak and faltering resolution of a people struggling to free themselves from the greatest curse that ever scourged to desperation the nations of the earth.

Personal liberty, absolute personal liberty, in the presence of the countless duties and obligations of civilized society! What a ponderous absurdity! How long, oh how long wilt thou haunt with thy grinning ghastliness the trembling quailing intelligences of this enlightened country? How long wilt thou go forth at the bidding of unscrupulous demagogues who would sacrifice all human happiness to the unhallowed objects of their vaulting, insatiate ambition?

Returning now to the question of right which I started out to discuss. The question "is it right to prohibit the manufacture and sale of intoxicating liquors by law," is about on a par with the question, is it right to do right. The very statement of the question in view of the experience of all mankind, in full view of the gigantic, widespread, and desolating evils which cry aloud for a practical remedy, not only suggests, but positively demands an affirmative answer. The many differences as to the manner of accomplishing the desired result, the speedy and complete suppression and destruction of the liquor traffic have nothing whatever to do with the principle innvolved in the discussion of this branch of the question. That will be considered hereafter. The ideas of duty and right are inseparable from each other. Is it our duty to do what we can to promote the happiness and welfare of others as well as ourselves? If so, then is it not right for us to use those available and effective means which are lawful to accomplish the result? If it is right to destroy a man's business by moral suasion and prayer can it be wrong to destroy it by law? The decision of the question of right does not hinge upon the character of the means. If the preachers and noble women of the country were to prevail in their fervent prayers to a sin avenging God to rain down liquid fire and brimstone from heaven upon all the saloons in the country and destroy them from the face of the earth, as was done in the days of Sodom and Gomorrah (which with all of their wickedness could not have compared with a dozen or so average saloons of the present age of the world,) would the saloon keepers not think it a flagrant interference with their personal liberty? Would they not likely object to the constitutionality of the measure? It is clearly to be seen that there is no possible difference in point of the principles involved. Is it a more flagrant interference with personal rights to force a man to do what is conceded to be right, through the instrumentality of law, than to forch him into measures by main strength and by putting him in fear? If a man deserves hanging ought we not to have a law by which he can be hung decently and in order? Or ought we rather to poison him or bore him to death with moral suasion and if that should not be effectual, swing him unbidden into a fearful eternity on the summary order of Judge Lynch? I care not to pursue this argument any further. I will next take up and discuss the question of expediency.

It is said by a great many people that prohibition does not prohibit. Some of them will pretend that they believe that prohibition is right in its objects and purposes, but that "it won't work," that they are fully satisfied that "it won't work." As a reason for this conscientious conviction they will say that drunkenness and intemperance generally is a kind of disease, and that when it gets clutches on a man, he will have whisky or blood. They will go on to show how easy it is for a man to send off and get whisky, and that the law will be so defective that it can not be enforced; that as provision is made for its sale for medical and mechanical purposes, unscrupulous physicians and druggists will conspire together to violate the law without the fear of God or his satanic majesty before their eyes. Therefore, prohibition is a farce and a practical failure. Under the chapter on local option I have already answered these arguments, I think, to the satisfaction of every unprejudiced reader. Prohibition, either local or general, is not intended for the reformation of confirmed drunkards. No reasonable prohibitionist expects it. Of course there are some men engaged in the cause who have never doubted that the adoption of any sort of a prohibitory law will absolutely put an end to drunkenness, that it will destroy the very appetite itself, and every latent inclination of the transgressor to trample upon the laws of the country. That no murders or robberies or other high crimes and misdemeanors can possibly occur in a town, county, precinct, or State where prohibition prevails. But, as is well known, the foolkiller may find plenty of work to do in other quarters. While he would slay off a few fanatical fools who could be very well spared in the contest, he would make a clear sweep of the opposition, and not one would be left to tell the tale of their violent taking off, or to sing the requiem of their folly and shame over their dishonored remains. They plant themselves upon the established and immovable impediment to all human progress, the fool's motto, "daddy did." The idea, if idea it can be called, that if "daddy" carried his grain to mill, or to the still-house with a big rock in one end of his sack to balance the end filled with grain, it would be disrespectful to his memory to do otherwise, if acted upon, would put an end to all human progress. It would drag the race down to a position far below the brutes. These people, and they constitute the great, unthinking, non-progressive masses of the world in all ages, are the ones who are particularly fond of the word "crank." Like the man who cried out "Beef! Beef!" at a certain perilous time during the great struggle of our ancestors for constitutional liberty, they cry, "Crank! Crank!" every time a man discovers and attempts to put into practical operation any kind of an improvement whatever.

Like the greasers of Mexico, who destroy every agricultural implement that is attempted to be introduced among them through the efforts of an advanced civilization, these "numbskulls" do and say every thing in their power to impede and effectually stay the onward march of moral and intellectual progress. They delight to mock at every effort of Heaven-born genius in the discovery of hidden truth and to clear away the thick, dark mists of popular ignorance and prejudice which have veiled them through the countless ages of the past. They pursue the pale, sickly form of the young dauntless pioneer in the fields of valuable discovery with that hell-born epithet " crank, crank," which has just enough of conventional meaning and disrespectful import to inflict a terrible wound upon the feelings of a sensitive nature to make him feel miserable, but not sufficiently pregnant with personal insult to justify an outbreak of personal resentment. I have heard this word "crank" as applied to the progressive element of mankind, to men who are unwilling to sleep away their lives in intellectual inactivity and idleness, not daring to question the accepted follies of their "daddies" or to make even a feeble effort or to attempt one solitary step in the discovery of truth and the destruction of "time-honored" folly, or the explosion of "constitutional" error, until I am heartily tired and disgusted. If there is one spurious word in the English language or its derivatives that I would expunge in preference to all others, that I would sink so deep into the voiceless gulf of oblivion that it would never more rise to the surface to mock the aspirations of rising genius struggling against popular error and prejudice, that word would be no other than "crank." To those of my readers who are conscious of the rectitude of their course who have in their warfare against whisky kept aloof from bitter personalities and personal vituperations, but who have had nothing in view but the redemption of our people from the curse of drunkenness and intemperance, I would here say be strong in your purpose and in your determination to conquer. Let those huge incubuses who have about as much energy and intellectuality as a jelly-fish cry out, "Crank, crank," to their heart's content. It will not hurt you in the long run. I would rather be a crank on the subject of prohibition than to be counted wise in the camp of the ungodly followers of Bacchus. Though I should be crowned with every possible honor they could bestow, I could not escape from myself; I could not escape the conviction of my own mind that I would be a consummate fool, if not for the want of sense I would still be a fool. But I now find that I have unconsciously strayed away from the subject under immediate discussion—the expediency of prohibitory laws and particularly of State prohibition.

Is it expedient to have laws of any kind for the government and regulation of the conduct of the people? If not, then it must follow that the prohibition of the manufacture and sale of intoxicating liquors is expedient, and if not, then it ought not to prevail. If we cannot prevent a man by punishment from manufacturing and selling the vile stuff, we can sometimes punish him for doing it just the same as we are now and then able to put a man into the penitentiary who has an inordinate fondness for horseflesh, just the same as we can once in a while force a man who overdraws on his personal liberty to do all sorts of mischief in violation of positive law to contribute quite liberally of his substance to the support of the government and to keep the wheels of justice greased for such cases.

It is doubtful if you can head off from the hell to which he is rapidly drifting, the poor, pitiful, helpless inebriate who is but a mere puppet in the hands of his master by the terror of law, however rigorous and severe the penalties may be for its violation. A drunkard laughs at consequences however direful thetr character. The fearful result following protracted debauch, the terrible sufferings he is forced to endure pending the efforts of nature to restore him from the burning effects of alcoholic stimulants, and the certainty with which they are inflicted, it would seem ought to be sufficient of themselves to deter him from a repetition of the offense against the laws of his own physical nature, but we all know from common observation and experience that they are wholly ineffectual. The infliction of the ordinary pains and penalties of the law would not be more so. They would be worse than a failure. They have ever proved such so far as I know. But that fact does not in the least argue that the manufacturer and seller who is generally sober and possessed of average self-control, can not be made to respect the laws which put an end to his nefarious traffic, just as the same man is forced to respect and obey other laws enacted for the benefit of society. These men as defiant of law as they threaten to be in the event prohibition is carried are I think sensible of the law's efficacy in the prevention of theft, robbery or murder. They say that they will sell whisky in defiance of the law. They ought to give us an earnest of their good faith by robbing somebody *in open daylight* as an evidence of their utter disregard for the law.

CHAPTER IX.

PROHIBITORY LEGISLATION.

CONSTITUTIONAL VIEW — PROHIBITION AND THE DEMOCRATIC PARTY. THE LOSS OF REVENUE AND DESTRUCTION OF PROPERTY. IMPORTATION OF LIQUORS. AN OPEN LETTER DISSECTED.

Under our peculiar system of government every citizen of the United States is protected by two constitutions and amenable to the laws of two seperate and distinct governments — the State and the Federal. It was the purpose of our representatives in the conventions framing these constitutions to so clearly define the powers and limitations of each that there would be no conflict of authority between them. To do this required a degree of statesmanship and political wisdom and foresight, almost amounting to prophetic inspiration.

While impossible to frame two such systems of laws to operate contemporaneously upon the same subjects without producing some conflict, the founders of the Federal Constitution came very nearly accomplishing that result. Of course the erroneous constructions of the various provisions of the State and Federal Constitutions and the laws emanating from and under their authority could not by any possible foresight have been provided against by the founders of the government. To these erroneous and often absurd constructions may be attributed much of the trouble that has sprung up in the administration of these two systems of laws. Much of this threatened conflict of authority has been obviated by the two different rules of construction applied in the determination of the respective powers of the two governments.

In construing and passing upon the constitutionality of a law enacted by Congress, the courts study the Federal constitution to ascertain whether the power is expressly given by the instrument to Congress to make such a law. If the power is not clearly granted by the terms of the Constitution, the law ought to be declared void and inoperative. The Democratic theory demands a strict construction of these powers.* The Republican theory is, that they ought to be liberally construed, even to the extent of usurping many of the long recognized powers of the several States. For instance, the Republicans take in the whole scope of government when expediency demands it under that sweeping provision of the Federal Constitution which gives to Congress the power to provide measures for the common defense. Every conceivable sheme that may tend in the remotest degree to contribute to the purposes of national defense, though it be apparently foreign to the purpose is embraced within the scope of that omnibus provision, and is held to be constitutional by the leaders of the Republican party. And this is substantially the difference between the two as national parties. The courts in construing a statute with reference to our state Constitution consider only the limitation of the powers of the legislature, and if they nowhere find in the organic law of the State a provision clearly prohibiting the Legislature from the exercise of the power assumed it is held to be constitutional. On this point there is no difference between the two parties as I understand them.

Having said this much upon the two rules of construction as applied to the powers of the State and Federal govern-

---

*The powers not delegated to the United States by the Constitution, nor prohibited by it to the States, are reserved to the States respectively or to the people. (Const. United States).

ment, I now come to the discussion of the main question before us, the constitutionality of prohibitory legislation. The idea of the Federal government's interfering with the police regulations of any State never could have entered the minds of the framers of its constitution. Neither could it have been intended by them to hamper the State governments in the execution or enforcement of such regulations as *exclusively* pertain to the internal affairs of the States. For men claiming to be Democrats of the Jeffersonian or any other school, to insist that the Federal Constitution ought to be so construed, is an inconsistency that I am wholly unable to reconcile or explain. Even the Republicans, as liberal and latitudinous as they are in the construction of the Federal Constitution, do not claim that there was any such intention on the part of the framers of that instrument. Then, how can it be that a man who claims to be one of the recognized oracles of Democracy, will contend that any law enacted by a State, either by its Legislature or by a majority of its qualified voters, as in cases like the one now being considered by the people of Texas, having for its sole object the regulation of its own police affairs is inimcal to the provisions or limitations of the Federal Constitution? This, to me, is a conundrum. I do not attempt its solution. These latitudinarian Democrats talk eloquently about the repeated infringements of the general government, upon the rights reserved to the States and to the people, and especially with reference to its judicial usurpation, and yet they make an argument against the constitutiunality of prohibitory laws, and unblushingly stultify themselves by assuming that the Federal Constitution in terms, limits and restricts the rights and powers of the States to attend to their own domestic affairs and that, too, in matters in which the general government has not the remotest concern. How on earth does prohibition affect the administration of its affairs, I would like very much to know.

If the people of other States composing the Union dislike prohibition in Texas, they can certainly stay away; they are not bound to come here and submit themselves to the privations it attempts to enforce. If they do not wish to surrender their personal liberty to manufacture, sell and drink whisky, they can stay in a country where they can. But they say that the Constitution of our fathers declares that no man shall be deprived of life, liberty or property without due process of law; they claim that prohibition does, or attempts to do these things, or, at least some of them; therefore prohibition is unconstitutional. This is the argument and all there is in it. Now let us examine and see what it leads to. The first question to consider is: What is due process of law? Who is to prescribe the mode of procedure?

True democracy says the Federal government can not do it without violence to the rights of the States, and as is known, even the Federal courts are bound to respect the general rules of procedure and practice of the States where they are sitting. Suppose, for instance, that the laws of Texas were ever so tyrannical and oppressive, and suppose that the proceedings of her courts were summary, vague, or indefinite in their character? Suppose a judge should by virtue of his authority to punish for contempts, sentence without a trial by jury an innocent man to imprisonment for life, for an alleged contempt of his court, assuming, of course, that the State law gives him such power: will any respectable lawyer in Texas; will the able and distinguished Senator, and the honorable gentleman of Navarro who occupies with so much distinction and credit a seat in the lower house of Congress from Texas, who has taken high constitutional grounds in opposition to prohibitory laws, claim that the Federal government has the power under that provision of the Constitution to relieve him from imprisonment? If such a proceeding is not depriving a citizen of his liberty without due process of law, I am unable to imagine such a case. If the general government can constitutionally relieve him from a life-sentence, it can, most assuredly, relieve him of any shorter time. We have some peculiar statutes in Texas relative to property rights, laws which are strange and perhaps unreasonable and unjust in the estimation of some persons who have been raised under the ægis of the common law of England. We have some few rules of procedure and practice which are peculiar to our own system of jurisprudence. Suppose one of our citizens or any body else who has invested in property in Texas, should take it into his head that there is no such thing as due process of law in the administration of justice in this State, and appeal to the Federal government to enforce the plain provision of its Constitution above stated. What would all Democrats think if "Uncle Sam" should send a commission down here to Texas with instructions to establish an authority to compel our courts to adopt and enforce some new-fangled due process of law? We would secede from the Union. To bring the absurdity right up to the question at issue, suppose the Federal government should say to the people of Texas either through a harsh construction of the Constitution or by a law of Congress enacted for the purpose of enforcing the letter and spirit of that provision, "You shall not prohibit the manufacture and sale of whisky, liquid fire, dynamite and other dangerous, destructive, and demoralizing substances or commodities, although they are destroying the lives, health, and property of your people and threatening the ultimate overthrow of society itself? The very ghost of liberty and the much-slandered and misrepresented spirit of old-fashioned Democracy would rise up in their terrible fury, and cry out, "Scourge them back," with thunder tones that would echo and re-echo throughout the length and breadth of the Union. We would not submit to it. We would not have to submit to it, because it would be recognized as the signal of the approaching dissolution and complete overthrow of our long-cherished Republican institutions. "O, Shame, where is thy blush?" Such Democracy has not been handed down to this wicked and perverse generation of professional demagogues by our honored forefathers. This same question has been decided time and again by the higher courts, not only of our own State, but of the Federal government. So has the objection that prohibitory laws are sumptuary in their nature.

Such laws were decided constitutional by the Supreme Court of the United States at a time when that court was composed of unquestioned Democrats. It was decided by Tany, by McLean, and many others whose personal views of the constitution were in strict harmony and accord with the ablest expounders of the Democratic theory of government. It has been decided time and again, and, so often, that the courts of the country everywhere regard it as a settled question, and refuse to go behind the long line of decisions establishing the constitutionality of prohibitory legislation by the states in their sovereign and independent capacity. It is not necessary to discuss the constitutionality of the proposed amendment with reference to our own State Constitution. If the amendment should pass and become a part of the organic law of the State, it would, I should think, harmonize sufficiently with other parts of the State Constitution.

I propose now to discuss an objection to prohibitory legislation which is perhaps of more practical importance to the people of Texas at this time than any other which suggests itself for our consideration with reference to the subject before us. An objection that has done and is now doing more to stay the impending revolution on the temperance question, particularly in the southern states, than all others combined, and yet it is in truth and in fact the most frivolous and untenable of them all. That objection is, that prohibition is undemocratic.

Such are the political prejudices of the people at large, such is their devotion to the empty sound of a meaningless name, that they will cling to its memory; the mere shadow of a long departed substance in spite of every effort of reason. Go ask the great mass of the people (and I say it in all kindness) what is Democracy? What are the peculiar principles and theories of government which distinguish it from other political organizations? With the fewest number of exceptions they will tell you Democracy is Democracy. "My father was a Democrat of the Jockson school, or of the Calhoun type; I have been raised in the Democratic ranks, and, 'like Mrs. Macauber,' I 'never can desert it'." Let an unscrupulous demagogue—and Texas is full of them—(no personalities are intended) raise the war whoop against any measure for the relief of the people "It is un-Democratic," and they respond, "Down with it, crucify its advocates," and that, too, without reference to its merits. We all know this too well to require further reference to those political prejudices, and we must not fail to recognize them in every attempted improvement upon the "time honored' follies of our "daddies." If I can get the patient attention of my readers for a short time, I believe that I can establish to every one who is open to conviction, that prohibition is not only Damocratic, but that it is very decidedly so. Whatever slanderous misrepresentations have been made by its inveterate enemies; however much injustice its pretended exponents have done in their insatiate desire for political preferment, true Democracy "and undefiled" means nothing more nor less than a government by the people, and that the majority shall rule in all matters when the individual rights or preferences of the minority are not guarded and vouchsafed to them by constitutional inhibitions upon the legislative will. These constitutional barriers are themselves but the chrystalization of the popular will which is the only solid and safe basis of all positive law.

The will of the majority under the guidance of intelligent leadership is ever supreme. It makes and unmakes constitutions; one day it may establish a government, and the next day pull down and destroy it. What the majority of the people do in the majesty of their power in the very nature of things cannot be undemocratic, whatever may be the opinion of the minority. I am now speaking of pure and undefiled democracy, without reference to the ever-changing policies which have at different times in the history of the democratic party, constituted its distinguishing features in the contest for ascendency with other political organizations. I have ever supposed that the democratic party was in favor of the enforcement of the law, that it favored the suppression of crime, that the grand object of its mission has been to secure, as it professes to desire, "the greatest good to the greatest number." If I have been misled in this important particular, I am anxious to know it and know it at once. I never could conceive that a political party could possibly flourish or succeed without at least making some pretense that its object is the amelioration of the moral, social or financial condition of the people. I do not believe that any party can exist very long whose avowed purpose is to encourage crime, to cultivate vice, to sow the seeds of anarchy, to unbridle and turn loose upon a helpless and unoffending peasantry all of the furies of a material hell. If such is the mission of the great democratic party, the party of free government and constitutional liberty, it is a self-convicted nuisance and ought to be abated at once. But that I may not be misunderstood, I repeat that such is not the mission of the great party of the Constitution. Those men, it matters not how high their position in the government, who have undertaken to commit the democratic party to whisky, have spoken without authority. That distinguished gentleman who not long since declared upon the floor of the Senate of Texas that it was as "impossible to run the Baptist church without water, as to run the democratic party without whisky,"* represented only the besotted element of the party for which he attempted to speak.

I cannot believe that this gentleman duly considered the import of this humiliating confession when he made it, or rather when he assumed to do so in the name of a party which he has so much dishonored. I am charitable enough to believe that he said it in jest or that it was a mere slip of the tongue unbridled by ordinary prudence and discretion. The time has certainly come when the law-abiding and peaceable citizens of Texas should rise up in their majesty and rescue the fair name of this daughter of constitutional liberty from the mire and disgrace into which she is being led by the cringing demagoues, who would barter away every jewel she possesses for a single mess of political pottage. I call upon every true lover of his party and of his country to rally once more, and in the name of constitutional liberty and free, sober and honest government to wrest the soiled and tattered banner from the polluted hands of such leaders, before it forever trails in the dust. We may as well know the truth at once, however painful it may be, that if the democratic party alligns itself with the reeling, slimy, and seedy hosts of the whisky element, it is doomed to an early disolution, and it ought to be thus, however much we may regret its decay and demise. Young Democrats, whose bosoms are throbbing with ambition whose hopes are gilded by the brightest rays of political aspirations, let me warn you as one who feels a deep and abiding interest in your welfare, as he does in the lasting glory and prosperity of his adopted State, which he loves as his own life, to forsake at once the leadership of those men who would commit the people's party and the people themselves

---

*Senator Burgess speech against the submission of amendment, Twentieth Legislature of Texas.

to the loathsome service of the liquor traffic. Whatever bright aspirations you may have, whatever prospects and deserts, I tell you that they will be forever engulphed in disappointment and despair and speedily at that, if you stake them upon the liquor traffic in this, the struggle which is now going on between order and disorder, constitutional government and murderous anarchy. Plant yourselves upon your honest convictions of right, and whatever may be the result, however much you may be sneered at by demagogues and timeservers, you will succeed at last, and you need not doubt it in the least althogh overpowered and repulsed at the first onset. But whether you should succeed in the object of your ambition or not, it is better by far that you should be disappointed than to accept transitory honors from the corrupting hands of the whisky influence.*

---

*Hon. Jno. H. Reagan, U. S. Senator elect from Texas, and a Democrat of the old school, in reply to an invitation from a number of anti-prohibition leaders to join their side of the question, writes as follows:

"If I had liesure to engage in this discussion, with all respect for opinions of the meeting you represent, I could not concur with the views expressed in your letter. While I have heretofore felt constrained to oppose prohibition because its friends sought to make it a political issue and to antagonize and overthrow the Democratic party, that reason does not now exist; and I am not inclined, by speech or vote, to countenance the evils flowing from the selling and drinking of intoxicating liquors as now practiced, or to give to them the moral support of public opinion or the protection of the state government.

In every community we find men, once honored and respected, reduced to poverty, wretchedness and dishonor by spending their money and time in drinking-saloons; wives weighed down with grief and sorrow and want, and heart-broken, and helpless children growing up in ignorance, beggary and vice, because husbands and fathers have been made drunkards and vagabonds by patronizing the drinking saloons. Millions of dollars are invested in this business of making men drunkards and in producing the desolation and ruin of women and children, which if employed in agriculture, manufacturing or commercial pursuits, and directed by the talents and time wasted in these drinking houses, would add untold millions to the aggregated wealth of the state, and make as many thousands of happy families as are now made miserable because this money and time are given to the selling and drinking of intoxicating liquors.

The framers of our State Constitution, having reference to these evils,

A favorite and often effectual argument against prohibitory laws of any character is, that they deprive the State of hundreds of thousands of dollars annually contributed by saloon-keepers and whisky-sellers to the support of the government in the way of taxation or license. It is further claimed that thousands of men are thereby thrown out of business, and left with their families to suffer and die for the want of legitimate employment. The great loss resulting to the State from the enactment and enforcement of such laws is piled up and exaggerated until it transcends the bounds of possible computation. This argument is intended to reach the mercenary impulses of selfish human nature, and is often stronger than the powers of reason and moral suasion in influencing mankind in their action upon matters of the greatest concern. Convince a man whose avarice predominates over

provided that "the legislature shall, at its first session, enact a law whereby the qualified voters of any county, justice's precinct, town or city, by a majority vote, from time to time, may determine whether the sale of intoxicating liquors shall be prohibited within the prescribed limits." It would be no great innovation upon this principel for the people of this state to adopt a constitutional provision declaring that the manufacture, sale and exchange of intoxicating liquors, except for medical, mechanical and scientific purposes, is hereby prohibited in the State of Texas." The State Democratic convention, which met at Galveston last summer, inserted in its platform of principles a declaration, in substance, that a citizen might be a local optionist or a prohibitionist, and at the same time be a Democrat.

The present legislature wisely determined, in submitting the question of the adoption of the prohibition amendment by a vote of the people, that the election should be held at a time when no other election was to be held, in order that the people might pass upon that question unembarassed by any other political questions or elections, so that the election should be non-partisan. In view of these facts, with all respect for the meeting at Austin, and its committee, I must express my regret that any effort has been made to make a party question of it; and especially do I regret that Democrats should seek to identify that great and grand historic party with the fortunes and fate of whisky shops, drunkards and criminals.

There is a broad difference between laws which interfere with legitimate trade and with such as would interfere with the purchase and sale of necessary food, drink and raiment, called sumptuary laws, and laws which have for their object the prevention and punishment of crime and the preservation of public morals and decency. And I think it hardly just to the mem-

the moral sensibilities of his nature, that a certain line of conduct is conducive to the promotion of his own interest, and he will pursue it in spite of every consideration of morality and justice that can possibly be brought to bear on his mind. He can not be made to consider any corresponding evil or disaster that may result to his neighbor. Rather than pay a few cents more in the way of increased taxation, he would see the complete destruction of social order, and especially if he felt assured that his pecuniary interest would not be involved in the disaster. He would be perfectly willing to submit to every other evil that might result from the act, provided his accumulated store of filthy lucre did not suffer. And all for what? "Gold, the admiration of fools and knaves."

But do not understand me by this slight digression from the main question to admit that the adoption of prohibitory

---

ory of Mr. Jefferson to assume that he would not have recognized this distinction.

I have, during all the years of my manhood, been a Democrat of the straightest sect, and an earnest and enthusiastic disciple of Thomas Jefferson, whom I regard as the greatest political philosopher and statesman this country has ever produced. And I would be as far from desiring to see laws passed which would interfere with the freedom of legitimate commerce or which would undertake to control the purchase, sale and use of necessary food, drink or apparel as any one could be. But I believe it to be the duty of the people, in a lawful manner, to protect themselves and society against the evils of the improper sale and use of intoxicating liquors. If I have not always so felt, it has been in a great degree because I was unwilling to allow any outside issue to subvert or cause the overthrow of the Democratic party whose principles I believe necessary to the preservation of our free constitutional system of government. We now have the opportunity to promote sobriety, thrift and happiness without endangering the success and perpetuation of the principles of the Democratic party, and I am in favor of doing so; and I shall at the coming election so vote, not because I believe prohibition the most efficient remedy which could be adopted for these evils, but because in my judgment it favors a policy which will do much for the improvement of the condition of our people pecuniarily, socially and morally, and to-ward placing them on a higher and better plane of civilization. I hope you will not consider it a breach of propriety for me to make this answer through an open letter, as I may have no other opportunity to state the reason for the vote I shall give on this question. And I beg to assure you, gentlemen, of my great respect for you individually and collectively

laws, however widespreading and stringent in their operation, results in financial loss to the State or to the people. In the first place, the whole license system is wrong, but that branch of the question will be pretermitted in this connection, to be taken up and thoroughly discussed in a future chapter of this work. We will suppose that in a county of twenty-thousand people we have as many as ten saloons, each paying to the State the sum of three hundred dollars, and to the county and city together, three hundred dollars more each, making the sum of $600, and the tax upon all aggregating the sum of $6000; half of this goes into the coffers of the State government, one-fourth, or $1500, to the county, and when the business is carried on in incorporated cities, the remaining fourth

and of how much I regret that I have to differ from you in your opinion on this question."

Dr. B. H. Carroll of Waco, Texas, in his celebrated sermon in reply to U. S. Senator Coke's speech in opposition to prohibitory laws has the following to say:

"But to return to the first point. Constitutions are not political platforms—voting for the local option clause in the Constitution does not stop us from taking position against it in our county. Granted. But should it stop you from denouncing it as anti-Democratic. Our position is just this, as repeatedly expressed. There is no necessity for the Democratic party to put in its platform a plank *pro* or *con* on this subject. Just relegate it to the people as a side issue. Then there will be no split in the party here in Texas.

Let men vote as they please on this subject and quit cracking the party whip. Allow ministers of God to preach against what they regard as a great moral evil without calling upon the people to "scourge them back and stop their rations." The Senator proceeds to ridicule the idea that Prohibition proposes to step only the *sale* of whisky.

To our minds there is no just ground for ridicule here. The law does not seek to prevent men from injuring themselves, provided they do not thereby injure society. The distinction is obvious: *Sic utere tuo ut alienum non laedas,* (so use your own as not to injure another,) is a proverb applicable to both Common and Divine law.

Prohibition is a war against the *business* of selling liquor; against the *saloon* as a *public educator of the young,* against a licensed wrong operating under the sanction of law. But he objects that this is "class legislation, in favor of the rich, and against the poor, in that a rich man can send off and get his whisky, while a poor man must take a drink out of the Brazos."

Without classing this as demagogism, let us put the shoe on the other

contributes to the municipal government. If there is no such incorporation, the last named amount remains in the tills of the whisky sellers. Now, I am not going to take time to dig up statistics gathered from the records of the different courts of the county and city, (if there be one), to show the large amount of money that is annually paid out and worse than wasted in the prosecution and punishment of crime and misdemeanors, traceable directly to the infamous traffic in liquors. It is wholly unnecessary to do so, as the appalling fact stands out in bold relief before the experience and observation of every intelligent reader, that the amount realized from the licenses will scarcely be a drop in the bucket compared with the necessary expenditure in keeping open the

---

foot. What about high license as class legislation? It would only take a small sum to send off for a gallon of whisky, but where is the poor man's chance to engage in this good business of *selling* liquor? How many of them have the $500 necessary to make them equal before the law? But the Senator at last comes to the true position for an anti-Prohibitionist. He plants himself on it squarely. If he sustains himself here, there was no need to introduce [any other argument. Hear him: "The greatest people that have ever lived have had the strongest whisky. When the Romans overran Great Britain, the early Britons had only a drink made of honey and water; hence they were easily conquered. But since they have consumed more ardent spirits in England than any other country, you see they control the finances of the world, and theirs is the greatest maritime power in the world. We have descended from those people, but we have improved in drinking whisky, but we sell some of the best that ever was put in a man's face." There we have it at last. I give you his exact words. Here we have the reason why Persia, Greece, Rome, and Switzerland conquered while they were abstemious and temperate, and the secret of their downfall when they became civilized wine-bibers and liquor guzzlers. Shades of Sallust and Juvenal! Here we have the secret of Moslem conquest, their superiority in art, science, and literature, while they obeyed their prophet and drank no wine, and the secret of their downfall when they lapsed from original simplicity and temperance. Here is an explanation — why ours is no maritime power. Oh. — Roach, — Roach, persecuted martyr! — why didn't you razee Secretary Whitney by showing that it was a lack of strong whisky that kept that ship from going faster? Why didn't you employ our senator to show that it was the temperance society that ruined our navy? O, lapsing civilization that now refuses to issue daily rations of grog to soldiers and sailors, thus destroying their martial spirits and undermining their fighting powers.

courts the increased length of time for the punishment of such offenses.

In this estimate we do not, indeed we can not, include the vast sums of money squandered and wasted by the unfortunate victims of the curse and which are not only lost to them, but to their dependent and impoverished families and to their bona fide creditors. How many helpless, miserable families have suffered for bread and for clothing; how many have been cast hopelessly adrift upon the charities of the world by the demoralizing influence of these gaping portals of destruction? How many merchants and business men have been left in the lurch by the same hellish influence and forced to levy a tax on other customers in the way of an increased per cent on the average selling price of their goods, wares and merchandise to make up for the amount squandered by their drinking and drunken customers? Attempt to count up the necessary loss annually sustained by our law-abiding people, leaving out the miserable drunkards and the pitiful sum paid to the State, county and city, will pale into utter insignificance. Besides this, a loss in the way of domestic happiness, the peace and quietude of society, the innocent, priceless blood of unoffending citizens sacrificed upon the altar of this insatiate demon, reaches out far beyond the circumscribed limits of human calculation. No system of arithmetical computation has yet been invented and given to the world, with which to measure the depth of human woe, or to suggest to the mind the faintest idea of just and adequate compensation for the bitter tears and voiceless heartaches that whisky produces. They can not be estimated in dollars, though piled up into golden pyramids until their glistening spires reach the blue vaults of the starry heavens. Oh, no, you can not wipe away the bitter tears of the disconsolate widow, or charm away the corroding sorrows of her stricken heart, by the magic powers and enchantment of the "vile dust of this world's wealth and grandeur." Neither can you, with all the dazzling and costly things of earth, dry up the fountains of the mother's grief whose young, thoughtless and misguided boy, dearer to her than the "apple of her eye," yea, than her own life, has been allured by the temptations thrown around him by these deadly and villainous dens, into a life of shame and disgrace. Do you think you can? If so, go seek out one from the scores and hundreds who may be found in every nook and corner of this "wide, wicked world," and learn how much of the glittering wealth of the globe will lift from her broken and bruised heart the pent-up sorrows that are crushing her down to earth? From her you will learn how false the word of England's profligate poet, "But pomp and power alone are woman's care." You will learn from her grief the vain emptiness of this world's possessions when compared with a mother's love. It is useless to say more in refutation of this mercenary argument against prohibition which is entirely sufficient to convince a large class of our people of its inexpediency.

The other objection, that it throws so many persons and so much capital out of employment may be answered by the following practical illustration: Some years ago there was a man living in a certain quarter of the county of Kaufman in this State, which was well adapted to the very lucrative business of hog-stealing, in which pursuit this enterprising man was largely interested. He had about all that he possessed invested in the business and gave regular employment to several thriftless individuals who were not fit for anything else.

He had succeeded well in evading the clutches of the law, and had attained sufficient respectability and standing among his neighbors to be called colonel. That my readers may not know to whom I refer, I will call him for, for short, Col. Swine-stealer. His hospitality was without bounds, and there is no question of the fact that he relieved many hundreds of vagabonds on the meat he had stolen—the legitimate profits of his business. I will not do the courts and the people of that county the injustice to intimate that they were influenced not to prosecute the Colonel by a consideration of the fact that he would be broken up in business, that his capital would lie idle, and that his worthless and villainous hirelings would thereby be deprived of access to the flesh-pots of the Colonel. This illustration, will, I think, suffice to show the absurdity of the objection to which it relates. I do not, of course, intend to class those who are engaged in the sale of liquor under a license from the State with hog-thieves. Many of them are not only generous and kind in their natures, but are scrupulously honest in their dealings. They would be as far from stealing a hog, or anything else, as the best citizen to be found in the community, but the business they follow is more destructive and damaging to society than the hog-stealing occupation.

It is objected by some of the anti-prohibitionists, after vigorously opposing prohibitory laws because subversive of personal liberty and contrary to the spirit of our Constitution and of the government, that the amendment is not strong enough, and that it is totally defective in not prohibiting the importation of spirituous liquors into the State. They claim to be better prohibitionists than those who favor the adoption of the amendment, because they want a much stronger document, one that will absolutely prohibit the introduction of the article into the State under any circumstances whatever. These are the prohibitionists of the "straightest sect." It is rather surprising, however, that we have never heard of them before. Why was it that they did not speak out about the time the senator from Gaudaloupe was heard from on the subject? Why did they not urge this objection at the proper time? They, with all others, have had their day in court, and it is now too late to object to the form or effect of the judgment. But, aside from this, I desire to show that the objection is wholly without foundation. All who are posted upon the State and Federal Constitution understand well enough that the power to regulate commerce between the United States and foreign countries and between the states is exclusively given to Congress,* and any attempt on the part of the states to usurp this authority would be unconstitutional and void; and had such a restrictive provision against importation been embodied in the amendment, it is quite probable that it would have vitiated all of the legislation passed under its authority. However, it is not necessary to discuss that proposition at this time.

One thing we may be assured of from experience and observation, and that is that it would be tested by the whisky dealers as soon as an attempt should be made to enforce it. The question was virtually decided in the License cases by the Supreme Court of the United States in 1847. (5 Howard, 505). The appellants in those cases insisted that a State or local prohibitory law was obnoxious to that provision of the Federal Constitution which gives to Congress the right to regulate commerce, as its effect was to prevent the importation of the prohibited articles into the State or districts adopting such laws. The court held that such laws were in the nature of police regulations and within the scope of the power reserved by the States and while their effect necessarily interfered with the business of the importers of such liquors, they in no way affected their right under the Constitution and laws of Congress to import such articles if they were disposed to do so. The right to sell them after importation was another and a different thing, and a matter within the control of the States. By an examination of those cases,

---

*Con. U. S., Art. 1, Sec. 8.

it will be seen that the court clearly and unmistakably recognized the want of authority in the States to prohibit the importation while they had the power to regulate, restrict, or entirely prohibit the sale of such articles after they are imported. In a recent case decided by the Supreme Court of the United States, involving the constitutionality of the drummers' tax, the principle was reaffirmed and the tax decided unconstitutional, because it was an invasion of the exclusive right of Congress to regulate commerce. The case has not yet been reported except through the newspapers and law journals, and hence I am unable to cite it that it may be easily referred to by those who may desire to pursue the investigation further.

If, as was held in that case, the States can pass no law imposing a tax upon persons engaged in selling goods, wares and merchandise to be imported into them from other States of the Union, it necessarily follows that they can not pass laws absolutely prohibiting such importation. If they were permitted to enforce a law prohibiting the importation of spirituous or intoxicating liquors because their introduction is alleged to be destructive to the moral, social, or material welfare of their people, they could likewise inhibit the importation of any other article by declaring it in some way detrimental to the interests of their people, and in that way they could shut out all commerce from the other States and all other countries, thereby severing all of their commercial relations, regardless of the Federal Constitution and the regulations of Congress under its authority. It is unnecessary to elaborate the proposition.

Not long since a very prominent and promising young politician of Texas,* published an open letter accepting an invi-

---

*Hon. Horace Chilton, of Tyler, late Assistant Attorney-General of Texas. Hon. Seth Shephard, of Dallas, makes substantially the same objections in his open letter on the same subject.

tation to join the anti-prohibition "pow-wow" at Dallas, in which he urges some objections to the adoption of the constitutional amendment, to which my attention had not been directed until the chapter on State prohibition had been, as I thought, completed. Proposing as I did in the outset to discuss the subject in all its phases, I can not pass unnoticed the objections urged by this distinguished young statesman whose prominence in the eastern part of Texas is such as to give much force to the position he so boldly and confidently assumes, in the estimation especially of the people of that portion of the State, when he is so favorably known. It is first insisted that the last Legislature in the enactment of a stringent law requiring heavy bond and prescribing increased penalties for violations of the law against illegal sales, with the removal of screens, pictures, music and games of chance, went as far as the urgent necessity for the further regulation and restriction of the liquor traffic demands at the present stage of our social advancement. That the better policy is, to make haste slowly in the effort to suppress this universally recognized evil. That the adoption of the proposed constitutional amendment striking down the traffic at one decisive blow would be a radical innovation upon the present order of things that might prove disastrous in its results, particularly to some interests and to certain classes of our people, who would justly regard it as tyrannical and oppressive. The usual appeal is made to time-honored principles and the customs of our fathers as a criterion by which we should be governed in the important crisis which is now upon us. It is objected that if the amendment is carried, " a man can not make his own wine from his own grapes for his own table;" therefore it ought not to be adopted. In answer to that objection, we will admit that it would be a great hardship upon all of the wine-makers in Texas, and that they would in all their after-years weep over the loss of that privilege, and, like Rachel of old, "refuse to be comforted" because of their dire misfortune and bereavement; and we may admit further, that a few of them would dig up their vines and transplant them into the soil of a neighboring State where there has been no attempted interference with such privileges. I do not think the State would hereby suffer any material damage or detriment. Say she should loose every manufacturer of wine "for his own use" or other purposes, the loss would hardly be perceptible if it should be felt at all. On the other hand, the benefits resulting from the law would be seen and felt in every nook and corner of the State in more ways that one—in ways that I can not undertake to point out and describe. Is the State, then, to neglect all classes of her people for no other purpose than to secure to an insignificant number of persons the small privilege of "making wine for their own use out of their own grapes for their own table?" I follow this flimsy objection no further. The second objection is, that we must not interfere with the Germans and their lager.

While Texas has opened her doors to immigration from all quarters of the globe, and sent out far-reaching and cordial invitations to all sober, honest, industrious and self-supporting persons to come and make for themselves happy and comfortable homes upon her broad and fertile prairies, she has never guaranteed to them exemption from any law, either organic or statutory, which her people may in their wisdom, see proper to enact, having in view the promotion of the public good." She has not guaranteed that the laws and customs of any other state or country shall be specially respected, or stand in the way of the adoption of any policy which may seem to the majority consistent with, or conducive to the welfare of the whole people. While I respect our German citizens, who are honorable and worthy of respect, as highly as any other man, I do not hesitate to suggest to them and to all others who are unwilling to submit to the will of the majority and to our laws generally, and govern themselves accordingly, that they are at perfect liberty to go somewhere else. The people of Texas cannot afford to let such considerations as these stand in the way of their moral, social or material advancement for the sake of a class of persons who threaten to defy the law and override the majority. The will of the majority must be allowed to prevail, else we have no such thing as Democracy. "The greatest good to the greatest number," although some hardship results, is the only true criterion by which we can be governed. To save the minority we can not afford to destroy the majority. The idea that "fifty-five per cent of our people ought never to assume to make that a crime which the other forty-five per cent esteem as among their rights," is novel indeed. If fifty-five per cent of the people ought not to prevail in the enactment of any penal law, then I would like to know exactly what per cent of the people constitutes a large majority, or a quorum to do business in the name of the whole people? Suppose that in a newly settled state forty-five per cent of the people "esteem it one of their dearest rights" to carry pistols, commit assaults, destroy property, steal hogs, or to do anything else inconsistent with the personal safety, and subversive of the dearest rights of their neighbors; according to this new fangled logic and latter-day statesmanship, nothing could be done in the premises. The absurdity is apparent.

But it is urged that the amendment ought not to go so far as to make it obligatory upon the legislature to pass laws absolutely prohibiting the traffic. That if any amendment had been submitted at all, it should leave the matter optional with the legislature to prohibit or not to prohibit, to restrict or not restrict, as may from time to time appear to be to the best interests of the people at large. We are not called upon to decide any such question. The legislature after, as I suppose, a thorough consideration of the subject in all of its phases, decided to submit the amendment in the form in which we are authorized and required to act upon the question, and it is useless for us now to find fault with it, or attempt to remedy its apparently objectionable features. The question is, which shall we have, saloons, or no saloons? whisky, or no whisky? license, drunkenness and disorder, or prohibition, sobriety and general domestic peace and social tranquiliy?

I shall not burden my readers with what I conceive to be a fruitless and worse than useless discussion in order to answer an objection, though apparently seriously urged by a most prominent young Democrat, who has held high official position, whose name has been favorably mentioned in connection with Congressional honors, and who by some has been thought good material for the United States Senate. When such an amendment as is suggested in the open letter referred to is in good faith submitted to the consideration of the people of Texas, if I am living, I may have something to say upon its merits, and it is quite probable that I would favor it, if "the best that could be done under the circumstances."

Until then I prefer to be silent and non-commital. My impression now is, that the policy of the State will be settled by the adoption of the amendment as proposed in a manner that will entirely supersede the necessity of the submission of the optional amendment preferred by the honorable gentleman whose recently published open letter suggested to the author the propriety of making this addition to the chapter after it had gone into the hands of the printer.

SUPPLEMENT TO CHAPTER IX.

REVIEW OF THE ANTI-PROHIBITION PLATFORM.

Without extensive preliminary observations giving the reasons prompting me to supplement what has already been said on the subject of State prohibition as contemplated in the amendment, soon to be voted upon by the people of Texas, I propose to discuss *seriatim* every proposition set forth in the platform or declaration of principles of the anti-prohibition, or "True Blue" convention held in the city of Dallas, Texas, on the 4th day of May, 1887, as unanimously adopted by that august body representing the intelligence of the opposition in the State.

"1. We oppose the pending prohibition amendment because it is a proposition to change our form of government from a free republic of sovereign and independent citizens to a species of paternalism hateful to our people. It will take from the citizen his most sacred and inalienable rights and add to and augment the powers of government, and is therefore undemocratic and anti-republican."

"Because it (State prohibition), is a proposition to change our *form* of government from a free republic of sovereign and independent citizens to a species of paternalism hateful to our people." I would like to know exactly what is meant by the expression "to change our *form* of government." If it is meant that a majority of any State or community have no right to change the form of their government when it ceases to protect those for whom and by whom it was established, I respectfully refer to the first article in the Declaration of Independence, the charter of American liberty and of our free institutions. The contrary doctrine is there laid down as plainly as the language of patriotism can express it. In what respect does the adoption of the proposed constitutional amendment tend to change our *form* of government? If I have studied our form of government to any purpose at all, I have learned that its present form is democratic, and that means that the majority shall rule in all matters in any way affecting the public welfare. In the organization of our State and Federal governments, a majority of the people were expressly given the right to amend the organic law when deemed advisable. Does the legitimate exercise of that power tend to change the form of government "from a free republic, etc.?" A few years ago slavery was protected by the Constitution, both State and Federal. We of the South thought that it was right; but it is not necessary to consider that question in this argument. A great many people of the Union thought differently, and an amendment destroying slavery was engrafted upon the U. S. Constitution, and forced upon the people of the Southern States. If that act did not *change the form of our government*, then I am at a loss to know how it can be done by the voluntary adoption of the prohibitory amendment now submitted to the consideration of our people.

Our Constitution has often been changed in important particulars, and in no instance, so far as I know, has a change been made without interfering with somebody's supposed inalienable rights and pecuniary interests. Under the Constitution of 1869, the passage of usury laws was in no way enjoined upon the Legislature, and the bankers and moneylenders all over the State loaned their money at the enormous rate of 5 per cent a month. A slight change was, (unfortunately for the bankers, who clamored for personal liberty to make their own contracts), made in the Constitution of 1875, which prescribes 12 per cent per annum as the highest rate of interest a man may legally charge for his money. If this is not "a species of paternalism hateful" to some of our people, then I am at a loss to understand the meaning of the word. I can not see that the form of our government can be greatly changed in that particular.

"We oppose this amendment because it is sumptuary and will vex the citizens and interfere with individual liberty."

This objection has been fully answered in another place.

"We oppose this amendment because it is at war with the fundamental principles of Anglo-Saxon civilization, and will destroy that inalienable right of the citizen to determine for himself by what method he shall pursue his own happiness without interference with the rights of others, which principle is the basis of our liberties and the sole hope of the perpetuity of our institutions."

"At war with the fundamental principles of Anglo-Saxon civilization"; that is the idea, and by it is meant, I suppose, that Anglo-Saxon civilization is opposed to all moral, social, and material progress. If so, then we will try some other stamp of civilization. If the Anglo-Saxon "brand" is to be supplied by the great whisky monopolies and beer-dealers' associations of this country, and is to be "rectified" through the refining influence of saloons and low doggeries, then it is certainly high time we were trying another "civilization" market. The "inalienable rights of the citizen to determine for himself by what method he shall pursue his own happiness, etc.", has already been discussed in the main chapter. (ante page). By "the perpetuity of our institutions" is doubtless, meant the perpetuation of *our* saloons and *our* places of business and amusement, and specially refers to the vested rights and personal proclivities of the members who composed the Convention.

4. We oppose the amendment because its inforcement will entail upon the government the necessity of promoting a system of spies and informers detestable to our people, and the

achievement of extreme legislation of doubtful constitutionality, and under the sanction of which our homes may be searched, our property seized and our dearest rights invaded. Texas cannot hope to escape these curses which have invariably attended similar experience in other states.

That "it will entail upon the government the necessity of promoting a system of spies and informers detestable to our people, and the enactment of legislation of doubtful constitutionality," is only the hap-hazard opinion of the members of the convention, or rather the committee that reported the resolutions. That matter is yet to be tried. Besides, honest men do not object to being watched, and those of our citizens who do not propose to manufacture and sell whisky contrary to law can very well stand the "spies and informers," they can very easily protect themselves from this hateful class by transforming themselves into honest law-abiding citizens. There need be no fears of unconstitutional measures to carry out the objects and purposes of the amendment. Such measures have already been tested time and again by the highest courts of the country, both Federal and State, and their constitutionality invariably recognized and upheld by those courts.

5. Its adoption will suppress the general use of milder stimulants and encourage the use of the strongest drinks and thus retard the advancement of genuine temperance. It will stamp as criminal the manufacture of wines from our domestic grapes for family purposes and will degrade drug stores into dram-shops and elevate our doctors into autocrats over our appetites.

It may have "a tendency to suppress the use of the milder stimulants," but I am unable to see how it can possibly "encourage the use of stronger drinks, and retard "the advancement of genuine temperance." If it will only do this, the liquor dealers ought to favor its adoption. In answer to the destruction of grape-culture, I refer to the closing paragraph of the last chapter. (Ante page.)

6. It will enable the rich to import and use their liquors without taxation or restraint, and will prohibit only those of our people who are too poor to buy their liquors in unbroken packages, and under its operation the saloon will give place to the guilded club room for the rich, while the poor will be forced to make their purchases at low dives and in violation of law. Such a class of legislation is odious to our people and contrary to free government.

If the first part of the above proposition is correct, and it is absolutely necessary for our people to have whisky, it will certainly have a tendency to make all the poor drunkards of the State strive to get rich so they can import liquors in unbroken packages. When they get able to do this, they can take care of their families; pay all of their old whisky bills as well as other financial short-comings; and if they get drunk and violate the law, they can contribute something to the coffers of the State and their counties; or to the decent support of the lawyers who may be employed to keep them out of more serious trouble.

7. It proposes by the preponderance of a majority in certain sections of the State to fasten by force on other sections a theory of moral and social conduct and habit distasteful and repugnant to the latter. The varied interests of these sections in our State have been a prolific source of care and thought in our statesmanship, and if this amendment is adopted it will engender a hostile sentiment in localities fatal to its enforcemet. Thus we get a disreputable law and a disregard of constitutional authority, and will produce a lasting and permanent evil to our people and tend to disrupt the State.

If the amended is adopted, as it certainly will be, the legislature will, at its next session thereafter, pass laws similar to others upon the statute books prescribing penalties for their violation. These laws will be administered by the courts and juries of the different sections of the State, and enforced by the officers precisely like other laws are enforced, and if a man does not wish *to be forced* to comply with their provisions, he can do so voluntarily. If he is determined to be forced to comply, he can make a trial of his strength in a contest with the State government in its effort to carry into execution the provisions of the law. If a whisky, or beer dealer finds himself unable to live under the new dispensation, he can sell out and leave the State, and no objection whatever will be raised. No writ of *ne exiat* will be resorted to for the purpose of preventing his speedy removal.

8 "It proposes to confiscate and destroy without compensation large property interests of our people. It will unsettle business and impair property values, paralyze, for a period at least, the commercial interests of our State, and destroy great industries already in operation for the manufacturing of the milder stimulants. It will abolish the source of public revenue fully one-third, and increase to a corresponding amount the burdens upon our lands and the necessaries of life, already overburdened with the exactions of government.

It has always been regarded as within the province of legislation to provide for the abatement of nuisances without regard to the property rights of persons attempting to maintain such nuisances, in defiance of the protest of the people affected or damaged thereby. Besides, the proposed amendment makes no such intimation, and it is certainly to be presumed that the legislature will have wisdom and virtue enough to provide for the enforcement of the law without the necessity of resorting to so harsh a measure as that of confiscation. "It will abolish the source of our public revenue." What is the source of our public revenue? Is it the saloons? If it can be shown that the saloon is the source of our revenue, or anything else than vice, personal, social and moral degradation, disorder and depravity, then I will concede that the amendment ought not to be adopted. The saloons a source of revenue! What a glaring absurdity! It is in deed and in fact the very canker-worm of the public revenue, which eats into and destroys the germs of material prosperity, the only true and living source of public revenue. That congressmen and reputed statesmen should attempt to palm off such an absurdity upon an intelligent people is truly surprising.

9. The zealous advocates of the prohibition idea have already established and organized a third political party, and have waged relentless warfare upon the principles and organization of other established parties. Instigated by foreign emissaries, they have by agitation for years secured from the Legislature of our State the concession of this proposition to change our organic law, and by studied purpose and concerted movement, they now seek to stifle political expression from our people, until their own political designs are fully accomplished. We warn our people of this threatened danger and call upon them to rebuke at the polls this sinister conspiracy against their political organization and fundamental principles of American liberty.

What are you anti-prohibitionists doing in the way of organizing third parties? The Democratic party of Texas in convention assembled no longer ago than last August, decided that a man's views upon the subject now being considered should not interfere with his good-standing in the party. While there were a few overzealous prohibitionists, who were dissatisfied because the convention did not think best to go further at that time, split off from the party and undertook to revolutionize the politics of the State in a few days. The great mass of the prohibitionists of Texas adhered to the old party and carried the State by an overwhelming majority. Had it been announced in the platform of the Galveston convention that the prohibition democrats would have to surrender their views upon that subject or abandon the Democratic party, the new party would have been much stronger than it was. However that may be, it was certainly established in the convention that a man may be a Simon-pure Democrat and a good prohibitionist. Acting upon that view, the prohibitionists have done nothing more than assert their right and intention to vote and work for the adoption of the amendment. They have not questioned the wisdom and patriotism of the recognized exponents of the Democratic party in the last State convention in the course they pursued in dealing with this important question of State policy. They have not so far as I have been able to learn, attempted to override the action of the convention by alligning the party organization on their side of the question. They have not attempted or threatened to read any one out of the ranks of the party, because he opposes the amendment. While they have invited everybody regardless of party affiliations to join in the effort to "squelsh" the liquor traffic, they have not assumed to be the only "true blue" Jeffersonian Democrats in the State. Nor have they as the Simon-pure Democrats invited and received into the fold of the party of constitutional liberty a motley host of recruits who never voted a Democratic ticket in their lives, and who never felt a Democratic impulse since they were ushered into existence. It is truly humiliating to a true disciple of Jefferson to behold these pot-gutted, hypocritical, pretended apostates of Republicanism going about with "true blue" Democratic (?) badges pinned to the lapels of their coats hurraing for Jefferson and Roger Q. Mills. "*O tempora, o mores!*" If the immortal Jefferson could rise from the dead and behold these "True Blue" disciples who are casting out prohibition devils in his name, he would not only say, "Depart, ye cursed, etc., I never knew you," but, like the author of those memorable words to the money-changers in the temple, he would walk in and say, "My house shall be a house of prayer, but ye have made it a den of thieves," (politically speaking, of course.)*

The word, thieves, is used because the quotation puts it that way, and I can not substitute another, and not because all of the "True Blues" are really and in fact thieves, although a large per cent of them are life-long Republicans.

---

*Since the above was written, Gov. Ross has published an open letter, in which he makes known his intention to vote against the amendment. The first reason he gives is, that our fathers in establishing our present system of government were infallible, and, as they did not see proper in that day to provide against the liquor traffic, it must be wrong in principle. The argument of his Excellency would lead us to question the wisdom of every constitutional amendment or statutory enactment which has been engrafted upon our jurisprudence since the adoption of the first Constitution in 1845. He speaks of the vast improvements that have taken place, with the unprecedented increase of population (the 20,000 then and the 3,000,000 now): of the schools, colleges and churches, which have sprung up all over the country with their civilizing, refining, and christianizing influences. The inference to be drawn is, that the people at large have nothing whatever to complain of and to make them unhappy. In other words, that the social condition of the State is perfect and, therefore, could not be improved by the prohibition of the liquor traffic and the suppression of saloons. He speaks of the "abuses" of the traffic, which of course presupposes that it is a good thing in its place. He compares our condition with that of Maine, and assumes, without giving statistics, among other things, that we have fewer criminals in proportion to population than that State where prohibition has been the policy for nearly forty years. The Governor finds nothing in the Bible discouraging drunkenness, but intimates that that infallible book rather endorses the views entertained by its Anti-prohibition expounders. His Excellency, I fear, has not been a regular attendant of the Sunday Schools nor a very close and critical reader of his Bible; otherwise he must have long since arrived at a different conclusion as to its teachings. (See chapter XII).

CHAPTER X.

NATIONAL PROHIBITION.

GENERAL DISCUSSION—U. S. SENATOR BLAIR'S SPEECH.

This effort would not be complete without a chapter devoted to the subject of National Prohibition, although it has not yet assumed an attitude which addresses itself to the practical consideration of the people for whose benefit the measure is intended. There has for some time been pending before Congress the following resolution, proposing an amendment to the Federal Constitution similar in its objects and effect to the measure now being submitted to the people of Texas, except that it is designed to be general in its operation, taking in all of the states and territories of the United States:

"Resolved by the House of Representatives of the United States of America in Congress assembled, (two-thirds of each house concurring therein), That the following Amendment to the Constitution be, and hereby is, proposed to the states to become valid when ratified by the legislatures of three-fourths of the several states, as provided in the Constitution:

ARTICLE.

"SECTION I. From and after the year of our Lord 1900 the manufacture and sale of distilled alcoholic intoxicating liquors, or alcoholic liquors any part of which is obtained by distillation or process equivalent thereto, or any intoxicating liquors mixed or adulteratey with ardent spirits, or with any poison whatever, except for medicinal, mechanical, chemical and scientific purposes, and for use in the arts, anywhere within the United States and the territories thereof, shall cease; and the importation of such liquors from foreign states and countries to the United States and territories, and the exportation of such liquors from and the transportation thereof within and through any part of this country, except for the use and purposes aforesaid, shall be, and hereby is, forever hereafter prohibited.

"SECTION II. Nothing in this article shall be construed to waive or abridge any existing power of Congress, nor the right, which is hereby recognized, of the people of any state or territory to enact laws to prevent the increase and for the suppression or regulation of the manufacture, sale, and use of liquors, and the ingredients thereof, any part of which is alcoholic, intoxicating. or poisonous, within its own limits, and for the exclusion of such liquors and ingredients therefrom at any time, as well before as after the close of the year of our Lord 1900; but until then, and until ten years after the ratification thereof, as provided in the next section, no state or territory shall interfere with the transportation of said liquors or ingredients, in packages safely secured, over the usual lines of traffic to other states and territories, wherein the manufacture, sale, and use thereof for other purposes and use than those excepted in the first section shall be lawful: provided, That the true destination of such packages be truly marked thereon.

"SECTION III. Should this article not be ratified by three-fourths of the states on or before the last day of December, 1890, then the first section thereof shall take effect and be in force at the expiration of ten years from such ratification; and the assent of any state to this article shall not be rescinded nor reversed.

"SECTION IV. Congress shall enforce this article by all needful legislation.

It may be expected that all who may favor State prohibition upon principle or expediency or both would, in order to be a consistent "dyed in the wool" prohibitionist, certainly favor the proposed amendment of the Federal Constitution on the ground that if it is good for the people of each State seperately that it would be good for them all in a bulk. In other words, that the more of a good thing we can have, the better for the people. That the amendment would work well in the utter destruction of the accursed liquor traffic throughout the length and breadth of the Union, there is no reason to doubt. In some respects I believe that it would be more efficient and satisfactory than State prohibition. It would prevent the serious trouble and difficulty which exist along the borders where it is almost impossible to enforce the provisions and penalties of the State law. Large towns and cities situated near the lines of anti-prohibition States must necessarily experience all but insuperable difficulties in keeping out interlopers and professional smugglers, but it is acknowledged that, while such is the case, prohibitory laws do much good in the border towns and cities. But while, perhaps, National, or rather Federal prohibition would be more efficient in such cases and perhaps more rapidly and completely destroy the evil than would State prohibition even in the same State where called into operation there is a different principle underlying the two measures or propositions. In another chapter I endeavored to draw the distinction between the respective powers, duties, and objects of the State and Federal governments and the different rules of construction as applied to the two constitutions. It is unnecessary to go over what was there said. It must clearly appear to every one who has had occasion to study the genius of our peculiar system of government, which is representatives rather than strictly democratic in its character, that all the power Congress is constitutionally permitted to exercise is expressly delegated to it by the States and by the people. Ever since the adoption of the constitution and the organization of the Federal government there have been two parties irreconcilably divided upon the great question which has been the chief bone of political contention and strife in all human governments, so far as I have been able to understand them. This difference of opinion and sentiment lies deeply imbedded in the natural conceptions of two different orders of mind and in the constitutional inwardness of the great masses of the people in all ages of the world with reference to the idea of personal freedom.

There is found to exist in every form of government a large class of the people who are submissive in their nature to the powers that be and while they are ever ready to take up arms in the defense of their rulers, they join and support them without questioning the right in every attempted usurpation upon their own liberties and those of the people at large. They are ever clamoring for increasing prerogatives and a stronger government without much regard to its tyrannical tendencies. In England this class of people are called Tories, and the same appellation was given to them in the earlier history of our own government. The other class, formerly called Whigs, but whose name has frequently been changed as occason or necessity demanded, have at all times opposed every attempted encroachment upon the recognized rights and liberties of the people by the sovereign authority under whatever guise it may assume. This restless, impatient, chafing under restraint is innate and incorrigible and it ever carries the torch with which revolutions are kindled in the overthrow of tyranny and oppression. These same opposing political forces are to-day battling with each other in the struggle for the mastery just as they have ever done in the past ages of our own history, and in the history of the world. They will continue to struggle till human governments shall be no more upon the face of the earth. No power save that of an omnipotent Creator in the regenerating influence of his spirit, can reconcile those two opposing political forces to each other. They are as diametrically and uncompromisingly opposed to each other as are the centripetal and centrifugal forces of the physical world.

Having laid this predicate, I will proceed to the argument and endeavor to apply the principles evolved from the foregoing apparent digression to the question before us for practical consideration; that of (1) the right of the general government to interfere with the internal affairs of the States, and (2) the expediency of such a measure. As substantially stated in the chapter on State prohibition, the idea of the interference of the Federal government in matters exclusively pertaining to the internal affairs of the States, those pertaining especially to their police regulations never could have been contemplated for a moment by the framers of its constitution. Such an idea or purpose is in direct conflict with the democratic theory of government, and, although the adoption of the proposed amendment by the people of the several States, as provided by organic law. would set at rest every question of the constitutionality of Federal prohibition, it would be a flagrant departure from the recognized principles underlying our dual system of government and would eventually lead to irreconcilable conflicts of authority and jurisdiction which would tend strongly towards the ultimate disruption and overthrow of the government.

It is best that the general government should be permitted to exercise no more power than is absolutely necessary for the accomplishment of the grand objects and beneficial purposes of its establishment. Otherwise, it becomes a trespasser upon the authority of the States who are ever jealous of their right to provide for the wants and necessities of their own household and ready to resent every attempted infringement upon this right by the general government. The results of such conflict of authority may be fatal to both. For these reasons I am not yet prepared to give my assent to the exercise of the authority assumed by the Federal government as contemplated by the proposed constitutional amendment. But while this is the case, and while I regard the exercise of such power by the general government over the people of the States as subversive of the objects for which it was created and contrary to the true genius and spirit of our American institutions, I am equally as firm in the opinion that State prohibition is in strict accord with the most ultra-democratic view of the true spirit and genius of our peculiar form of government. At the close of this chapter will be found the recent speech of Hon. H. W. Blair, the author of the proposed amendment before the United States Senate, in which will appear an able and exhaustive presentation of the merits of the resolution and of the opposite view of the powers and purposes of the Federal government. There are good men who would hail with delight the adoption of the proposed amendment, regardless of the principle involved, regardless of Democratic or Republican theories of government, and I am not disposed to quarrel with them on account of their views even if they should go so far as to say the necessity of effectually pulverizing the rum power is one of those necessities we read of in the book that "knows no law," that knows no party, that regards and follows no "time honored principle" or custom that stands in the way of the material welfare of the people for whom all governments are established and maintained. For myself, I would not destroy the constitution, I would not revolutionize our present admirable form of government for the purpose of engrafting upon the Federal Constitution an amendment, however grand and glorious in its purpose, that would interfere with the long-recognized right of the States to regulate their internal affairs; to make all laws which operate exclusively upon their own citizens, and in no way affect the interests or concerns of the general government. At least, I would not favor such an innovation until every other possible means was exhausted to accomplish the purpose. I am not at this time called upon to say what course I would take should I be forced to decide between revolution and whisky, and until that time shall come, which I hope will not be in my day, prudence demands that I should remain silent.

Favoring the resolution providing for the submission of the proposed amendment to the Federal Constitution, Mr. Blair made the following remarks upon the floor of the United States Senate:

"In order to justify legislation of any kind restricting the manufacture and use of alcoholic liquors, I believe it to be necessary to maintain these propositions:

"First. That it is the duty of society, through the agency of government, which is the creature of society, to enact and enforce all laws which, while protecting the individual in the full possession and enjoyment of his inalienable rights, tend to promote the general welfare; and especially whenever that welfare is impaired or threatened by any existing or impending evil, it is the duty of society to enact and enforce laws to restrict or destroy that evil. It may be proper to observe that no law can promote the general welfare which deprives an individual of an inalienable right, when that right is properly defined, or which impairs the enjoyment thereof, whether of life, liberty, property, or the pursuit of happines. But society has inalienable rights as well as individuals, and the right to such legislation as will promote the general welfare, in its true sense, is one of them; and the inalienable rights of individuals and the inalienable rights of society at large are limited by, and must be construed and enjoyed with reference to, each other.

"Second. While society has no right to prevent or restrict the use of an article by individuals for purposes which are beneficial only, yet if that use, beneficial to some, is found by experience to be naturally and inevitably greatly injurious in its effects upon others and upon society in general, then it becomes the duty of society, in the exercise of its inalienable right to promote the general welfare, and in self-defense to social life, just as the individual may defend his natural life, to prohibit, regulate, or restrict the use of that article, as the case may require. This principle is daily applied in laws which control the manufacture and use of gun-powder, nitro-glycerine, dynamite, and other things of great and dangerous potency, the unrestrained use of which, even for useful purposes, has been shown by experience to be destructive to the inalienable rights of others. This results from the common principle of law that every man must so enjoy his own rights as neither to destroy nor impair those of another, and it is the great end for which government is instituted among men to compel him so to do.

"Third. No person has a right to do that to himself which impairs or perverts his own powers: and when he does so by means of that which society can reach and remove by law to such extent as to become a burden or a source of danger to others, either by his example or by his liability to commit acts of crime, or to be essentially incapacitated to discharge his duties to himself, his family, and society, the law, that is, society, should protect both him and itself. A man has no more right to destroy *his* inalienable rights than those of another, or than another has to deprive him of his own. The laws restraining the spendthrift in the destruction of his inalienable right in property and punishing suicide (as the common law did, by forfeiture of estate, &c.), or *attempted* self-murder (as the law does now), are familiar examples of the application of this principle.

"These are elementary principles of law and of common sense. They are corner-stones of all just government. To these principles every member of society is held to have given his assent. They are unquestioned, so far as I know, by any one who believes in any law. They are axiomatic and indestructible as the social organization itself.

"Fourth. The use (unless medicinally) of alcoholic liquors to the extent of intoxicating or poisoning—which, as will hereafter be seen, is the same thing as intoxication—is an injury to the individual; it inflicts great evils upon society at large; it is destructive to the general welfare; it is of a nature which may be greatly restricted if not destroyed by the enforcement of appropriate laws; consequently such laws should be enacted and enforced; and this should be done in our country either by the States or by the General Government, or by *both*, if such laws can be made more efficient thereby."

GENERAL CONSIDERATIONS.

I desire at this time less to attempt a summary of fact and argument directly in support of the joint resolution than to offer a few considerations touching the present condition of the great debate upon the liquor traffic which for many years has been so active in all parts of the country ; and with the consent of the Senate I will venture a few suggestions which seem likely to compel attention, whether willing or reluctant, from politicians and statesmen and patriots and parties, as well as of this great nation, which embraces them all.

It must be conceded that the use of intoxicating (that is to say of poisonous) liquors as a beverage is the chief source and immediate cause of more hurt to society and to individuals than any other one agency which can be named. The war of the rebellion cost us fewer lives and less treasure year by year during its term of death and devastation than the nation has sacrificed annually to the Moloch of alcohol during the period which has elapsed since its close. Pestilence has not slain sixty thousand victims in any one year since the settlement of this country. If cholera and small-pox combined should sweep away one hundred thousand of our countrymen in a season, the nation would organize as one vast funeral procession and hang the heavens with the emblems of despair. Famine is with us unknown, or at least unnecessary, and whenever it exists is a crime either of the victim or of the community, and not an excusable misfortune in any case whatever; but in other civilized lands starvation, even during the last fifty years, has occasionally taught mankind that the terrible word can not yet be dropped from the human vocabulary as descriptive of an evil liability to which is extant among men.

Yet it may safely be said that since the battle of Waterloo, now the full period of the life of man, there has been no one year in which the combined suffering and pecuniary losses, inflicted upon the Caucasian race by war, pestilence, and famine has equalled the total of destruction chargeable to alcohol in the same lapse of time. Beyond this, the curse of alcohol has not been intermittent and occasional, but perpetual and inexorable, and I think on the whole increasing like the everlasting and unyielding pressure of gravitation and depravity. I have no heart and no time to repeat the familiar mathematical statements which come to us from municipal authorities, from the leading luminaries of all the professions, and from every source of authentic information, by which we learn that at least three-fourths of the pauperism, insanity, and crime, and of the public and private burdens which these great evils impose upon us directly chargeable to intoxicating drink. Such facts are as familiar as corpses upon a battle-field, and seem to attract no more attention.

I hazard nothing in appealing to the consciousness of every one who listens to me to attest that he has seen more of evil flowing from this than from any other cause during his whole lifetime, and I should hardly fail if I asserted that the personal sorrows and afflictions which he has most to bewail among friends, kindred, and the community where he may dwell are traceable to the same omnipresent curse. Those who preach, preach against it, and those who pray, pray against it. The press recounts its daily crimes and deviltries, and those who drink as well as those who abstain vie with each other in stigmatizing rum as the worst thing there is extant. Yet somehow the old king does most wonderfully hold his own. He is a popular curse. He has a round billion of money invested in his business, one-fortieth of the property and labor of the country producing and distributing death and misery to the American people. His market is as sure as that for cotton, corn, or beef. The unnatural appetite which constitutes the demand has become as insatible and almost as universal as the demand for healthy foods. This appetite descends with the blood, and the parent thus becomes bar-tender, even after death, for his child.

Multitudes bewail the evils of intoxication, attend temperance meetings, sing temperance songs, and pay a dollar a year to help along the blessed cause, and then lease their real estate for saloons, protest against the insertion of prohibition planks in political platforms, lest remonstrance against evil shall upset party supremacy, or, it may be, with upright purpose, influenced by profound discouragement and disgust, they break down and destroy an organization which they created and which they might control and save and use as a mighty power for the removal of the evils which they deplore. So it goes; and the evil expands, until we are told, no doubt truly, that the production which in the year 1862 was said to have been 16,000,000 gallons of distilled liquors and 62,000,000 gallons of beer, perhaps an exceptionally un productive year, was, according to the just-published report of the Commissioner of Internal Revenue, 69,000,000 gallons of distilled spirits, 19,000,000 barrels or 700,000,000 gallons of malt liquors, and over 2,000,000 gallons of wine, all gone into the consumption of this country during the fiscal year ending June 30, 1885. Really we do not seem to be getting ahead very rapidly, according to these figures; but I suspect that the returns of 1862 were imperfect. There is, however, I think, no doubt that the consumption of all kinds of intoxicating liquors has increased quite as rapidly as population in the United States during the last quarter of a century. This is especially true of malt liquors and perhaps of wines. I believe the rum traffic to be the great menacing danger of America and of civilization.

REVIEW OF PROGRESS DURING THE LAST CENTURY.

The thought which I have in mind for discussion upon this occasion is embodied in the question, What had we better do? I do not assume that I can answer this question. I can state what seems to my vision to be the better way—that is all that any man can do—and the Supreme Ruler of events will direct the pathway of action, as He has from the beginning until now.

Sir, we stand upon an elevation to-day at the end of the first century of the temperance reform. It is an hour of retrospect and of forecast. Something is revealed by the lamp of experience for the guidance of our feet in the century to come. What has been done in the last hundred years? By what means has it been accomplished? What remains to do, and by what means and methods shall the remaining work be wrought? In the first place, during the century just closed we have learned that the use of intoxicating liquors as a beverage—simply as a beverage and not as a medicine—is an evil always useless and hurtful. We have learned that alcohol is a poison and not a food; that it is not useful to the human system save under circumstances when a poison may be useful; never to produce or improve health only as it may remove an obstruction to the natural and proper action of this vital machine so fearfully and wonderfully made. Science has become our ally and fortifies our cause impregnably with her demonstrations. The Byronic phrase, "Rum and true religion," was hardly blasphemous sixty years ago.

A venerable Christian once told me that when he was six years old his sainted mother became converted and joined the church in one of the best towns of my own State. Among his most vivid recollections was the memory of the visit of the distinguished divine who came on two or more occasions to his father's house for the purpose of testing the theological soundness as well as practical piety of his mother during the probationary period which preceded her admission to the church, every such interview in the discharge of his sacred calling being opened by a liberal drink of New England rum, administered by the hands of the candidate for admission. It was not only the way of the world, but it was the way of the church. Drinking which did not result in actual helplessness was hardly considered an offense, while as a social custom its indulgence was as universal as it was delightful, and its dangerous tendency was overlooked most strangely and wickedly by the great majority of the best of men. Now the Christian ministry, Protestant and Catholic, is almost a unit against rum. The medical profession is against rum; the judiciary is against rum; science, religion, the learned professions as a whole, which one hundred years ago were for rum, are now against it. The substantial press of the country is against it; intelligence, conscience, all the great forces and agencies of society are against it.

Whenever and wherever any of them advocate its cause the work is accompanied by a concession of the evil, and the hypocritical or ignorant pretense that it can best be suppressed by some policy which increases the evil. You can not conceive of a political platform which advocates or justifies the liquor traffic because it does any good. All opposition to the evil is deprecated, or its license is sought only upon the ground that stringent and prohibitory measures increase the evil, or that such invasions of personal liberty are dangerous to individuals or to the State. It seems to be forgotten that the very essence of all government is an invasion of personal liberty to do wrong or injury, and there can be no personal liberty to perform any action hurtful to society and to the State which is beyond the jurisdiction and the power of the government established for the preservation of both. In short, this much, and it is everything in that it is the major premise of the syllogism whose conclusion is the destruction of the traffic, has been established by the agitation of the century just closed, that the manufacture, sale, and use of alcohol as a beverage is the greatest crime and curse of modern times. All the great conservative and preservative forces of society are now arrayed against it. That means its ultimate and inevitable extinction.

There never was an evil which has passed away that was not destroyed by public opinion. There is not, there never will be, an evil which can withstand the assaults of the enlightened condemnation of a free people who suffer from it. Then, Mr. President, we have this impregnable fact and supreme consolation which the past century has bequeathed to us—more precious to humanity than a diadem of morning stars—that the liquor traffic is doomed and shall be destroyed. The demon has been tried and condemned to death in the highest court, the court of public opinion. To us is assigned the work of execution. Let us proceed to perform that duty faithfully, relentlessly, and now.

FORMS WHICH LEGISLATION HAS TAKEN.

For a moment let us consider the means by which the achievements of the past have been won. There seem to be two agencies which influence human action, persuasion and force—the actions of individuals upon each other and upon the community, the result of moral suasion, embodied in law. The law itself becomes in its turn the fortress and re-enforcement of the moral sentiment and opinions of the community; and by the sanctions which belong to its administration and the reverence which a free people must always entertain for the laws which have once been enacted, even when the reasons therefor have become forgotten or obscured in the agitation of fresh issues concerning the public weal, the law preserves and maintains the good to secure which it was enacted. After popular enthusiasm has passed away the enemy comes in again like a flood. Then it is that a vigilant and determined minority can rally under the ægis of an existing law and summon its sanctions as a means of recalling the former acuteness of a now blunted public sentiment, as well as to directly suppress or restrain the evil prohibited.

True it is that when a law is really wrong or by the nature of things has become obsolete, the reason thereof failing, it is impossible for a minority long to enforce it; but on the other hand if the evil remain and the law be right, the fact that it is on the statute-book is a very great advantage, especially in times of declension in public zeal for the right. Both these forces, moral suasion and public law, have been employed in the promotion of the temperance reform during the century past. It is so patent that moral suasion, by education and argument, has been and always must be the great preliminary all-causing and controlling agency in moulding public opinion, which alone makes laws and gives permanent efficiency after their enactment, that for my present purpose I need not press its importance to the future, as well as the past further, upon your attention. I wish to speak, however, for a few moments upon the character of the legal enactments which in the past have been relied upon to promote the temperance reform. These have been by license, or by prohibition of the traffic or immidiate consumption, either by the State or by some supervision of the State, as a town or county, by authority derived from the State. The General Government has never passed, as it might do, for the District of Columbia and the Territories, any form whatever of prohibitory law against the rum traffic.

All license laws are based upon the idea of taxation for revenue, and imply a sanction of the trade as well as participation in the profits thereof by the whole people, who, for the general good, alone can execise the taxing power. A license gives the right to sell in consideration of the fee paid to the people, and prohibits such right to those who will not or are not permitted to pay the tax. The same sum imposed as a penalty for selling in violation of a prohibitory law is payable for each and every sale, and there is no consent to the act on the part of the public whatever. The fact that the penalty, like the fee for the license, goes into the public treasury is of no consequence at all.

These license laws, or excise laws, although for a while they may restrain, are of no ultimate help to the temperance reform. They are, in fact, one of the chief defenses of the traffic, and whether high or low are of most pernicious final tendency. They bribe the public conscience, they bewilder the public intelligence, and they never are long enforced in those provisions which are sometimes honestly, but more generally with bad design, attached for the apparent purpose of restriction. The licensee soon violates all these restrictions, and then is as liable to prosecution at the instigation of the common seller without any license at all as is the latter at the suit of the licensee himself. One violator of law will not prosecute another violator of law.

Then where is the motive for prosecution on his part, the creation of which is said to be the great excellence of the license law as a means of regulating the trade? It has disappeared and the license law is no law at all in its practical effect, save only as it does the general coffer fill with the price of blood. So far as it promotes the gilded saloon by closing the low groggery I have only to say the latter is far more respectable and a lesser curse in the community than the former. Ten groggeries will not work the ruin wrought by a single palace of strong drink. Every lover of his country should vote for the groggery as against the gilded saloon. The license law, high or low, is no device of the temperance reform nor of the temperance agitation. It was not developed by it. The moral sentiment of the community had nothing to do with its origin, nor, unless under a grievous misapprehension, with its present support. It has existed ever since there was a traffic, and for the sole purpose of getting money out of it for the public pocket, and might just as well be applied to the commission of any other offense against the public welfare by those who would pay for the liberty as to the trade in rum. A license law seems to me to be radically wrong in principle, pernicious in practice, and, so far as I know, no such law has ever imposed any real or permanent restraint upon the gigantic evil with which civilization is now called upon to contend. There remains to be considered only the State and local option laws, which have assumed to prohibit the sale of alcohol for drinking purposes. The amendments to State constitutions have as yet become hardly an operative force.

These prohibitory laws have partially succeeded and they have partially failed. Why have they so far succeeded? Because they were found on the right principle, and hence rallied conscience and humanity to their support. Why have they so far failed? Because they were, save in the principle involved, in no just sense prohibitory laws at all. They did not and they do not and they can not, when enacted by a State only, prevent the traffic in intoxicating liquor. The liquor traffic comprises vastly more than the retail sale, or even the wholesale and retail transaction. The liquor traffic is practically independent in a large degree of any State, and in an absolute degree of most of the States. True, if the drinking habit were not so powerful and universal, it might be somewhat different. But now every little hamlet, not to say almost every house, sends forth its cry and holds out its money to the whole land and to the whole earth, begging for strong drink. The supply can be made everywhere, and under the protection of the armies and navies of the nation, and of the world if it come from beyond the seas; alcohol, in the original packages, can be rolled into every cabin as well as every palace in the country. But how inadequate and what a misnomer as a prohibitory law is that which can only forbid the sale to the consumer in a State, and how much more so one which is operative only for the same purpose in a county or town. Even the State constitutional amendments, which prohibit the manufacture as well as the sale, must fail —inevitably fail. In the very nature of things there is and there can be no adequate and permanent remedy but in a national constitutional prohibitory law. It will be time enough to cry that prohibition does not prohibit when prohibition has been tried.

The State of Maine has very greatly improved the condition of her people by the operation of her quasi prohibitory law; so of New Hampshire and Vermont. Ask any old resident of any one of these States and he will tell you yea. A politician with a flask in his pocket or a liquor-drummer from Boston might bewail the failure of the prohibitory law in those States; but these laws in their practical operation are miracles of good; and considering the existing appetite, which antedated the law and the existence of which was the cause of the attempted reform, the enormous and concentrated capital and action protected by nearly all State, and the overwhelming power of national law which makes the stuff anywhere and carries it everywhere, I say deliberately that not even the law against murder is any better enforced than these poor halting paragraphs of infantile legislation, nicknamed prohibitory laws.

THE SITUATION NOW AND ITS REQUIREMENTS.

We have been one hundred years convincing science, religion, the professions, the judges who administer the criminal laws, and the great mass of the people that alcohol is poison, and that its manufacture, sale, and use is the organized destruction of individuals and of the body-politic. The nature of the legislation which is to remove and renovate all is now to be considered and enacted and enforced. Whoever believes that the destruction of the liquor traffic is not a national issue has made a mistake. Whoever does not comprehend that the removal of that evil is a duty which the nation is about to perform fails to discern the signs of the times. Everywhere the question is up. In the North and in the South; in Massachusetts, New York, and Ohio; throughout the West and Southwest, and all over the sunny South; in every State the agitation is irrepressible, because the evil is gigantic and omnipresent. It is impossible to suppress these convulsive efforts of the social system to free itself of this foreign and destructive element. It must be eliminated or society will die. It is of no use to cry peace, for there is no peace. Peace without a complete cure would be the most dangerous symptom. It would indicate the destruction of vital power, presaging decline and death.

The American people must do something. What shall we do?

The Washingtonian movement swept over the country some forty years ago like a tidal wave from the sea of life. That movement was moral suasion in its most powerful manifestation. The great wave subsided and the enemy came in once more like a flood of fire, and there be those who believe that the last state was worse than the first. Was, then, the Washingtonian movement wrong? Nay, verily, but it was incomplete. The tremendous public opinion which the discussion evoked should have been crystallized into the enduring forms of State and national law. The triumph then would have been complete and the work secure. We have at last learned something, and we are still learning more and more, that it is what we save that makes us rich. Deposit all savings in the solid banks of constitutional and statutory legislation, State and National, and the liquor traffic will not pauperize this generation of laborers in the field of temperance reform. We shall have a most precious inheritance to leave to the generation which comes after us. We shall not repeat the mistake of our fathers. Whatever we advance we shall hold by the authority of law. The one all-essential thing to be done is to put forth every effort to secure political action. All political action is partisan political action where there is opposition. State political action is important, but National political action is all-important.

I have endeavored to indicate why it is indispensable, and the only action which can render that of the States either permanent or efficient. If either should wait for the other, by all means let the States wait on the nation; let all the people of all the States concentrate upon one grand effort to amend the National Constitution so as to prohibit the manufacture, the sale, the importation, the exportation, and the transportation of alcoholic beverages anywhere within the limits of the National domain. That is the way to rescue and preserve the States. It is easy thus to create the popular sentiment which must exist within the States in order that legislation may be secured in their several jurisdictions. The evil is National, and the war which saves the nation must be fought by the nation. The Constitution, now the charter of the rum power, is to be amended by securing a two-thirds vote of both Houses of Congress, submitting a proposition for that purpose to the States for their action, and its approval by three-fourths of the entire number of the States. The President has nothing to do about the submission of the proposed amendment to the States, because he legislates only by veto, which is nullified by a two-thirds vote of the two Houses, and a two-thirds vote must be secured in its favor in the first place. Between the submission to the States and ratification by three-fourths of the States a considerable period might, undoubtedly would, elapse, but we should succeed in the end. All the energy of the reform throughout the Nation could be concentrated upon the States one after another, and I sincerely believe that, once before the people, we can complete the work in five years' time. Nationally nothing comparatively important can be done now but to get two-thirds of both Houses of Congress to vote to submit the proposed amendment to the people. It is nothing to us whether a Senator or Representative be a Democrat or a Republican, a St. John man or a Greenbacker, whether he is for license or prohibition, provided that he will vote to take the sense of the people upon such a proposed amendment. That is what we want of him now. Only this and nothing more.

What honest man can say that this request is unreasonable? What political party which cares for political freedom can deny to the millions who desire to be heard upon this tremendous question of the amendment to the Constitution of the country, so as to preserve the existence of our nation and of our civilization before the only tribunal which can decide it, the exercise of this fundamental right? We ask no man or party now to pledge himself to advocate the amendment before the people; we will take care of that when we get to the people. But we demand that he shall give to us, and that political parties shall give to us a chance to be heard in the proper forum—the forum of the people—which is our right. It is our concern, not now his or theirs, whether we are defeated or successful when we reach the people of the several States. This amendment might be thus submitted to the people in 1888, or at the latest by 1890, and the amendment itself become a part of the law of the land before the close of the century. But, sir, how long before a third party can elect a single representative against the old parties upon this issue or any other? When shall we get our two-thirds vote? When shall we get the Senate, if we postpone all until one or the other of the great political parties is destroyed, and its rival is in a minority with the triumphant prohibitionists in control of the Capitol? You and I will die without the sight.

It seems to be the fashion among our third-party friends to find all the fault possible with the Republican party, and to excuse the Democratic party, which is its only real antagonist for the control of national affairs. A Republican might retort that this is natural and all right if the Republican party sustains the same relation to politics which the church does to religion. If any party does good we must look to the Republican party for it; and it is, I suppose, a consciousness and concession of this fact which enables public opinion to hold the Republicans to that higher standard of conduct in politics which in morals and religion is enforced by sinners against the church. We must accept this responsibility or abandon "the grand old party" and return to the beggarly elements of the Democratic world. That we can not do. Therefore it is that the Republican party must and will promote the great temperance reform in that way and with such rapidity of aggressive action as shall be deemed consistent with successful results. As others speak from their several standpoints, so do I from that of a Republican who is in the party and proposes to stay there. If I can accomplish nothing in the party I know very well that I can nothing out of it. I helped to create the Republican party. I have in my humble way participated in its great deeds. I have shed my little share of blood in its career of glory, and there I am at home. Parties can not be made to order, and this great organic force is ours. I realize its tremendous power, and believe that under God it holds in its hands the better fate and higher destiny of America and of the world.

Flaws and specks there be on the sun; they would be invisible but for his own supreme effulgence. What light save his own could reveal his imperfections?

This great work is easier than it seems. I made a serious effort to secure the adoption of a proper plank for the purpose in the Republican platform at Chicago in 1884, and draughted a resolution to that end, which was introduced at my request by Hon. E. H. Rollins, my late colleague in the Senate, and referred to the committee upon resolutions. In its terms it was perfectly satisfactory to Miss Willard, the president of the Woman's Christian Temperance Union, the chief agency in all this temperance reform, simply pledging the party to take the sense of the people upon the amendment of the national Constitution, as I have already indicated. Miss Willard talked for thirteen minutes to the committee like an angel from heaven, and we retired. The committee gave no sign, and the platform was as dumb as a block of wood, and the party was beaten, as I fear it will be every time in the future until that plank is inserted along with other great issues which concern the welfare of the American people and mankind.

But you are not to infer from all this that no one on that committee was in favor of the adoption of the proposition. A member told me that many of the committee were for its adoption there and then, and more than a majority favored the proposed amendment in principle and believed that by 1888 the Republican party would go to the people with the resolution for submission to the people in its platform. I think the failure to do so then was the one fatal mistake in that campaign. There was no trouble with the German vote. Half of the Republican German vote is for such an amendment to-day, and the all-important industrial issues would have kept the whole of that intelligent suffrage with the Republican party so far as it ever is with us in any campaign. God and conscience would have been for us, and they count for something in a close campaign. The whole camp-meeting element of the country would have been aroused for Blaine and Logan, and we should have carried all the Northern and more than one of the Southern States.

No more such mistakes should be made. The working people of this country are naturally with the Republican party, and substantially the whole temperance vote will be with the party which adopts this issue the next time. Should there be wisdom in the councils of the Republican party the division of forces fighting for a common cause will be over, and for the all-sufficient reason that the Democratic party is on the other side, and that there are but two sides to this temperance question possible, the right side and the wrong side; the Republican party, if true to itself and to its high mission, will in the next general election favor taking the popular sense upon this all-important proposition. I can but hope that many individual Democrats will cast their influence and their suffrage in the same direction. It ought not to be a party question; there should be unanimity in a matter like this, but perhaps we can not hope so much as this for our country. It would be the millenium.

Let the temperance people of this country consider how

the labor organizations, with their one great purpose—the amelioration of the condition of those whose lives are spent in manual toil, by dictating nominations inside the two great parties to which they belong and one of which must always succeed—have obtained in the past and are certain in the immediate future to obtain in the nation and in the State legislation most promotive to their welfare.

I have thus endeavored to answer the question, what had better next be done in the temperance reform. Every man, woman, and child is interested in the answer; future generations depend upon that answer for their destiny of weal or of woe. Without undervaluing local and State agitation and legislation, let us concentrate every energy and effort upon the one great work of securing the submission of a proposed National amendment to the people of the States. Then we shall have before us a period of agitation in the States for its ratification there. That accomplished, we shall have regenerated the Constitution, and the tremendous powers of the Nation will soon throttle this giant Despair, who is feeding by day and by night upon the bodies and souls of our countrymen. Let us wisely conserve our forces and our votes. Let us be misled by no false analogies between this struggle and the great transition which destroyed the slave power. The analogy is an unfortunate one, which can only be realized and made pertinent by consummation in a terrible war. Peaceful agencies, if wisely employed, will accomplish the grand result. Numerous issues essential to the public welfare are always pending, and great parties which are intrusted with national control must embrace and simultaneously deal with them all. We most influence those with whom we are in harmonious relations. The man who owns an interest in the machine gains nothing if he throws it away, especially if it be a good one, and he who abandons the church has a poor chance to reform it. Stay in the ship and help to sail her to the port of joy.

But, after all, each man must decide for himself the method of his action. Let us, however, at least concentrate on the things to be done, that the tremendous forces now dissipated in the sand may become a mighty torrent of beneficence and sweep away the nation's curse. Abating no whit of effort in the way of instruction or persuasion, increasing the activity of all the agencies now employed to influence individuals, municipal organizations, and States, let us lift up the mighty banner of national constitutional prohibition. Let us ourselves contemplate the subject from this higher elevation.

The nation refuses to permit the importation of criminals; then let us prohibit the importation of the cause of criminals and of crimes; we refuse to receive the paupers and outcasts of surrounding nations; then let us repel from our borders the primal source of poverty, wretchedness and despair. What we refuse to receive from abroad, shall we continue to manufacture and export? What we refuse or ought to refuse to import or export because of its malignant and destructive work, shall we as a nation continue to manufacture, distribute and consume among ourselves? Shall we longer divide and destroy the result of our most zealous efforts among the people and in the States by permitting the National Constitution and National power, within their sphere the supreme law of the land, to protect the manufacture, the distribution, and the wholesale trade in this merchandise of death? Nay, verily, if the new century is to complete the temperance reform there is but one way to accomplish it—national prohibition must be our watchword.

Let this issue be carried into every caucus and primary for choice of delegates and into every Congressional Convention of every party which has any chance of success at the next Congressional election—the election of 1886. Let the same issue be made in the caucuses which nominate the Legislatures who make Senators of the United States, and thus choose members of both Houses of Congress, who will demand for the people whom they represent the opportunity to be heard in the forum of the States for the amendment and regeneration of the Constitution of the country, so that this sacred instrument shall become the warrant for destruction, and no longer the charter of life and liberty, to the most terrible curse and crime of civilization. This seems to me to be what we had better do next.

Sir, I will beg your indulgence to repeat the recapitulation and conclusion of my remarks upon the joint resolution made in the House of Representatives ten years since, which constitute a summary of considerations to which I respectfully ask the attention of the Senate and of the country.

RECAPITULATION.

"Sir, I only wish further to say that by the indulgence of the House I have thus at great but I hope not at unnecessary length endeavored to call the attention of Congress and of the country to the vast and increasing public evils which exist in the land, whose origin lies in the excessive use of that most powerful poison, known as alcohol. I have not dealt in specific instances, but in masses of fact, as they have been gathered and accumulated here and there by the statistician, the census-taker, the official investigator, and most of all by that noble profession which comprises so many of the ablest and best of men—a profession whose theory is the gospel of man's physical and mental nature, and whose practice is philanthropy applied to the details of all human woe—the medical profession, which by its researches in the chemical world and its incessant and protracted pursuit of the recondite origin of disease and of the philosophy of suffering and despair, as well as of the sources of vigor and hope and happiness to mankind, has placed civilization under the largest debt that is due to any of the learned orders of society; that profession, sir, has not failed to stamp upon alcohol the mark of Cain among poisons. It is the murderer of men. That noble profession has brought it to the doors of the Capitol, and charged it with the wholesale death of our people. They assail it as the pestilence which walketh in the darkness and which wasteth in the noonday—as the parent of every crime, as the cup of misery ever full; the prolific source of ignorance, poverty, squalor, idiocy, insanity in all its dreadful forms, personal ruin, social destruction, national ruin—the prime agency of hell on earth. And with them come all classes and conditions of men. These are not witnesses whose testimony can be denied or gainsaid. I will not speak of women in rags and disheveled hair, with her van cheek and hollow voice, nor of her children shivering on the corners of the street, starving within the shadow of churches built to the Most High with the price of their blood. It is not fitting here to be sentimental, not would I attempt it if permitted. The gravity of the occasion has passed beyond all necessity of resort to touching tales and strokes of pathetic imagery. The evil is before us. Its infinite extent must be admitted. There is nothing to be considered but the remedy and its application. I have endeavored to present one that seems to me to have been born of hope.

"This measure is not proposed by any party that now exists. I trust that it will encounter opposition from no party whatever. It has been prepared with the knowledge of scarcely any one. I am alone responsible for it. It is not the project of "temperance men," as they are sometimes called, whether derisively or otherwise. On the contrary, mistaking its true character and misconceiving its far-reaching consequences and its avoidance of conflict with the interests and passions of the present time, "temperance men" have complained that it is an evasion of the conflict. I fear that fifteen years of agitation will convince such of us as may then be alive that this objection does not recognize the great power of existing forces woich must be overcome. It should be remembered that no battle is won until the enemy is driven from his position. He is now intrenched in the Constitution of this country. The battle may go on, as it has gone for fifty years, without one single blow being struck at the manufacture of alsohol. And, as hitherto, "men may come and men may go," and thousands may continue to fall on either side, yet the battle remain forever undecided, because the struggle, however violent, is renewed forever by the recruits of successive generations. There is no concentration of forces upon the main position. Effort is lost because misdirected. Much of it, to be sure, is not wholly lost. Moral suasion—that is, argument and precept and exhortatlon, from the pulpit, the rostrum, the press, and private admonition—molds public opinion and accomplishes wonders for individual men, but it lacks the powerful re-enforcement of national law. That it can never get until it asks for and demands it.

"This revolution in national law can be wrought only by years of agitation and effort. Local sentiment must be awakened almost everywhere. In at least two-thirds of the country existing opinion must be reversed before the Constitution of the country in this respect can be changed. Meanwhile each state retains all the power it has over both fermented and distilled liquors, and as soon as this measure has been ratified there would be conferred upon the States largely increased control over both. Discussion and effort would demand the attention of the nation as such, and a concentration of the whole army upon a comprehensive plan of battle to carry the citadel would be substituted for isolated and sporadic warfare. And when the battle is once gained it is won for all time. This form of effort is infinitely the best way in which to accomplish local reform. The facts and arguments upon which the temperance reform is based are the same, whether urged to influence the action of the individual, the local opinion, or legislature of a single state, or the nation at large; and the modification of the national Constitution involves that universal local effort and the creation of that public sentiment everywhere which will result in the enactment and enforcement of Prohibitory state and territorial laws.

"Temperance men object because the first clause of this amendment if adopted does not become operative until 1900. They fear that they will die without the sight. So they may, but how can they object until they have tried to see whether they can obtain even *this?* Consider the past. Be admonished by history. Do not lose everything by attempting the impracticable. Remember that this is an effort to procure the enactment of *law*, which must carry the heads and hearts of conservative jurists, of dignified and unconvinced legislators, and the *popular vote*. This is a different thing from enthusing a popular assembly under the magnetism of Mr. Gough. Do not forget either that it is to be the act of the *nation;* that, however it may be as between God and alcohol, however it may be between the maker of alcohol and the higher law, yet *we* as a *nation* have assured the maker and dealer in liquor that he might vest his capital in permanent forms, that he might manufacture this article for all purposes whatever, and that we would protect him in the enjoyment of his capital and the production of his still. We take from his industry vast sums in the way of taxation for the support of the Government. True this legalized destruction of national wealth infinitely transcends the advantage of the tax, but nevertheless we have *legalized* the traffic for a century. Now, have we as a *nation* any *right* at once to destroy this industry and turn the distiller and his family upon the street to starve? Is he not entitled to reasonable notice of the change in the national policy, that he may gradually divert his capital and turn his business capacity in some other direction and train his son in some other employment? And if this view does not strike you with force, then consider the further fact that there are more than $500,000,000, probably $1,000,000,000, invested in this traffic to-day in the United States, and that such an interest will for many years to come have sufficient *power* to defeat any measure which destroys it at once.

" But liquor-makers and sellers are *men*. Great numbers of them are respectable and honest men. I have no sympathy with the wholesale denunciation of them as a criminal class. Many of them recognize the dreadful consequences which flow from the business in which they are engaged; yet it is a lawful business. Circumstances over which often they have no control have identified them with it just as others have found their way into the pulpit, into Congress, or into other avocations of life. It is no more just to denounce them as cold-hearted villains, intent upon nothing but the destruction of mankind, than it is to assail the personal integrity of every man who ever owned a slave. If approached in a proper spirit with a proposed reform in which they should be recognized as men and invited and urged upon considerations which must influence any human being, and which would give them a chance to save themselves and their families, I believe that the actual *co-operation* of many liquor makers and sellers could be secured.

"Since the introduction of this resolution it has been attacked as a palpable effort to curry favor with the prohibitory sentiment of the country and at the same time avoid offense to the 'beer element.' It is no such thing. This measure is not of that radical nature to command the vehement approbation of what are known as prohibitory men, though it must and I trust will command increasingly their approval. But the question of the manufacture and use of fermented liquors is left where it now is, with the *States*, because it is *medically* still an open question whether the restricted use of such liquors is not beneficial to the people, although their use is fast becoming excessive and an abuse. But there is very slight difference of opinion as to the destructive tendency of *distilled* liquors as administered by the "laity," and all agree that the great mass of the evils of intemperance arise from their manufacture and use as a beverage. And if the ban of the law can be placed upon the manufacture and use of distilled alcoholic liquors as a beverage, the minor abuses resulting from fermented liquors can well be left wholly to the restraining powers of the States, as enlarged by the second clause of the proposed amendment. While by no means of a callous organization, I certainly do not complain of criticism which attacks my personal motives, some of which has been brought to my attention. Those motives are not relevant to the measure itself. And whatever may be said by others, I am consoled by the consciousness that this step is taken after long reflection, that my motives are satisfactory to myself, and that they will be judged by the only tribunal to whom they can be surely known, and whose approval is of much consequence.

"The opposition of the consumer to any national measure which should at once deprive him of his beverage would be found to be very serious and I fear decisive. But there is no class of men who have a stronger desire to see their children saved from the chains which hold them to their own dreadful doom than the drunkards of this country. This measure has been sneered at as a proposed reform—*for posterity*. So it is; and as such it ought and I think will enlist the overwhelming force of parental feeling in its favor whenever the public mind has studied its peculiar features and elements of strength.

"I think that existing parties may well hesitate to oppose this measure. The cause it represents is one of moral reform, and it must be re-enforced by legislation. In due time it will be. If neither of the great parties now dividing the country sees fit to antagonize it, this measure will force its way without being made the source and object of political strife. Becoming operative so long in the future, it ought not to provoke the opposition of any political organization, and all men should be able to consider this subject calmly and to decide upon its merits.

"If it is a measure enlisting the moral convictions and humane sentiments of the people, and especially of that nucleus of able, conscientious, and aggressive men who are ultimately the ruling power in every progressive nation, although for years they may struggle on, fighting and dying under the banner of defeat, it will be well for all parties that would live to beware how they oppose this proposition. At least let it have fair consideration by the House and the country, for it is a subject which *will have* consideration. It is not a ghost, nor will it "down." I ask for it the considerate attention of all men now, for the time is coming when it will be forced upon them. The political exigency which absorbs and distracts the country will pass away, but this evil will not pass away. Its extirpation will be imperiously demanded long after the question of the succession to the Presidency shall have been settled whether by peace or by war. Public men will be destroyed who touch it, but the cause will survive. Stronger arms will uphold and advance the banner until victory floats on its ample folds; and the Constitution of the country shall yet become the pledge of sobriety and temperance among the people, the ally of virtue, and not the charter of this great source of ignorance, misery and crime."

IMPORTANCE OF STATE AND LOCAL-OPTION MOVEMENTS.

May I be pardoned a further word? The movements of the present time for prohibitory amendments of State constitutions and for statutory prohibition and regulation, including the system of "local-option" effort, are of great importance, especially as the means of temporary restraint and as the centers of agitation and means of creating enlightened public opinion; but such is the nature and scope of the evil and such are the relations of the general and special or State governments to each other, that nothing but a movement based upon the national idea presents a clear prospect of permanent success. The same and greater difficulties arise in all action for the permanent or even temporary suppression of the liquor traffic that does not include aggressive co-operation of the Nationel Government which ruined the country under the Articles of Confederation, and which did not abate until the whole subject of commerce, foreign and between the States, was placed under the control of one sovereign power. The combination of local and national effort is indespensible to the desired end. Neither can prevail without the other; neither can be postponed for the other without harm. Let everybody throw a stone at the liquor traffic, each in his own way, when he is so organized that he can not or will not use prepared amunition nor shoot with the regulation gun.

But still the fact will remain, that to ignore or delay the movement for a prohibitory amendment of the national Constitution so that it may be reserved to be a Yorktown rather than a Bunker Hill—that is to say, a crowning rather than a preliminary battle—is to decide to fight as a mass of individuals or an isolation of States rather than as a trained army with a general plan of campaign and a national concentration of organized power for the destruction of an organized national curse.

It is a division and misdirection of power, where combination and definite aim are required to give substantial success It is time that the probibitory idea should assume that control of national parties, at least of the Republican party, which belongs to a sentiment that is the conviction of three-fourths of the people in that party. The Republican party can not remain permanently three-fourths for prohibition and one-fourth against it. That is less possible than it once was for the nation to remain permanently half slave and half free. Ideas never compromise. They contend for mastery, but they never conciliate nor coalesce. We are at the divining of the ways—

>   The crisis presses on us,
>   Face to face with us it stands,
>   With its solemn lips of question,
>   Like the Sphinx on Egypt's sands.

ACTION.

But I feel like indicating my own inclination for action on the subject. For one I have been down here in this hole long enough. Sooner or later, and I trust not much later, I hope we may come to ourselves, like the prodigal, and proceed to climb up and out. I will remain here so long as I think I can persuade others to climb with me, in order that we may stand on each other's shoulders, and that those first out may lift the remainder with proper tackle—for the hole is very deep. Only for this will I remain longer in the hole, and for this I will remain, if need be, a great while. Others may, if they will—and they will—stay here permanently; but, sir, they will find that the masses of the Republican party and of the American people of all parties prefer to be on top of the ground, where there is less dirt, plenty of fresh air, something good to eat and fit to drink, and one can see across the country. Besides, it may interest some to observe that this hole has already begun to cave in, and that the gravel is disagreeable in one's mouth and eyes.

Why not let the order be given to rally on top of the ground? But there are too many who like, or at least think it best, to stay in the hole, and are even now busy drawing the hole in after them.

To this in their cases I do not object. It is well that the dead be buried, and if they can be induced to perform the work for themselves it will prove that they can still be useful to mankind.

But who that is alive desires to be buried alive?

Emerson advised the young man to "hitch his wagon to a star." To follow such advice might be dangerous for conservative parties like us, but to mortals who still breathe even this would have advantages over a permanent location under forty feet of soil. All the great living issues of the day—industrial, social, educational, political—are one; they stand or fall together. Temperance is one with them, and they are one with it. It is even now the chief practical remedial issue for the working men and working women of this land. The temperance reform and the labor reform are the same reform, and you can not long separate the agencies which promote them, nor prevent the inevitable union of those whose salvation depends upon them—the common people of the world.

It may be suggested in reply to this that it is better for the party to eject these pestilent fellows at once, that peace may return. But I know of some who are not thus to be disposed of and who are inclined to claim their rights to remain, and to insist that if anybody is to quit they shall go who would use the party as a means to curse and not to bless mankind. Besides, the issue is not raised by individuals, and no matter who is driven from the ranks the evil is the same; the issue is open, and must be met and decided by the American people all the same. On this occasion I have spoken partly as a Republican. But, sir, I do this only because I believe that thus do I speak most as an American, most as a man. That party, with all its faults and shortcomings and failures to reach unto its own ideals, I revere as the great agency which, under God, saved the country and secured its future. That party will yet, from the laws of its superior being and unfinished mission, concentrate its tremendous energies and perfected equipment upon this gigantic national evil until it is destroyed and for the promotion of every other cause which concerns its national welfare.

But, sir, we must advance. Our generation is passing away. Let not those of us who have chiefly done our work forget that the nation will survive us, and that the tree of liberty will be full of sap after we have passed away. Let us die in the direction of hope. If the victory come not in our time nor to our advantage, let those who bury us have reason to embalm our hearts, that in the thick fight which is between us and the holy land chieftains who command our children shall, like the crusader, cast the sacred relics far forward into the ranks of the foe. So may the armies of the Cross win victories from the memory of our devotion to the right.

Let us, at least, leave behind the examples of unflinching and unselfish valor put forth in a sublime cause—a cause which it is duty to uphold even though complete success may linger until our warfare is ended, and our sacrifices and calamities, if any there be, endured for its promotion, shall be long overpast. •

I have given Mr. Blair's speech in full notwithstanding its great length, not only because it presents the subject of national prohibition from the standpoint of the Republican party, of which Mr. Blair is a distinguished leader, with reference to the theory and purposes of our Federal compact, and the nature and scope of the powers which may with safety be delegated to the general government by the people, but also because it contains an able presentation of the facts and a thorough survey of the perilous situation which must impress upon every reasonable and unprejudiced mind the necessity for prompt and vigorous action. Mr. Blair is of opinion that the Federal government may with safety and propriety be trusted by the people through the instrumentality of the proposed constitutional amendment, with the execution of such power as seems to those who hold to the democratic theory of the government to pertain exclusively to the regulation of the internal police affairs of the several States, the exercise of which power ought to be retained by the State governments or by the people of the individual states. The difference is only as to the means of suppressing the evil; there is no disagreement as to the necessity for immediate and decisive action in the premises. For my part, I would prefer that the States first make the trial, and if they, after a fair test of their strength in the struggle with this gigantic evil, should fail to come off victorious, then I would say, regardless of pet theories of government, though they have been my own; let us suppress it by any available means and through any agency on earth that will be most effectual in the accomplishment of the desired result. We already have a provision in our Federal Constitution which gives to Congress the power to declare war; and even the chief executive without the aid or advice of Congress, may call out the militia for suppressing insurrection or repelling invasion. It is doubtful if a liberal construction of that provision would not of itself authorize Congress to declare and prosecute a war of extermination against this, the worst enemy the nation has ever had since the organization of our government. No insurrection or invasion however fierce and destructive can compare in its blood-curdling terrors to the blighting sway of the liquor traffic. If the people of the several States, acting in their sovereign capacity over their own internal affairs can not with their militia triumph over this enemy; then let us call out the regulars and move on to glorious victory.

CHAPTER XI.

THE LICENSE SYSTEM.

HIGH LICENSE, LOW LICENSE, FREE TRADE IN WHISKY.

So far as I am informed, in all states where general prohibition laws do not prevail the license system is in vogue.* I am not now aware that there is one state in the Union where no special restrictions are laid by the State on the manufacture and sale of intoxicating liquors. While men are permitted everywhere to engage in other commercial pursuits without such restriction, they can not sell whisky in any of the states without paying large sums for the privilege, in addition to the ordinary taxes imposed upon dealers in the harmless commodities of the country. If the right to traffic in whisky, or rather, intoxicating liquor, is absolute and inalienable, then, by what authority does the State impose *any restriction* upon its exercise which is not imposed upon the traffic in other goods, wares, and merchandise recognized as legitimate articles of commerce? Can any man who makes the least pretensions to capacity for logical reasoning give an idea of the distinction between the right to restrict and the right to destroy? There is not, and in the very nature of things, cannot be, any half-way ground in the argument. If the State can lawfully restrict in the slightest degree, then where must it stop before transgressing the boundaries of legitimate constitutional authority? If any advocate of license who denies the

---

*See Appendix. Some of the states collect taxes, but refuse to license.

right of the State to prohibit, will draw for me the line where the right of restriction by taxation or otherwise shall stop, then I will take back all that I have said in advocacy of the majority to absolutely prohibit not only the manufacture and sale of intoxicating liquors, but anything else that is found to be detrimental to the welfare of the people at large, I promise that the next book I write will be in favor of the destruction of all human governments, the abrogation of all laws, the complete overthrow of all sovereign power and legislative authority. I will be ready to accept the inevitable result. I will be ready then to admit that anarchy is not only right, but that it is conducive to the establishment and maintenance of good government. The right of a state to restrict by special taxation or positive law the exercise of any calling or business whatever is as palpable, inconsistent, and irreconcilable with the personal liberty contended for by the opposition as Egyptian darkness with the burning rays, of a mid-day sun. No reasonable mind can contemplate for a moment the idea of the contemporaneous exercise of these two inconsistencies without being overwhelmed by the grandeur and sublimity of this monstrous absurdity. And yet how full is the world, how full is this great state of Texas, of men, and men too who have been honored by the very highest distinctions within the gift of the people, who, in one breath, advocate high license on principle, and in the next breath overturn and destroy the whole basis of their argument, denying the existence of any such principle by assailing the right of the government to prohibit. When the argument is complete, and stands out in bold relief upon the stage of human sophistry where it belongs, it is something like "the play of Hamlet, with Hamlet left out." The argument turns upon and destroys itself. Indeed, it is well enough that it does, for the reason that common sense and good logic have more decent and difficult work to perform. But I leave this self-emasculated propositinn to the further contemplation of the reader, who can not fail to appreciate the absurdity.

The next question I shall consider is, What good can high license accomplish in the suppression or correction of the evil? Will it have the effect to diminish the sale and consumption of this demoralizing fluid? Such is not the purpose of high license. It diminishes one thing and one thing only, and that is competition. When the whisky business of a town is carried on by ten saloons, it will probably reduce the number to five, provided the license is doubled. If it is multiplied by three or four the number of good healthy, thriving saloons will likely decrease in inverse proportion. They will not have to sell their liquid insanity for any greater price by the drink and if they did, it would not make a particle of difference, as drinking men do not stand on a nickle. The increase of their trade by the suspension of those which are unable to pay the increased license for the privilege of competing with them in the corruption of humanity, more than repays them for the increase of taxes and by reason of their wealth and magnificence, they become if possible, more respectable and perhaps less loathsome in their appearance and surroundings.*

---

*Rev. DeWitt Talmadge, D. D., in his sermon on High License says:

Now, this high-license movement is the property qualification in the most offensive shape. Why do you not carry it out in other things? Why do you not stop all these bakers until the bakers can pay a $1,000 license? Why do you not shut up all the butchers' shops until the butchers can pay $1,000 or $500? Why do you not stop these thread-and-needle stores and the small dry-goods establishments, except that a man pay $500 or $1,000? "Oh," you say, "that is different." How is it different? "Well," you say, "the sale of bread and meat and clothes does no damage, while the sale of whisky does damage." Ah, my brother, you have surrendered the whole subject! If rum selling is right, let all have the right; and if it is wrong, $500 or $1,000 are only a bribe to Government to give to a few men a privilege which it denies to the great masses of the people. Why do you not carry out this idea of licensing only those who can pay a large license?—give them all the privilege."

Hence more attractive. Their music is more delightfully bewitching, and their games more varied and enticing. High license, if it has any perceivable effect upon the liquor traffic, has a tendency to make it more respectable, and consequently increases rather than diminishes man's inclination to drink. There is no necessity to consume time and space in the discussion of the effects of low license and medium license; the principle is precisely the same.

There is no small number of people who are, or profess to be of opinion that the best way to prevent drunkenness is to take the bridle off of the "critter" and turn him loose upon society. They speak of the good old days of our unsophisticated ancestors when our fathers and our grandfathers took their corn and their barley to the still-house, the grain in one end of their homespun sacks and a big rock or log chain in the other to make them balance across their saddles, had it ground up and distilled into whisky, which was so good, pure, and free from adulteration that it never made any one drunk, though he poured it down by the gallon. That these good old men, every one of whom took a bee line for the pearly gates just as soon as the spirit left him, always kept an old-fashioned decanter "dearer to their hearts than the old oaken bucket which hung in the well," which "dear old decanter" was kept full of pure, unadulterated corn or rye whisky, and that all the family drank to their heart's content, and none of them "flickered." Ah, those good old days that we read about when every body was honest, when every body was moral, when every body was righteous, and belonged to the church, and when nobody talked about his neighbor.

When there were no drunkards, no thieves, no murderers, no traitors to their country. What if those saintly personages were to come down from their lofty seats beyond the starry hosts and behold for a moment the moral depravity of their degenerate sons and grandsons who are moving heedlessly along the road to a drunkard's frightful eternity? Would they recall with delight and satisfaction the recollection of those "dear old decanters" which sat upon the mantle? If those saintly old grandfathers are now permitted to look down from the shining portals of heaven upon the rich harvest of drunken vagabonds which sprang from their loins and those " dear old decanters " of unadulterated whisky, would they not in all probability recall that good old passage of scripture they used to read while their boys were enjoying the decanter: "Be not deceived; God is not mocked, for whatsoever a man soweth, that shall he also reap?" In those days of sinless perfection, free whisky might do, but it would be a very dangerous experiment in this corrupt age of the world. But the real truth of the matter is, that the people who lived in the days of our grandfathers' unadulterated whisky, "old oaken buckets," and "dear, old decanters," were not any better than we are to-day. Neither were they any more sober, if all of the truth could be known. The bad things they did in those days were not so easily found out as they are to-day when railroads, telegraphs, daily papers, and all other contrivances for the spread of evil reports are everywhere in the land. The report that a neighbor or his young boy was drunk at a certain time, if thought to be a matter of sufficient importance to start out on a journey could not get beyond the immediate neighborhood or vicinity of its occurrence until it had become too old and stale to excite the least degree of interest. And so with all of the other short-comings of our grandfathers and their neighbors. It is, moreover, absurd to suppose that our unskilled ancestors understood better the art of making whisky than those who are at this time engaged in the unhallowed business, and while it may be that many poisonous substances are put into the stimulating decoctions of to-day in order to make them kill quicker and at a greater distance, there is no law which compels a man to drink them, and if he is able to afford it, he can get as good an article of spirituous liquor to-day as he could have obtained at any age of the world. Will any man doubt or dispute the proposition that as perfectly pure and harmless whisky can be made now from the same materials as could have possibly been manufactured by our forefathers who made no pretensions to chemical science? If such scientific knowledge has infused into the whisky of to-day a more active and more dangerous property than it possessed in olden times, do you suppose that the manufacturers would not throw aside the science and return to the simple methods adopted by our ancestors for the manufacture or production of pure, unadulterated whisky? Adulterated whisky! What an idea! What ingredient on this wide earth can be found that could be termed an adulteration of this deadly product of the still?

Having said this much in regard to the adulteration of whisky, to which so much of drunkenness is attributable by these people who are always pining for the good old days of our "grand daddies" and free whisky, I desire to submit another proposition, and that is this: you simple minded sons of a sanctified ancestry, bring me one single decanter of that pure, holy, unadulterated whisky that will not make a man beastly drunk if he drinks enough of it, and I will at once change the positions I am now contending for and advocate with all the feeble powers of my mind the abrogation of all license laws and every legal restriction; and instead of wasting the energies of my mind upon the study of methods to suppress and destroy the evil, I will boldly advocate its free and unfettered manufacture and sale. When whisky is bereft of the demon which lurks in every drop of its constituent elements then its production and sale will need no restriction or regulation whatever at the hands of the government. It will then cease to produce insanity, death, misery and despair, and all the catalogue of indescribable evils which now cry aloud for a practical remedy. What need would there then be of attempting to suppress it?

But I cannot close this chapter without recurring to the Constitution, to some of whose misconstrued provisions and limitations of power the opposition to prohibitory laws are constantly appealing. If I am not mistaken, I believe that the Federal Constitution declares that taxation shall be equal and uniform. To construe this provision according to the same rule demanded by some of our Democratic leaders for the construction of other provisions or limitations of the same instrument referring to sumptuary laws and the depriving of a man of life, liberty and property, without due process of law, and make all of them apply directly to the acts of the individual states, or their people, would force the State government to abolish the disproportionate taxation on the traffic in whisky. If the sale of whisky is as legitimate and harmless within itself as traffic in other commodities, as is strongly insisted by the advocates of license, then, how can we reconcile the action of the State governments in imposing such burdens upon the business, with that provision or requirement of the Federal Constitution, the supreme law of the land, which declares that taxation shall be equal and uniform? But the true construction of these provisions, as has long since been established by authority, is, that they are intended to limit and restrain the powers of Congress and have no more application to the legislatures of the states in the enactment of laws for the regulation and government of their internal affairs than they have to the sovereign power of a foreign country. The State of Texas can lawfully impose taxes *ad libitum*, whether altogether equal and uniform or not, if not prohibited by the plain import of her own Constitution, provided it does not operate to the prejudice of the rights of persons which are specially protected by the positive terms of the Federal Constitution.

The drummer's tax was recently declared unconstitutional because it was held to be in conflict with the provision of the constitution of the United States, which gives to Congress the exclusive right to regulate commerce between the States, and not because of the objection that such taxes were not equal and uniform: (Constitution U. S. Art. 1, Section VIII). From this and what has been said in a preceding chapter, it is, I think, clearly to be seen that the provisions, limitations, and positive requirements of the organic law of of the Federal government have no application whatever to the power of the states to tax, license, or destroy the traffic in liquor or anything else detrimental to her people. If such construction can be placed upon the Federal Constitution as would abridge the rights of the different states to pass laws for the suppression or prevention of crime within the limits of their several jurisdictions, then is the Democratic theory of our system of government untrue, and the people of Texas ought to know it at once. They ought not to be kept in the dark. The pretended leaders of the party who are harping on constitutional limitations ought to fall into the ranks of the opposite party, where they belong. Those men, however high in authority, who go about over the country appealing to the spirit of our American institutions as interpreted by the founders of the Demoaratic party, ought to get for their own use a political primer, and study the rudiments of Democracy, the first principles of constitutional government.

As stated before, the question of constitutionality with reference to the organic law of our own State is fully solved by the fact that the authority for the proposed prohibitory law is to become a part of the Constitution itself; and being the last expression of the people, (the Constitution makers), upon [the subject, it would prevail over any existing provision which might be construed to be in conflict with the amendment. The license system has perhaps had the effect to diminish the evils of drunkenness, but it has proved itself powerless to destroy it. Local option has done much good in some localities of the State, but State Prohibition is the grand effort which must accomplish more than them all.

Before closing this chapter I desire to notice another objection to the passage of prohibitory laws by a State which is frequently urged by the opposition. That objection is, that the passage of such laws by the State or by the people of a subordinate division of the same under the provision of the local option law in noway interferes with the right of the United States to issue licenses in accordance with the internal revenue laws of the general government; and I have within the last few months heard the advocates of whisky make use of that argument, and that too with wonderful effect. Within the same time I have read a lengthy article in a respectable weekly newspaper of Texas, for whose editor I have the very highest regard, in which it was insisted that as the Federal government would not, and could not, be prohibited by State law from issuing licenses to whisky dealers, such law was practically inoperative by reason of the conflict. That there are some people in the world so ignorant of the general principles of our government as to be influenced by such a fallacy, is by no means surprising; but that men who make any sort of pretension to a knowledge of public affairs to entertain or express such an idea is truly an intellectual phenomenon. Aside from the long line of decisions of the higher courts of the country, it would seem that ordinary common sense would suggest the absurdity of such a proposition. It is true that there is such a law enacted under the authority of that provision of the Federal Constitution which gives to Congress the power to collect taxes for the support of government which makes it incumbent upon every man who wishes to engage in the liquor traffic, to provide himself with an internal revenue permit or license for which he pays an amount fixed by such law, the object of the law being to raise money to carry on the machinery of the general government. This law is general in its operation and takes no cognizance whatever of the restriction by way of license or otherwise imposed by the several States. Suppose a man is too poor to take out the license required by the State, county and municipal authorities within the limits of which he proposes or desires to do business? Suppose he should think that these laws are unjust, oppressive, and subversive of his personal liberty ; and ignoring the right of the State, county, or city to interfere with his business by their exorbitant taxation, should take out a license from the United States government and open his saloon in defiance of State law? If the payment of this internal revenue tax gives him an absolute right, independent of the State, county, or municipal authority, to "go on with his rat killing," then he can go on with impunity, in spite of prohibition, whether local or general, statutory or constitutional. It is not very strange or unaccountable that the United States government, will accept a man's money and issue a license if he is fool enough to risk the ability of the State and local authorities to punish him for a violation of their laws.

All the general government can do when he pays his internal revenue is, to say to him, "So far as I am concerned, you may sell enough mean whisky to destroy every home and blast every ennobling aspiration in your State, and you will not be molested by a prosecution in my courts. I have nothing whatever to do with any controversy that may arise between you and your State or your municipal government. That is none of my business, and if you get into the jail or penitentiary, it is no fault af mine, and I have no power under the Constitution or laws to relieve you from the consequences of your folly. To make the proposition more clear by way of illustration; here are two persons who have an interest, or supposed interest in some tract of land; a third party comes along and desires the privilege of cutting off the timber which is of value. He goes to one of the part owners and purchases his interest or secures his permission to enter upon the premises. When he gets into possession, instead of taking such a proportion as is covered by his privilege, he attempts to take it all. Now it is plain to be seen that the man who had consented to the entry without regard to the consideration he receives, can have no cause of complaint and has no right to object to the trespass. But the other part owner may prosecute his action of trespass and damages, and in some cases may have a writ of injunction against him. To apply the illustration to the three parties concerned in the matter before us; the United States government claims, and we assume justly, an interest in the blood-money of the traffic in liquor, and the several State governments also set up a claim to an interest in the same unholy price of so much of the social, moral and material prosperity and happiness of their people. The saloon-keeper compromises with the general government and undertakes "to stand off" the agents of the State when they come around to demand her share of the spoils. In this whisky-selling business it must be evident that it takes three to make a bargain. Perhaps I may say four, and sometimes it takes five.

First, a man must make a bargain with the devil, and his conscience, if he has one, for the price of the excellent service he is to do in the promotion of his cause. He must, in the next place, make a bargain with Uncle Sam for the privilege of drumming for his satanic employer. Then, before he can begin his ungodly work of destruction he must settle with the State and if he lives in an incorporated city he must pay to its government a hundred or so dollars to aid in the prosecution of increased crime, to punish and maintain in the city prisons the poor, pitiful drunkards he has made in the pursuit of an occupation made lawful by the sanction of three seperate and independent governments. And yet they say that to engage in this business is a natural and even inalienable right when it absolutely requires the combined sanction of three distinct systems of civilized government to secure to a man, covered all over with the glories of American liberty — personal liberty — this God-given, blood-bought, inalienable right to traffic in whisky. But for all this there is one government established before the origin of human dynasties or republican institutions from whose transcendent authority no license to make drunkards, vagabonds, and criminals can ever be issued. The penalties it inflicts upon the conscience of the dealer in the elements of death and social disorder and ruin may never be known to the public; he may crush during the whole of his worse than useless existence every compunction of the silent monitor within his casehardened breast, but there will come a time in the not far distant beyond when he will certainly appear before a court, not to answer a prosecution for a failure to pay occupation taxes and to take out license, but for a whole catalogue of murders and other high crimes and misdemeanors of which he may perhaps never have heard during life, but for which he finds when too late that he is to be held criminally responsible before a court where all secrets are made known.

CHAPTER XII.

PROHIBITION AND THE BIBLE.

Deeply and firmly implanted in the human consciousness there is found in every age and social condition of mankind an idea or realization of dependency coupled with a feeling of respectful awe and reverence for some superior being or intelligence. Man in his most barbarous and unenlightened state falls down and worships at the shrine of some sort of object which he deems superior to himself. Whatever of goodness and virtue and all else that constitutes the highest qualities he may in his crude notions conceive as belonging to the best of his race, he attributes to that superior being in the highest degree. In a state of profound heathenism, when brute force and courage are supposed to be the highest traits of character and most worthy of emulation, the mind ascribes to that being which it worships and adores, those estimable qualities in a degree beyond its own comprehension. In more advanced ages of man's civilization, when his mind becomes developed and expanded, when he learns more of wisdom and of virtue and how to read the foot-prints of God in the light of his infinite goodness and mercy, he loses sight of those sterner attributes of his maker which terrify the ignorant and the barbarous and delights to contemplate his milder majesty and to the beautiful order of his works, learns to conform the order of his life. This respect and veneration towards God and his revealed word to-day exercises, and justly so, more influence upon the human mind and affections and upon the thoughts and actions of mankind, than all other instrumentalities combined.

So strong are the religious feelings and so deep-seated and inexorable the religious prejudices of mankind in general that if you can only engage them upon the prosecution of any work, however hazardous, or in the support of any proposition, however absurd, when properly understood, you can overcome all opposing forces and all opposing arguments, however deeply founded upon reason and experience. The reader will readily call to mind from well-authenticated history at least a hundred illustrations of the truth here asserted. To illustrate extensively is not within the scope of this work, which is intended to be brief and strictly practical. If you can convince the masses of the people that prohibition is in the least inconsistent with the teachings of the Bible, and that Christ, while on earth, was a wine-bibber and taught that intemperance was a virtue and drunkenness was no crime; if you can get them to believe that this immaculate exemplar of the truths of his own precious gospel favored the establishment and maintenance of saloons, then there is no use to go on with an effort to adopt prohibition in the State, or even in a county or a precinct. When the advocates of whisky gain this point, which they are making a desperate effort to do, they will have accomplished their work and the advocates of the measure may as well surrender at once. Nor am I disposed to say in view of the high estimate I have ever been taught to place upon the beauty of Christ's spotless character and example, that the people would not be right in voting against prohibition or against any other human institution if it should be established as a fact that he when on earth had set a precedent for their action by his great and glorious example.

And this brings me to the discussion of the question: Did Christ, by precept or otherwise, put himself on the record as opposed to prohibition? In other words, did He, the acknowledged Son of God, by his works declare himself in favor of saloons? If He did, and I can be made to believe it, then I am just so much of a good christian, although I make no extravagant pretensons, to follow the precedent and to take back every word I have said in the preceding pages, and taking up my cross, I will fall into the bloated, staggering ranks of the anti-prohibitionists and fight a good fight; at least, I promise that I will fight to the very best of my ability. I should not consider a man a good, consistent follower of the meek and lowly Lamb, if he could not afford to stay with him at all times and under all circumstances, through fiery trials and "through evil as well as through good report." Not only will I align myself with the opposition, but I will do all in my power to persuade others to do likewise. And why should I not? If we imitate Christ, can we be far in the wrong? I think not. And right here I desire to notice, rather by way of parentheses, that the saloon-keepers and their spokesmen, whom I am not disposed to personate, while they are proposing to follow Christ in this one particular, in selling, drinking, and advocating whisky, at all times, studiously avoid following him in any other of his teachings. Count up, if you can, what other things they have or propose to do to show forth the glory of his name, or to advance the cause of his kingdom on earth. Let us right here demand of them that if they propose to follow Christ and His teaching in the matter of selling and advocating whisky (?) they must show their consistency by accepting and following Him in all others. If they will only do that, society need not trouble itself about the whisky they may sell while in the act of imitating Christ. We would have no need for prohibitory legislation either statutory or constitutional. No more necessity for them than there was in Christ's day.

But having carried that branch of the argument to a legitimate absurdity, I will go back a little farther and see if there is any authority in the Bible for the assumption that its teachings are in any way opposed to the principle of prohibition. The example of Lot is often referred to by these latter-day followers of Christ and exponents of the truths of the Bible. We are nowhere commanded to take Lot as our criterion. On the other hand, his character suffers the greatest disparagement in many other particulars. Take every one of those old Testament characters who drank to excess, and you will find that the act was clearly disapproved and generally punished. In not a solitary instance do we find that God ever bestowed a special blessing on a man because he got drunk. There is one peculiarity about the old Testament biographies, and that is, that they show up the bad as well as the good side of their heroes or subjects. If one sinlessly perfect life is given throughout the whole Bible including both the New and the Old Testaments, except that of Christ, I am unable to call it to mind. Take Abraham, Moses, David, and Solomon — take all of the old prophets and patriarchs whose histories have been written, and we find them covered all over with blemishes, blemishes recognized and severely condemned by the inspired historians themselves.

Come down to Christ's time and take up the personal history of his disciples and immediate associates, and you will find evidence of the weakness of the flesh, though walking in the shining light of the divine presence. Thomas was a sceptic and Peter a coward. Judas, though a traitor, was not the only one of Christ's companions who had faults. Because Thomas had his doubts, does it follow that we all should be sceptics? Because Peter got scared and denied Christ, does it authorize us, nay, even require us to do likewise in the face of the commandment which informs us of the fact that he who is ashamed of Christ before men, of him will Christ be ashamed before his father which is in heaven? Because

Christ for no other purpose on earth than to make a demonstration of his power converted water into wine, does it follow that he intended thereby to set an example to the world which would lead to the practical abrogation of all of his teachings? It is not material whether it was fermented or unfermented wine as some of our prohibition friends and advocates have labored so hard to establish. Put the very harshest construction upon it and admit that Christ made the very strongest of wine for the use of the guests at the wedding and that they drank it even to drunkenness, of which I believe, we have no account, the act must be construed with reference to the context of his life.

In construing a law for the government of human action we are bound to construe it with reference to the objects it was intended by the legislature to accomplish, whatever may be its literal import. Shall the actions of our precious Redeemer be gauged by a harsher and less liberal rule of construction? Shall we leave out of our enquiry into the rectitude and moral significance of any isolated action of His while on earth, the object and purpose of His glorious mission, to make men nobler and better, to redeem them from a lost, ruined and hopeless condition? In view of the matchless consistency of His life, with its sublime purposes and objects; of the life which He sacrificed upon the altar of man's possible redemption, is it charitable—is it not sacriligious to even suggest that He intended by the first manifestation of His divine power over the elements around Him to lay the foundation of a power and establish a principle that would finally work out the complete overthrow of His kingdom on earth? It is unjust to Christ. It is shameful to humanity. I am surprised that a man who pretends to even a shadow of reverence for the christian religion, who has the least regard for the Bible, or respect for himself, would stand up before an audience in a chri tian land, composed even of drunkards, fresh from the slime of the gutter, and charge Christ with being the author of so foul and blighting a curse as the infamous liquor traffic. Or to say that He, by any act of His, wilfully encouraged this debasing and destroying evil which has done more to thwart and impede the progress of the cause than the devil and all of his angels operating through all other mediums.

Solomon, the strongest in mind, though probably not so strong in other respects, of the old testament writers, wrote many centuries before Christ: "Wine is a mocker and strong drink is raging, and whosoever is deceived thereby is not wise." Christ was aware of the fact that the writer of those words, bristling with experimental truth, had been king of a great nation, the nation from which He himself had descended. He knew that with all his faults he had written with the hand of inspiration, and that what he had written was a part of the scriptures, when He spoke those other memorable words; "Search the scriptures for in them ye think ye have eternal life, and they are they which testify of Me." He did not say You must not accept as the truth as they were a part of the law and inspired words of his Father, the writings of Solomon and especially that part which positively declares that "Wine is a mocker, and strong drink is raging." He also knew that there had long existed a class of people, or rather an order or society of persons who called themselve Rechabites, who had ever been faithful to their vow of total abstinence, and who had been rewarded by authority for their fidelity to their obligations, and yet we nowhere find where He rebuked them or expressed the least disapprobation on account of their abstinence and the honor they had received. The order, I believe, existed in His day. Others of the same character were in the same land, but yet He nowhere commands or advises them to turn from the alleged error of their way and patronize the saloon-keepers.

I must pass on to something else, but before leaving this

innocent man who has been wickedly and falsely accused of encouraging the liquor traffic, I desire to return to the event of the marriage at Cana of Galilee. Christ did not go there to interfere with the established customs of society. His "time had not fully come." He did not go there as an invited guest to disturb the customary joys of a wedding occasion. His surroundings, His authority, His influence were not such as would permit Him to assume the unenviable and generally obnoxious position of a public censor. He had up to that time done no extraordinary act which evinced in the slightest degree that He was God in the flesh, and even if He had been so recognized at the time it is doubtful if He could have prevailed by the use of ordinary means or persuasion upon the host or the guests to have laid aside the long established custom of having wine upon wedding occasions. Suppose you are invited to a wedding or any other ordinary social gathering; you have peculiar tastes which prominently develope and bring to the surface your likes and dislikes either in the matter of diet or apparel. You go to the table and you yet something you don't relish? Is it the part of good breeding to complain? Suppose that some lady's dress is not made in a fashion to suit you; would it be very good manners for you "to speak right out in the meeting" and say what you thought upon that very delicate subject?

Suppose, furthermore, to thoroughly meet and answer this question, that there was a scarcity of some article that, by the ordinary custom of the country, was thought indispensable, although you might think entirely otherwise, even that the article was positively, though not fatally, injurious. Suppose that you had it within your power, even by the potency of a word, to gratify the supposed wants of the company, and thereby complete the happiness of the occasion, you would be very apt to do it for no other purpose than to fill up the measure of the happiness of the guests.

We can not at all times ignore conventionalities, especially when no great injury is done, but, ah, suppose if such a supposition is at all allowable, that you felt within you the impulses of a deity waiting for a fit opportunity to manifest itself in the performance of a miracle? Here I draw a veil over the scene and leave the balance to the serious contemplation of the reader.

But an anti-prohibitionist orator, we will call him for short, "Orator Puff"—asks, "Does not St. Paul, or Solomon, or some of the prophets say somewhere in the lids of the Bible to a man named Timothy, or Clover, "Take a little whisky or brandy, or something of the sort, for your headache, or sick stomach, or words to that effect?" Then, if it is admitted that something of the sort was actually said by St. Paul, the conclusion naturally follows, in their estimation, and according to their false logic, that the saloon business is not only a legitimate occupation, but specially recommended by the scriptures.

God made every thing for a noble purpose.

The alcoholic principle, whatever we may call it and whatever form it may assume, has not only its proper place in the physical universe, but in all probability is as indispensable in its place as any other however apparently useful. That wine, whisky and brandy are sometimes beneficial in cases of actual sickness as arsenic, morphine, strychnine, and even other preparations known to *materia medica* may safely be conceded. Indeed, in every law that has been passed, or proposed, I believe that provision is made for sick stomachs and such bodily ailments, as the one from which Timothy was suffering when St. Paul advised him to take a little wine for his stomach's sake and his often infirmities. According to every construction of human language and inference from the same, I would suppose that Timothy was not only sick at the stomach but that he was often subject to such attacks. Suppose, however, that Timothy was not sick, Paul evidently thought that he was. Perhaps he looked pale and depressed in his spirits, and Paul, not being a physician, but belonging, I believe, to the legal profession, thought that a little wine would be beneficial in restoring him to his usual vigor and spirits. It would be rather natural for a man who had for years before he was converted engaged in the practice of law, to have given a similar prescription. Did Paul anywhere in his varied writings advise Timothy or any one else to quit preaching and go off and start him a saloon? If he did I have no recollection of the passage.

Moreover, I do not believe that there can be found in the Bible, either in the Old or in the New Testament, a single expression which endorses drunkenness or even intemperance in any of its forms. Neither do I believe that a solitary line can there be found, which indicates in the slightest degree that the people of any State or government may not without violence to the spirit or letter of God's word entirely and absolutely prohibit its manufacture and sale within its limits. One thing we must learn if we have not already learned it, and that is, that while the elementary principles of law as found in the Bible are sacred and constitute a safe basis for our own enlightened jurisprudence, those laws by themselves would fall far short of meeting the demands of the present advanced age of our civilization. There are hundreds and perhaps thousands of good, wholesome laws upon the statute books and in the constitutions of our own and other States, for which we find no sort of authority or precedent in the scriptures.

"But," says Orator Puff, "did not Christ in instituting the Lord's supper not only authorize, but positively enjoin upon His followers the drinking of wine as a token of His own death and sufferings upon the cross? Did He not by that, the last act of His life set an example to justify mankind in making beasts of themselves throughout all generations? Did He not thereby bequeath to posterity a legacy in the guise of a dispensation to get drunk, which can not be taken away by human authority? Did He not in that one act lay the corner stone of personal liberty to drink wine and other intoxicating liquors, which can not be taken away by constitutional majorities." We recur once more to the true rule of construing a law or an action. For what purpose was the Lord's Supper ordained and established? What object did Christ have in view when He blessed the bread and the wine, and gave them to His disciples as a token of His broken body and shed blood and commanded them to take them in remembrance of his death and his sufferings for the sins of the world? I have not time to speak at length of the manner in which the important events of history, both sacred and profane, were commemorated in those early periods of time, when the art of printing was undreamed of, and that of writing was understood by none other than the priests and the scribes. It is unnecessary to speak at length of the custom of the people in the erection of monuments, in establishing feasts, and in setting apart days for the purpose of reminding themselves and their posterity of important historical events, which should not be forgotten.

Christ had, almost from the beginning of His mission, used a beautiful figure to explain or portray to the minds of His disciples the true relationship that existed between them and Himself. He compared Himself to the vine, and His disciples to the branches. "I am the vine, ye are the branches." Who will say that the figure is not beautifully designed and expressed? Who will dare say that the relation existing between Christ and His true disciples was not well represented by the vine and its branches, ever entwining themselves around the parent stem, intertwining with each other, and reaching out and clothing in verdure and beauty the nude and unshapely objects of the vegetable kingdom, by which they are surrounded? The juice of the grape represented the blood and the life of the vine. As the branches drink of the blood of the vine, so the disciples, carrying out this beautiful figure, are commanded to drink it as a token to ever remind them of the sacred relationship represented by the figure. Nothing but the juice of the grape would have sufficed or could have been used without destroying the beauty of this figure of speech, so aptly representing the true relationship existing between Christ and His disciples; "the vine and its branches." They could not take this appropriate emblem without recalling the figure representing the sacred and important relationship.

I trust that this is sufficient to satisfy such of my readers as may have been led by demagogues into the erroneous belief, that Christ chose the wine as the representative of His shed blood, for the purpose of putting the stamp of His approbation upon the indiscriminate and excessive use of intoxicating liquors. Such a construction, if allowed to be placed upon the actions of Christ would lead mankind, whom He came to redeem from the curse of sin, into a state of moral depravity more loathsome and at war with His own teachings, than any example or precedent ever set or established by the great author of the whole catalogue of evils known to sin-cursed humanity. Again, I say that such a charge is unjust to Christ; sacrilegious and blasphemous in its character and overwhelmingly demoralizing in its tendency.

The teachings of the good Book can not be at war with the best interests of mankind. They cannot be subversive of good morals. If they should appear to establish such an inconsistency the fault must necessarily be in the feeble and perverted understanding of the finite mind, struggling to comprehend a subject beyond its limited capacity. While it may be impossible for the human mind ever to fully understand, harmonize and thoroughly appreciate all of the grand and glorious truths contained in the Bible, if unfettered by prejudice, scepticism and infidility, it must conclude that its teachings are ever consistent with good morals. A contrary view would overturn, utterly destroy its influence for good.

CHAPTER XIII.

PROHIBITION AND NATURAL LAW.

A strictly systematic and logical arrangement of this book would have placed this chapter at the opening, instead of the conclusion of the argument. Rather by accident than otherwise it falls into line as one of the last chapters of the book. It is usually supposed and asserted and that too, by persons of a high order of intelligence, that all human laws have their foundation in the Bible, and this idea has become so generally prevalent, especially among the christian people of the country, that it is with some degree of hesitation that I proceed with an argument that has long since led me to a different conclusion. And in saying this I desire it understood that I do not mean to detract in the least from the authority of that book, nor the importance of the truths it contains. I would rather reverse the popular notion and say that the rules of human conduct which are contained in that book are derived from a law that antedates not only the Bible but all authentic profane history. It goes far beyond Moses, far beyond Abraham, far beyond the flood. The Mosaic code was written, I believe, about fifteen hundred years before Christ, the principles upon which that law was founded, were laid down at the creation of the material universe. Nothing, either animate or inanimate, nothing belonging to either of the three kingdoms of organized existence has ever been created and placed in this universe without the simultaneous enactment of a law by competent authority, the authority of its creator by which its existence and the peculiar work it is to perform in the unerring economy of nature, are to be governed.

The simplest and the sublimest of created entities have their appropriate laws; the stars which sang together in the morning of the creation, "The fountains of the great deep," as well as the tiniest, tenderest blade of grass which waves and flits in the breeze, each and all have inexorable laws for the government of their existence and their movement however grand, however simple they may seem to the human understanding.

The world could possibly exist in some condition without the Bible; mankind might perhaps be able to maintain his existence upon earth without the aid of the wonderful revelations which it contains, but it is impossible for this finite mind to conceive for a moment that the material universe could be kept together without natural laws, the will of God indelibly written upon the tables of his own handiwork. How it is, and what it is, when it originated, and how it operates, we do not, we can perhaps never know. But we are able to realize the existence of this law, this code of natural laws, and through the bare knowledge of their operation, which is unexplained and unexplainable, so far as the human mind is concerned, we are able to succeed in providing for some of our wants and necessities, and in the preservation of our lives. By this knowledge, which we do not know how to appreciate as we should, we are able to plant our crops in due season, and to calculate with reasonable certainty upon the harvest. It is the purpose of revelation through whatever instrumentality it may come; it was the purpose of Moses and the prophets, and of all of the inspired writers of the New Testament to make known to man such of these laws which are themselves eternal and unchangeable as may not be easily discerned from the operations of nature itself.

Such should be the object of all written law, whether human or divine. Such is the invariable object, purpose, and effect of every divine law; not always the object and results of human legislation and its authoritative construction.

But to discourse further upon natural law generally could add nothing to the purpose for which this chapter is being written. The above will serve as a major premise of the argument before me. I could not hope to reach the conclusion in view without saying thus much in a general way upon the subject of natural law. No elaborate argument is necessary to establish the proposition that man is subject to this law of all nature. Many of the requirements of this perfect law of his being he has already learned, others he has not learned after centuries of patient and persevering study and application; and still others, it seems, that he has studiously endeavored to keep himself from learning in the very presence of the infliction of their direful and disastrous penalties. The law of his nature which demands that he shall be temperate in all things, he refuses to understand and if accidentally found out, he persistently refuses to obey it. He does not have to search the Bible or human statutes and decisions to find out that he ought to be temperate in all things; the law of his own personal being is constantly reminding him of his willful or unintentional violations of this law.

And before going further with the argument I desire to examine into the true import of this word "temperance" as used by St. Paul and other inspired writers of the old and New Testament scriptures. I also desire to speak of the probphrase "temperate in all things."

It is sometimes supposed that the words "all things" embrace all sorts of things that can be enjoyed without reference to their moral character or tendency. That is to say, that a man is thereby authorized to do any "thing" the mind can conceive of, provided he does it in moderation. That view of the import of those words would soon lead us to assume that a man may not only get temperately drunk, but to engage in stealing, arson, burglary, profanity, and every conceivable violation of the laws of society or common decency, provided he does them in moderation. In other words he may with impunity do a little moderate or temperate stealing, swearing or housebreaking. The absurdity is too plain to require further notice. The passage must mean that a man must be temperate in all good things—the bad things he must let entirely alone if he desires to do right in the sight of God, and in the estimation of his fellow-man.

But going back to the argument, I have to say that there is one thing we all know without the aid of biblical inspiration, and that is that if we eat too much, even of such food as is specially adapted to our physical necessities, we suffer the penalty. We are thereby informed in a manner not to be mistaken that we have violated a law of our being, which is benignly intended as a warning not to do so again. If we are wise and if we have proper self-control, we will certainly heed these timely warnings and in the future govern ourselves accordingly; otherwise we will go on heedlessly eating to excess until struck down by the penalty of outraged natural law. When found to be incorrigible our Master cuts us down as the barren fig-tree.

In such instances we violate two natural laws, one of whose penalties is invariably visited upon our physical constitution; the other may operate upon our conscience. The results of the latter may, however, under ordinary circumstances never be perceivably felt and realized by the transgressor, but it may be dissipated throughout. God does not create any thing in vain. He causes the earth to produce a sufficiency of food, and if we could only come to a true understanding of the world's necessities, my impression from the idea I have of the divine economy, is, that there is not any too much, although it may be quite unequally distributed.* Suppose now that every man who has an abundance of such things should be a gormandizer and a glutton? Suppose he should at every meal eat two or three times as much as is necessary for his health and his subsistence; would there not in all probability be a scarcity of provisions and some people be forced to go hungry? Now, if there is no such natural law in addition to the one which operates on the individual himself, then he may eat to his own physical destruction and no one has any right to complain. Not even would the God who made him and provided him and the world with the means of subsistence have any cause to interpose a further objection than is manifested through the medium of a sick stomach. If one man can do this without violating this supposed law of his nature, then every other man who is able to afford it can do the same thing, and at least half of the world would have to go on half rations and some, no doubt, die of starvation.

But to proceed to the discussion of the relation between the prohibition of the sale of intoxicating liquors and the rights, privileges, and immunities of our natural law. I have already assumed or admitted that alcohol, in at least some of its forms, may be beneficial in the various arts which are useful, and that it is sometimes necessary as a medicine, just as other dangerously poisonous compounds are essential in the treatment of bodily diseases. It may possibly be good for the headache, backache, snake-bites, bad colds, influenza, and consumption for aught that I know, and if so, it would probably be the duty of a competent physician to administer it in small quantities, (never by the quart or gallon) in some

---

*This view is suggestive without reference to the Malthusian Theory of the relation between population and subsistence which Henry George assails in his "Progress and Poverty."

cases. But while this may be true the converse is equally true, that it should not be administered in any case when the patient is afflicted with the very best of physical health. If it should be, then by reason of what natural law? For what purpose ought it to be taken or administered? Does it nourish and strengthen the body? Does it add to its tissues? Does it, in any way whatever, add vigor to the brain or the nervous system? What possible good can it accomplish? I pause here for a reply. If it should be determined by the intelligent reader that it does no good whatever, the conclusion necessarily follows that it does harm. The human system naturally rebels at all foreign substances. You may as well hope to stick a thorn in your flesh and let it remain there without pain or uneasiness as to inject into your stomach a liquid not adapted in some way to its necessities or requirements.

Nature will not allow any loafers in her workshop. Those who venture to go there must work even though they should do no better than to break some of the wheels of the intricate machinery or even tear down the shop. It must be conceded by every fair-minded man that whisky is quite active and energetic in his work. He is of strong force of character. Indeed he is invariably "independent in all things and neutral in nothing." He was never known to lie idle even in a weak stomach very long at a time. He rushes at once to the office of the head-clerk or manager of the human system, turns him out of doors, seizes upon the passions, inflames them to their utmost tension and fury, and of the peaceable harmless machine that it was he makes a mighty engine of death and destruction. Do you think for a moment that whisky is neutral? That his influence upon the human system, except as is manifested through the abnormal activity of the brain, is neither good nor bad? If you answer that the influence is for good, I demand that you tell me in what respect and further that you prove your assertion by appropriate demonstration or experimental truth. If you answer that the influence or effect of whisky or other form of alcoholic stimulants upon the human system is bad then why not discourage its use, if for no other reason than for the sake of your love for humanity ? When it is admitted by the opposition that the physical results of drunkenness are bad, then have I not established the proposition that drunkenness is in violation of natural law? There can be no conflict between natural law and natural right.

If no natural right is invaded by the prohibition of the manufacture and sale of intoxicating liquors, etc., then what objection can be urged to the measure on that account, as is so often attempted? But they are now ready to say that prohibition undertakes to prohibit a man from killing himself which is one of those rights that we read about as having been guaranteed to us by the constitution of our revolutionary fathers, who fought, bled and died, to secure to their progeny the God-given right to commit suicide.

It is earnestly contended that if the State, or a majority of its peole, can interfere with a man's right to purchase whisky or his facilities for obtaining it, can, upon the same principle, interfere with his right to buy and eat bread or any other article of food. The falsity of the reasoning is in this, as has been already stated that the inordinate consumption of such food, though it be a mild stimulant, like coffee, however injurious its excessive use may be to the system, in no way deprives a man of the right use of his mental faculties, nor has it ever been known to make a man vicious in his disposition or dangerous to society. The use of intoxicating liquors is followed by all of these effects. It is wholly unnecessary to speak of these terrible effects and their consequences. I could not hope to do justice to the subject. If a State has a right to punish crime, upon what reason or principle shall it be deprived of the right to prevent its commission? The main object of the punishment of offenses is to prevent their recurrence, and as is supposed by some, to execute vengeance upon the transgressor, however flagrant and heinous his crime.

It is supposed that the example thus set before the people will necessarily have the effect to deter others who are viciously disposed from the commission of crime. However much some individuals may enjoy the influence of the penalties of the law upon their enemies, the great commonwealth does not share in the clamor for revenge. If the main object of the infliction of pains and penalties upon violators of the law to prevent the commission of crime, why can not the State make an effort to accomplish this same result without the shedding of blood? Besides, the punishment of the guilty can not blot out the consequences of the act; can not restore the life of the murdered victims; can not bring back to its owner the property destroyed by the torch of the drunken incendiary. It is folly to contend that the State has no interest whatever in the lives and happiness of its citizens. For the preservation and protection of these, the substantial elements of a State's own wealth and greatness, government is established and maintained. If not for these and other purposes having in view the promotion of the welfare and happiness of the people at large, then I would like very much to know what they are for.

If it is conceded that such are the true objects of governments and that it is right or expedient to have a government at all, then by what kind of logic can we escape the conclusion that the State has the natural right to use its authority and every legitimate measure to enforce it for the accomplishment of the objects of its existence? If the commission of crime is in the least wise detrimental to the best interests of society and destruction of the happiness of the people has not the State the right according to every principle of natural law and natural justice to prevent or suppress it?

Let the shining lights of the anti-prohibitionists of Texas answer this question. If they fail to do it to the satisfaction of the intelligent voters of the State, then let them forever hereafter hold their peace. If they should deny to the State the right to prevent crime by the timely removal of the cause or at least some of the most prolific causes of crime, then let them explain why the denial of such right should be limited in its application to the proposed effort of the State to suppress the infamous liquor traffic, the recognized hot bed of crime and social disorder? If the principle is to be applied to the effort of the State or its people to abate this nuisance, to pluck out by the roots this great moral cancer which is feeding upon the best interests of the State converting so many of its people into drunkards, paupers, and criminals, then let it apply to them all. Let it be said that the State of Texas has no right whatever to interfere with the personal liberty of its most wayward and God-forgetting citizen to commit any crime he may choose from the whole catalogue of offenses embraced in the penal code of the State.

But to return once more to a consideration of the natural law as involved in this great controversy. Let us consider the supposed natural right a man has to manufacture intoxicating liquors. As stated a few pages back, God has only provided a sufficiency of food for his people. No more and no less, and if ways and means could be devised and carried into effect by man for the proper distribution of the same, it would doubtless be found that there would not be any to much. The great trouble has ever been in effecting such distribution.

So many people are poor and unable to purchase, the rich are generally too selfish to send out much of their surplus on considerations of charity. The conversion of so much healthful food for which so many of the poor people of the country are clamoring into a commodity not possessing, so far as I have been able to find out, a solitary element of nutrition, does not seem to me to be in accord with the economy of nature and hence a violation of natural law. This leads me to a casual consideration of the process by which this unfortunate transformation is accomplished.

It is known that whisky is made by a process of distillation, or evaporation and condensation followed by what is termed a rectifying process by which the essence or spirit of a substance is extracted. This substance may be corn, rye, barley, sugar cane, and perhaps a great many others. Before the distilling process can properly begin it is necessary to produce an incipient stage of decomposition, or we may say, putrefaction. The substance is put into a form and condition most favorable for spoiling. After being ground up and mixed with water it is kept heated in a degree most favorable for the invasion of that implacable enemy of all organic matter called ferment, which eats into, sours, and destroys every nutritious and life-sustaining property that may be contained in such organic substance. When sufficiently rotten and soured by fermentation it is condensed by heat into vapor, then condensed and re-condensed into a worm "that biteth like a serpent and stingeth like an adder."

By what law of nature does man justify the conversion of so much of the food God has provided for a noble purpose into an insidious poison, which, being taken into the system, makes the poor poorer, and reduces the rich and self-sustaining to the condition of beggary? I desire it understood, however, that this latter suggestion is not intended to weigh much in the argument against whisky, and in favor of the legal prohibition of its sale and manufacture. I verily believe that the transformation of so much nutritious food which could be used in the relief of the starving poor through this artificial rotting process is in itself a violation of natural law. But whether this view should hold good or not in the estimation of my readers who are making an honest search for the truth, its unrestricted manufacture and sale is in direct violation of that general principle of law which underlies the organic structure of all government, the general welfare of the people, "the supreme law of the land." I close this chapter by a recurrence to the motto I have adopted expressive of the leading principles contended for throughout the preceding pages of this work: "Salus populi suprema lex," the welfare of the people is the highest law. The next and last chapter will be devoted to the press, whose power and influence can not be overlooked in the discussion of so great a question as the one I have been considering.

CHAPTER XIV.

PROHIBITION AND THE PRESS.

THE DAILY AND WEEKLY PAPERS—ANTI-PROHIBITION SPEAKERS AND LEADERS—CHEERING WORDS TO THE TEMPERANCE WORKERS, ETC.

I can not conclude this work without some reference to the power of the press, the general tone of which must necessarily exert a large and far-reaching influence not only upon the results of the canvass which is now agitating the minds of our people, but upon the great revolution which is rolling on towards the ultimate destruction of the liquor traffic in the land. The influence of the press, for good or for evil, is entirely beyond estimate; beyond the capacity of the human mind to conceive. I am not vain enough to attempt even a feeble portrayal of the majesty of its power in leading and directing the minds and the hearts of the people. Those who do not read the papers, are led by those who do read them, and they in turn are to a great extent influenced in their opinions by what they gather from their readers. This is indeed an age of newspapers. Time with a large class of our intelligent reading people is too precious to devote to the perusal of books. They read the daily and weekly papers and from them gather almost exclusively their practical ideas of life and its current affairs. The fewest number have time to study the classics or to pour over the old musty volumes of scientific lore or political economy. They read as they run, and run as they read, often without much thought as to the character of their reading. Many there are who take every thing they see in print for the truth. They accept as the best article of logic the very flimsiest specimens of moral, social, and political sophistry.

They do not take time to hunt down the fallacy even though it should establish a proposition in direct conflict with their own individual experience and observation. Indeed, they swallow it all, good, bad, or indifferent. It is this tendency of the present fast age to accept as the truth every assumption indulged in by the biased mind of the newspaper editor or writer, that gives to the press the great power it is known to possess. The grandest truths ever spoken, if conveyed only through the medium of unwritten language can exert but a limited influence as it reaches the understandings of but few. The most palpable falsehood when scattered abroad through the columns of the press may influence thousands to their detriment, possibly leading to their ultimate ruin. This is why the sayings of an editor however insignificant and unreliable he may be in his general character, are of more importance in the estimation of the public than those of any other, though he be as wise as was Solon or Solomon. What a man says "with his mouth" soon perishes; what he says with his paper is treasured up and may live for ages whether it be a truth or a falsehood. What a man says expends itself upon his immediate hearers; what he writes for the press may echo and re-echo throughout all the intellectual universe, and through all time, and its influence for good or for bad may reach into eternity. I speak of this to show why it is that these newspaper men have so much power and influence in moulding public sentiment. Indeed, no great principle can be promulgated among the people without the aid of the press.

We cannot now understand how many kind ever made any perceptible advancement in civilization before the art of

printing was invented. The progress of the arts and sciences
and the knowledge of the principles of human government
must have been slow. We may wonder how there could have
been any progress at all. But be that as it may, we now realize that the art of printing has not only been invented, but
that it has become a mighty engine of power. It is an instrumentality that ought to be used in the service of every righteous cause, in the establishment of every correct principle of
government and of every popular movement having in view
the promotion of the public good. It is a power that the
prohibitionists of Texas ought not to ignore. Every legitimate effort ought to be made, every instrumentality not in
conflict with right, ought to be brought to bear to secure the
co-operation of the press in the accomplishment of the purposes and the objects in view. It is folly to denounce the
country press as venal and corrupt.

It does no good whatever; besides, it does harm ; it makes
matters worse ; it does not in the least keep people from reading the editorial columns of their local papers and believing
every word they may say, however absurd it may be when
logically dissected. Every bad word that you may say against
a newspaper or its editor, however infamous he may be, only
brings him into notice, advertises his paper, and increases its
circulation. Hence, it adds proportionally to its influence on
the opposite side. I do not mean by this however that we
must not repudiate their absurdities, but that in our treatment
of the fallacies contained in their arguments we ought to be
temperate; we ought not to deal in meaningless personalities.

We ought to address what we have to say to the proposition
falsely assumed, and not to the man or to the instrumentality
through which he expressses himself. If the devil should
speak the truth, we ought not to reject it. If our best friend
on earth should give expression to a falsehood, either intentionally or ignorantly, we ought not to accept it because of

our respect and good feeling for the one who originates or propagates the false statement.

Having said this much, I shall proceed more directly to the discussion of the true relation of the press to the people. A failure to understand this relationship and to appreciate the great difficulties encountered by the country press in dealing with great, or even unimportant issues which come up for attention, causes almost, if not all, of the dissatisfaction that is so often and generally expressed by the people at the failure of the newspapers to speak out boldly and unreservedly upon all of such questions, and always to be found on the right side of the controversy. In the very nature of things, a newspaper can not be on both sides of a question at the same time without assuming a very awkward and unsatisfactury attitude in the eyes of the public. One side may be right, both can not be, while it is quite possible for both to be wrong. While every public journal, as well as every private citizen, ought to speak out boldly or fearlessly when public duty or obligation demands such expression, both ought to remain silent under all other circumstances. No one ought to shrink from the discharge of a duty when it is recognized to be such. The decision which he must make for himself of the question whether there is any such duty or obligation to the public as requires a public expression must necessarily depend upon ctrcumstances. While at one time, and under certain circumstances, a man would decide in the affirmative, there may be other times and other circumstances surrounding the case which would require a different decision.

The good book tells us that "He who provideth not for his own household has denied the faith and is worse than an infidel." This may seem to some strange doctrine, yet we can not reject it without irreverance for the teachings of that holy book. If it mean anything, it means that no man is justified in neglecting the imperative wants and necessities of his family without a better excuse than that he feels it to be a higher duty to provide for the public at large than for those whom God has specially entrusted to his care. Suppose we have a poor journalist, and we do not have to go far to find an actual *bona fide* example, who has been brought up to that profession and that he knows no other by which he can eke out a bare support for his family who are daily depending upon him ? Each day of his life he brings home the scanty proceeds of his toil, which is barely sufficient to procure bread and raiment for his wife and little ones ? An exciting local controversy springs up, and his patrons come to daggers points with each other. It may be a question in some degree, however great, affecting the material interests of his town, precinct, or county. Take a local election for instance, with two popular candidates in the field for the same office. The poor publisher may feel that it would be to the interest of all of his patrons that his favorite should be elected and he may further be of the opinion that the election of the other would be quite detrimental to the public welfare. If he espouse the cause of his favorite and advocate his election through the columns of his paper, the friends of the other are certain to withdraw their patronage from his paper. His family can not subsist without it. He is now called upon to make the choice to either be silent upon the subject in so far as the columns of his papers are concerned, or remit the care and support of his household to the cold charity of an unfriendly world. Now, which course ought he to pursue in view of the position and unmistakable teachings of holy writ as above quoted ?

There are times in every one of our lives when silence is not only excusable, but a posttive virtue, and that, too, when the very impulses of our nature would lead us to rebuke what we conceive to be error and folly. The aphorism that "all truths should not be told at all times," applies with peculiar force to the press. The laws themselves would not permit such a thing. No newspaper can lawfully publish the truth when it is destructive of private character unless such truth is a matter in which the public is in some way interested or concerned. But while I am a great advocate of silence under severely trying circumstances and surroundings, I shall not go so far as to say that the same circumstances or surroundings would justify the promulgation of a falsehood or the perpetration of a wrong, that any consideration ought to prevail with a journalist to traffic in his editorial columns. While such commercial transactions can not be punished as bribery, it sustains nearly the same relation to bribery as false swearing does to perjury. It is morally and socially wrong, and ought to be condemned by that portion of the press of the country which has not suffered such pollution. The idea of influencing a man's opinion with gold is an absurdity. Opinions are not made from such stuff, and the expression of such spurious opinion through the columns of the press or any other medium of communication is a cheat and a counterfeit and the very essence of the worst kind of hypocrisy.

But there is another class of newspapers that I desire to discuss, and that is the great money-making institutions known as the dailies, which are usually published by corporate capital. A dozen or perhaps a hundred or more individuals living in different sections of the country, and each perhaps of his own peculiar views upon leading political questions, organize themselves into a corporation for the purpose of establishing and maintaining a great daily paper in some favorable locality.

The stock is divided out and put upon the market just as is the case in other enterprises of a similar character. Officers and directors are elected from among the incorporators; editors, reporters, and business managers are employed, and it is not to be expected otherwise than that such officers should strive to make the enterprise a financial success. If they do not, they are very apt to be relieved of their positions at the very earliest, practicable moment. The exclusive object of the original investment may not be to coin money but the stock soon shifts around and gets into the hands of those who are disposed to make every dollar in sight out of their investment. The advice to the editor and manager will generally, if not invariably, be similar to that of the old man to his son when he started him out into the world: "My son, my advice to you is to make money; make it honestly if you can, but, my son, — make money," The editor and all of his assistants are impersonals. Their names do not appear at the head of any of the columns of such papers. The truth seems to be that the paper is edited by everybody in general and nobody in particular; and as a corporation is notorious for having no soul and no responsibility can be fixed upon any one connected with the enterprise for the unconscionable falsehoods it may choose to promulgate: "for revenue only."

The whole concern is operated on a blind tiger system by which an uninterrupted tissue of falsehoods and absurdities are rolled out upon the public, and nobody is able to find out who operates the internal machinery. Great corporations make very poor martyrs. When you start out to look for a victim to be immolated upon the altar of an unpopular movement, however righteous it may be when fully understood and appreciated, you need not fool away your time with "soulless corporations." They have no suicidal inclinations whatever, nor have they any principles upon which they are inclined to sacrifice their material interests, or for the maintenance of which they are likely to hazzard any portion of their annual dividends. With all due respect to such papers, and they are indispensable in the transmission and distribution of the current news, for which they have every facility, I am constrained to make the suggestion that their editorial columns ought to be abolished by law. It may be put down as a practical certainty that as long as they have editorial space it will be at the service of the highest bidder, and no body is responsible for the moral depravity of the bargain. But before passing from this branch of the subject I desire to say that these seeming reflections upon the integrity of that portion of the daily press as is conducted by corporations has no reference to any particular paper, much less to any individual connected with its management. How could I reflect upon the character and personal integrity of the man who manipulates the "blind tiger" in the unlawful dispensation of the elements of death and social depravity unless I could know "judicially" or otherwise who the manipulator is? How could I reflect upon the personal honor and unimpeachable veracity of the man who writes lies and false arguments for a daily paper when I have not the least idea who that propagator of falsehood and error is?

What I have said is intended to have general application. It is intended to take in every "corporation daily" in the United States and Canada. In their capacity as a medium for the dissemination of news and general intelligence they are indespensible to the welfare and progress of society. As moulders and leaders of public opinion they are totally unreliable, and the masses of the people ought to know better than to accept their mercenary opinions, if opinions they can be called.

But while this is the case with the editorial columns of that particular class of newspapers, it is not so with the great body of the country press. Nearly all of these papers are published by individual capital and labor. The average country editor is not only his own publisher, but his own compositor and his own "printer's devil." The responsibility of every department of the weekly paper of the country usually devolves upon a single person, who has no one to share with him the great volume of abuse and other incidental vexations of personal journalism. If the mechanical department does not come up to the standard he is denounced as a botch workman; if the local and general news items are sparse and of no interest; if the editorials are not sufficiently equivocal and uncertain to cover all sides of the question, he is cursed and bemeaned as a traitor to his country and the best interests of society. Truly the way of the average country editor and publisher is hard and especially so if he is not financially above the whims of his patrons, which is rarely the case. I have been a country editor myself and am prepared to speak from experience as well as from observation. There are many things that come up within the sphere of the circulation of his paper which circumstances prevent him from ventilating through its columns, although they would gratify a spirit of animosity and revenge in a large class of his readers, and who think he ought to notice them specially for their own personal benefit and satisfaction. He is constantly between two fires, and there is no safe way to escape.

When editing a paper at one time I conceived it to be my duty as the friend of a certain candidate for office, to show up the political waywardness and inconsistency of some of his opponents, and ,upon the advice of my colleague I wrote a whole column of personal history which had been furnished me, as I thought, by unquestionably reliable authority. The same day of the publication of the issue containing this scrap of history so interesting to those who were on my own side of the question, the party to whom it referred demanded an immediate personal interview. It so happened that I was in no particular mood for personal interviews at the time. However anxious I may have been at other times to be interviewed by parties desiring my political opinions for the benefit of the public, this was one of the times when I wished especially to be left alone " in the solitude of my own originality." But it was not for me to escape the proposed interview. Fortunately the difficulty was settled without a resort to the established code of honor, and I managed to come out alive and without any serious damage to the reputation of myself or my paper. It taught me a valuable lesson, and from that time till this good hour I have had an aversion to the publication of scraps of personal history, especially when I was to be the historian or responsible for its results.

During my brief and, as some say, brilliant career as an editor and publisher, I had occasion at one time to pay a very high compliment to the beauty and intelligence of a certain popular young lady, "without disparagement to others," of course. The next day I was waited on by a committee of those others for whom no disparagement was intended, and an immediate personal interview with the editor was imperatively demanded. Unfortunately the editor was in. Up to that time I had been vain enough to suppose that I had more courage than an average lion. I imagined that I could face cannon balls without the least trepidation. The idea of being scared by anything in the guise of humanity had never entered my imagination. In this I found that I was sadly mistaken. Suffice it to say that I was "weighed in the balance and found wanting." I surrendered at discretion. I was undone. I stood "speechless" in the awful presence before me. Indeed, I had nothing to say—nothing at all. I was thoroughly interviewed, and my readers "needn't to doubt it." I can not repeat what was said, but I can say one thing, and that is that ever afterwards during my journalistic experience I was mindful of the use I made of even as seemingly harmless a thing as a personal compliment. These were not all the difficulties I encountered, but these are sufficient to illustrate the point I am attempting to make, and that is the impossibility of an editor pursuing in the editorial management of his paper a thoroughly independent course in all matters, even though the principle or interests involved should be of the most trivial and insignificant character.

No man need to enter the profession of a journalist with the expectation of succeeding in accumulating money, or of even preserving intact his own personal safety and at the same time totally ignore the prejudices, and weaknesses common to humanity. It may be that it ought not to be thus, but human nature is an important factor to be considered in every undertaking, and we can not shut our eyes to its foibles. Whoever attempts to ignore them in making his calculations for the present and the future is not wise. Whoever attempts it will certainly fail in his undertakings.

Having said this much in regard to the difficulties in the way of independent journalism, I desire now to apply the principle, I have thus attempted to evolve, to the press and its relation to the question of prohibition. In every county, in every town, in every precinct of the State there are two classes of people; one class in favor of prohibitory laws, the other opposed to such legislation. In most of these subdivisions they are nearly all about equal in number and influence; especially is this true in the towns and cities. To these towns and cities the most refined and the roughest elements of our society seem naturally to gravitate; the medium classes usually prefer to remain in the country. These two elements are naturally antagonistic to each other. In many places, especially the smaller towns of the State, it requires the co-operation of both classes to build up and sustain their public enterprises.

But few country weeklies can live in the smaller towns without the liberal patronage of both, supplemented by the patronage of the intermediates and transients. The result is, that those papers whose very existence depends on the combined patronage of both elements of society are naturally slow to antagonize either. They may not be in sympathy with the whisky traffic. Their editors and publishers may be, and generally are individually in favor of moral and social improvement, and of the suppression of this prolific cause of social disorder; but they hesitate to take a course which they know will result in the early suspension of their business and the deprivation of their families of the ordinary necessities of life. They are not to be abused for such hesitation. The question now pertinently suggests itself, what ought to be done? What ought the poor dependent editor and publisher to do in such cases? What ought the people who favor prohibition to do to help him out of the inevitable dilemma? This last is the practical question for us to consider, and I shall address myself fearlessly to its discussion. If there is such a case as the one above stated in your town or city; if there is a newspaper proprietor in your place who is hesitating on account of these forcible considerations to enter the campaign against liquor with his paper, when his heart is in the right place and in sympathy with the cause, then let me call upon the friends of State prohibition to share liberally with him the pecuniary losses he must inevitably sustain by reason of his espousal of the cause of prohibition.

Don't understand me to suggest or intimate that you should attempt to influence his opinion with money, but let me ask you to increase your own patronage to an amount at least equal to that which he may lose "for righteousness' sake." You will find any number of them who are now neutral, that would come out boldly on the right side of the question and that, too, without violence to their preconceived opinions on the subject if they could only be assured that they will be supported in the glorious work. Those who run newspapers must live just as other people must live, upon the proceeds of their labor. It requires no small amount of money to keep on foot a very insignificant paper, and as much as I would delight to see every member of the press on my side of this question, I have not the heart to condemn those who are financially unable to assist in the work and maintain their independence of the traffic and its advocates. It is one thing to put forth a declaration of independence; quite another to maintain it, especially without the necessary war material, money included. Those who are naturally inclined to the other side of the question and to lend the columns of their papers to the opposition ought, if possible, to be convinced of the error of their way and brought over by argument and persuasion to the service of a nobler cause. If they can not be influenced by such means to forsake their errors, then there is no other alternative, I suppose, than to let them "go on with the procession." It will do no possible good to villify or abuse them. It might be very good policy to withdraw from them; "Let them alone; they are joined to their idols." It would be more charitable to suppose that they are honestly mistaken than that they have been bought up by the liquor influence.

It ought to be the policy of all temperance reformers to secure upon all legitimate terms the co-operation of the press, which is a great power in the land. With the solid support of the newspapers of Texas the amendment would carry by an overwhelming majority. With the press on the side of the opposition, there would be no hope whatever of its adoption. But before leaving this important branch of the subject I desire to speak further with reference to the great daily papers of the State. There is no use in wasting time with an effort to secure their support. Let it be everywhere known and understood by the people that their editorial opinions are but articles of legitimate commerce and are either knocked off to the highest bidder or let out by contract for the season. They are no body's opinions; they are any body's opinions who may be able and disposed to put up the necessary collateral at the rate of about twenty cents a line. In saying this I certainly mean to cast no reflection whatever upon the integrity of the daily press generally, nor even those run by great corporations strictly for the money there is in it; in other words, "for revenue only. I do not doubt that if you bargain for their opinion they will carry out their contract to the letter. If you should contract for a column of campaign "buncombe," I have not the least doubt but that you would get a full column. If you should bargain for more buncombe, you would certainly get the full measure, and that the quality of the whole would strictly correspond with the sample in every respect.

They will deal honestly with you in the matter of carrying out their part of the contract. They will treat you like a gentleman in other respects; they will say nothing whatever about such commercial transactions you may have with themselves as are of a private character. In other words, they will not be likely to give you away by publishing to the world the fact that you had consummated the purchase. They would not perhaps send forth a catalogue containing the established prices of political opinions manufactured to order. Their honesty and their courtesy is unquestioned. It is rarely ever the case that they sell out to both sides of the question. A few have been known to do such a thing, but when it has occurred all of the honest ones which confined their traffic to one side exclusively have promptly condemned such a flagrant violation of journalistic ethics. Lest I be misunderstood I desire to emphasize that they are scrupulously honest and sincere in everything except their opinions, which are not worth the time it requires to glance over their headings. They serve God with all the fervency of their nature; money is their God. To make money is their only religion. Not long ago the author dropped into the sanctum of one of those journalistic blind tigers. An idea had somehow struck the managing editor that I wanted to publish something on the subject of prohibition, although I had not made the slightest intimation upon the subject. Just as I got my head into the doorway of this "sanctum sanctorum," as they call it, the manager squalled out, "Twenty cents a line, sir; good morning, etc." My reply was, "Not any, I thank you; good morning." This self-important fellow, whose surname was "Aleck," and whose first name may be easily guessed, pounded upon me unmercifully, and in the course of his brief remarks he swore that prohibition was a farce and a misnomer, and that it seemed that all of its advocates were crazy and even doing their best to make everybody else non compos mentis, and that they were succeeding quite admirably; that prohibition was too small a matter for the notice of his paper, and that he would say or publish nothing about it for less than twenty cents a line. Anticipating that I had come there to dispute with him on the subject, he squared his chair around to the table, and as I walked out in disgust I thought I could hear him saying over to himself, "twenty cents a line, sir, twenty cents a line." So much for prohibition and the press.

This volume would perhaps not be complete without a passing notice of a particular class of persons known as anti-prohibition orators or speakers, and what I shall have to say of this class has no reference whatever to any particular individual. It would add no dignity whatever to a work devoted to the discussion of general principles to contribute to the notoriety of individuals, not the least of whose purpose, in publicly espousing so bad a cause, is to make themselves notorious. What other aim can they have? How can any of them hope to accomplish any good for their country or to contribute thereby in the least to the general welfare and upbuilding of society? What good results do they promise shall follow the success of the cause they are professing to advocate? What interest do they say can possibly suffer by the adoption of the constitutional amendment? How can society be worsted by the effort? In what respect can it suffer detriment? How can the progress of moral, intellectual, or religious advancement be hampered by the termination of the ungodly sway of King Alcohol? The people whom they would beguile by their sophistry; whom they would mislead by the delusive phantom of personal liberty, have a right to demand an answer to these questions. We must ever judge of the correctness of a principle by its practical results. If the practical results of the principles they contend for with so much hypocritical earnestness have not fully demonstrated the absurdity of the positions they assume, then expedience is a delusion; our own observation a deception.

Is there a man in all this broad land of ours who has sufficient mental vigor and acumen to form a conception from external surroundings, who will have the hardihood to say that the liquor traffic is a blessing, or even to deny that it is a curse to mankind? If so then I shall be ready to say that the magnitude of falsehood is beyond all human comprehension. Had such an individual lived in the days of Ananias, the name of that distinguished prince of liars would have never been recorded upon the pages of history. Joseph Mulhatton and Baron Munchausen would be brilliant and shining examples of human devotion to truth and veracity when compaired with such an individual. If the liquor traffic is not a blessing to mankind, then why should those pompous anti-prohibition advocates struggle so hard for its perpetuation. If it is a curse, then why should they oppose its removal or destruction? Why should they not rather labor to suppress it? If it is not a blessing and negative in its character, then there is no important principle involved in the controversy. It is a positive curse as evidenced by its results; then the principle upon which it is based is necessarily and positively wrong. A corrupt stream can not flow from a pure fountain, neither can a pure stream issue from a corrupt source. All nature teaches this truth and we can not ignore it, if we would. It is equally impossible for bad results to follow from the operation of sound principles of morality, and the reverse of the proposition is equally true. All of the bombastic and highsounding arguments can not establish the contrary doctrine. What logic can convince you that a corrupt and poisonous stream can issue from a pure fountain in the very face of your own and all human experience? And are you to stultify yourself by accepting and being led away by a sophism that brings you to a conclusion in direct conflict with your own personal experience and observation. I do not think so.

There is, I believe, a school of philosophers who deny the existence of all material things; who contend that all objects we see, feel, and hear around and about us are but the creatures of our own imagination. While that may be the true philosophy of nature, it has never been accepted as such by a sufficient number of human intelligences to make a respectable showing. The great mass of mankind are too fond of what they conceive to be the real pleasures of the world to turn loose their hold on reality and go off into the imaginary or spiritual as long as they can keep from it. The argument that establishes the conclusion that whisky is not an evil and a curse in the very presence of the facts which demonstrate to our own conclusion beyond any reasonable doubt the reverse of the reasonable proposition, necessarily leads us to the endorsement and acceptance of the doctrines of that school of advanced thinkers who deny the existence of a material universe. When led thus to repudiate the naked unvarnished truth as it appears to the mind and the conscience through the medium of every one of the senses, I will be ready to accept as the truth any thing that can be imagined.

however inconsistent with all human wisdom and experience. If told that daylight and impenetrable darkness could exist in the same place at the same time, I would not doubt it in the least. Why should I doubt it? Absurdities would cease to exist; physical impossibilities would become things of the past.

Assuming, then, as we must, that the prevailing system of licensing the sale of intoxicating liquors is baneful and destructive to the best interests of society, then, what reasonable apology can these champions of the opposition make to the intelligent mind for striving to perpetuate the curse? With what show of consistency do they cry out, "Personal Liberty," when there is no personal liberty or any other sort of liberty for the reeling, staggering slave of a consuming thirst, the fiery offspring of the liquor traffic? Do they hope to make men free by upholding the relentless sway of the meanest and most despotic of tyrants?

In the name of the good people of Texas and all other states which are struggling to free themselves and their children from this accursed tyrant; in the name of the thousands and millions of his miserable, dying victims who are powerless to resist; in the name of the countless throng of sorrowing women and helpless, innocent children all over the country, I demand that these loud-mouth champions of personal liberty answer these questions "or forever hereafter hold their peace." The idea of preaching temperance, and at the same time advocating saloons; the idea of preaching temperance reform, and at the same time sowing broadcast all over the country the seeds of intemperance, is an inconsistency that I can not account for or undertake to explain. I dare say they will not attempt to reconcile it themselves, as none of them, so far as I have heard, have claimed to possess omnipotent power, if indeed omnipotence could accomplish the work. Preaching moral suasion and temperance, and establishing dens of iniquity in every nook and corner of the State! Such purity of profession! Such delectable practice! Such delightful absurdity! Give them plenty of rope and they will soon put an end to themselves. No answer is demanded; they cannot possibly formulate an argument that does not inevitably destroy itself according to every recognized principle of logic. The wise man of the Old Testament once said, "Answer a fool according to his folly, lest he become wise in his own conceit."

I now come to consider briefly the duties of those faithful veterans of the cause and their gallant recruits who are marching to the field to engage this enemy of mankind in forensic discussion. Though you may feel intellectually weak and unable to cope with the adversary, you may go forth without fear. You may have a stammering tongue, but you have God and the right upon your side. Though your efforts may fall short of the full measure of their design at the first, they will continue to grow stronger and stronger with proper application to your work. Shakespeare beautifully and truthfully writes :

> "Thrice is he armed who hath his quarrel just,
> And he but naked, though locked up in steel,
> Whose conscience by injustice is corrupted."

When Christ sent His apostles out into the wide, wicked world He charged them among other things to "be as wise as serpents and as harmless as doves." No better text could be selected for the direction of your methods in the prosecution of this glorious work. Be wise as the strength of your intellect will permit; be as harmless as the least offensive of God's creatures.

In a former chapter I have written at some length upon the folly of attempting to convince men and turn them from the error of their way by the use of bitter words and personal vituperation. Legitimate argument, supplemented by timely persuasion is the only way to reach them. Any other course excites their passions and provokes their resentment which will be stronger than their judgment. Be kind, be gentle, be at all times conservative in your speech and in your conduct. If you have been able to gather any available truths from the foregoing chapters, you are at liberty to use them without giving credit to the author.

Indeed, I cannot see how any man can reasonably demand credit in a literary sense or otherwise for penning a truth of which no writer can, in the very nature of things, be the author. Truth is eternal. Those who act as the medium for its promulgation soon pass away. Such truth is at a par with the conclusion neccessarily reached by the arguments used on the opposite side of this question. If what I have written is, after being "weighed in the balance," found to be the truth it belongs to the world, and I have no right to claim a monopoly of its use and demand that every other person who may desire to use it shall squander his valuable time in informing the public that he received it from me or my book. In the preceding pages I have attempted to call things by their right names. I have tried to be plain, and to make my positions clearly and unmistakably understood. That some of the arguments may appear at first blush rather far-fetched and irrelevant, I have no doubt whatever. In formulating my arguments I have generally begun at the beginning, and from the starting point of fundamental principles I have endeavored to lead the unprejudiced mind by a logical process to a tangible conclusion, a conclusion, that the simplest mind can not fail to comprehend and appreciate. In dealing with the arguments of the opposition I have in every instance attempted to dash them to pieces upon the rugged boulders of their own glaring absurdity.

It has been my purpose to show up these ponderous absurdities in a way that may be seen so clearly and distinctly by the honest enquirer after truth that he may be able to avoid the shipwreck and save himself from its terrible destruction. Be assured just here that the unblushing fallacies of these apologists of crime, these advocates of the establishment and perpetuation of a "sheol" upon earth will in due time be shorn of their beauty and attractiveness, and the rottenness of their true character fully disclosed. Be further assured before it is everlastingly too late that the man who boldly attempts to palm them off upon the unskilful public will certainly come to grief; that he will be socially immolated and politically damned " without the benefit of clergy," if he does not "repent and be baptized" into the ranks of the reformers. It would also be well for him to understand in this connection that delays are peculiarly dangerous. For one, if I know my own heart, I rejoice not at the downfall of any human being. I envy no man on the topside of this earth. So far as I know, there is not a man standing between me and the goal of my earthly ambition. There is not a man within the broad range of my personal acquaintance that I would not rejoice to see become wiser, wealthier, and better; on account of whose social, professional, and political success I would not feel gratified, if in the least degree worthy of his triumph. And, ah, could I but know in the future that the influence of this little volume has in any way contributed to the elevation of my race, though in a slight degree, I would feel amply repaid for my study and labor without regard to the pecuniary fate of the venture.

Could I but realize in anticipation that the truths I have herein recorded, or attempted to record, shall sink deep into the heart and conscience of even the humblest of my countrymen and lead him safely to the rock of his temporal salvation, I would be happy indeed, and contented. That every line I have written will be put through the crucible of the severest criticism, I can but expect. That the positions I have assumed will be ridiculed and sneered at by those who feel and appreciate their inability to answer and refute them, I am fully and entirely assured. I know that there are many in the world who will not be convinced; who "will believe a lie and be damned" when the truth would answer even their own selfish purposes a thousand fold better. They are "joined to their idols," and there is no use to trouble them with argument or persuasion. They are of those of whom the poet spoke when he said:

> "Convince a man against his will,
> And he is of the same opinion still.

For such people this book was not written, and they are under no obligation to read it, and if they should do so through curiosity, or for any purpose, they are expected to criticise it, and the author would feel much disappointed if they did not do so. They are expected to ridicule and sneer at the truths it contains, and I promise in advance that I shall not get angry or complain. I here throw down the gauntlet to the opposition as I conclude the last chapter of my book. Let them take it up if they will.

APPENDIX.

APPENDIX.

Synopsis of the prohibitory legislation and license laws of the different States, with their history and practical results, compiled by the author from unquestionably reliable sources.*

MAINE.

STATE PROHIBITION.

Settlements began in the territory now constituting the state of Maine, in 1623, but politically it was a part of Massachusetts until 1820, when it became a state. Whatever legislation it had was that of Massachusetts, and the progress of events was similar. While Boston merchants were pushing

---

*For the material contained in this synopsis I am much indebted to Rev. T. A. Goodwin, of Indianapolis, and his "Seventy-six Years' Tussel with the Traffic"; General S. F. Carey, Cincinnati, O.; Samuel D. Hastings, Madison, Wis.; H. F. Chreistberg, of S. C., in "Hand-Book of Prohibition"; W. H. H. Bartram, in "The Voice"; Hon. Wm. Daniel, Baltimore, Md., in "Hand-Book of Prohibition"; John Russell, Michigan, in id; J. Wofford Tucker, Florida, in id; also J. C. Greeley, of same State; R. H. Whitaker, North Carolina, in "Hand Book"; Rumsey Smithson, Virginia, in id; Will C. King, Oregon, in id; Jno. Hipp, Colorado, in id; Hon. Neal Dow, of Portland, Me.; J. S. Hoagland, North Platte, Neb.; E. P. Augur, Middletown, Ct.; Kate L. Penniman and H. B. Quick, St. Paul, Minn. I am also indebted to J. N. Stearnes, Sec'y Nat. Temperance Society, New York; E. J. Morris, Grand Scribe Sons of Temperance, Cincinnati, O.; and Walter I. Crawford, G. W. C. T., of I. O. G. T., N. O., La., for valuable assistance rendered in the collection of materials; and to Mr. A. J. Jutkins, of Chicago, for copies of "The Hand-Book of Prohibition", which has been very serviceable to me in my work.

the African trade, sending out rum and bringing back slaves, enterprising citizens of Maine were sending lumber to the West Indies, bringing back some Spanish dollars, and much molasses, which was converted into rum and drank by the people. Accordingly general poverty existed. Outside of the "merchants" (rum-sellers) there were few men of wealth ; general coarseness and severe brutality prevailed. Few houses in the country towns were not ornamented with old hats in the place of broken panes.

A temperance society was organized in Portland, April 24, 1812, and in Bath the same year. These proposed to discountenance drunkenness. They had no higher aim. To be "sparing and cautious" in the use of liquors was their effort. (See Liquor Problem, Pape 202.) The advance towards total abstinence was similar to that in other portions of the country. The "Washingtonian" movement found a good field in Maine. It was a great awakening : earnest men all over the land had revelations.

Among these were Gen. James Appleton of Marblehead, Massachusetts, a member of the Massachusetts legislature. While listening to a debate upon a license bill in that body in 1831, he was suddenly seized with the idea that if, as appeared by the debate, the sale of liquor was so baneful to the public, it should not be licensed at all, but rather forbidden altogether.

He advocated this doctrine in the Salem *Gazette.*

In 1833 he removed to Portland, Maine. Here he advocated prohibition, and with such ability and success that he was elected to the Maine legislature in 1837. He presented petitions for prohibition which he secured from his neighbors. These were referred to a "joint select committee," of which he was chairman, and his "Report" was, according to the Maine *Temperance Advance* of Feb. 12. 1853, "the first announcement of the prohibitory principle and is the origin of the Maine law.

Meantime, in the same city of Portland, there was a young man whose growing interest in the question was destined to bear rich fruit. This was Neal Dow, "whose first public appearance as an advocate of prohibition was in 1839, when he appeared before the Board of Aldermen of his own city to induce them to refer the question of license or no-license to a vote of the citizens." He was then thirty-five, and the next twelve years put him into such relations to the History of Prohibition as to make him, though not the earliest, among the most conspicuous, of its advocates. He vigorously presented the doctrine, traveling in 1846 over 4000 miles in the State addressing the people. The legislature that year was elected on that issue. A prohibitory bill passed the house by a vote of 81 to 42, and the senate by 23 to 5. It was approved by Gov. Anderson, and stands as the first prohibitory law in a christian state.

But it was ineffictive; penalties were light. No one knew what it involved to fight the liquor traffic. In 1849 a more stringent bill was passed, but it was vetoed by Gov. Dana. In 1850 Mr. Dow introduced an amended bill containing the "search and seizure" clauses, but it was lost by a tie vote in the senate. The following year Mr. Dow appeared with his bill perfected: it passed by a vote of 86 to 40 in the house, and 18 to 10 in the senate, was signed by Gov. Hubbard, and became a law June 2, 1851. Meanwhile Mr. Dow had been elected mayor of Portland.

"All eyes were turned upon Maine to see if she would execute her law. Will the mayor of portland stand firm at his post and do his duty, or will he shrink in fear of mobs and riots? He speedily announced his purpose to execute the law, and gave venders sixty days in which to dispose of their liquors and get out of the business. The mayors of other cities issued similar proclamations. On the morning of the 4th of July the mayor of Bangor seized, confiscated and destroyed ten casks of liquor. Mr. Dow, according to promise, issued his search-warrant, seized about two thousand dollars worth of liquors, and publicly destroyed them." In other cities the same promptness and energy were exhibited, great concourses of people witnessing the destruction with respectful silence. It was demonstrated that a prohibitory law could be enforced.

On the 15th of January, 1852, seven months after the enactment of the law, the Mayor of Portland sent a Message to the city council, in which he said:

"The number of persons who continue to sell strong drinks in the city is now very small. They are almost all foreigners, and sell with great secrecy and caution. An open rum-shop or bar of any kind is entirely unknown. A barrel, keg, or other vessel of liquors is not to be seen in the city at all, except at the city agency.* The law has executed its mission with more ease, certainty, and dispatch than was anticipated by its most ardent friends—it has been most triumphantly successful. I think it not an exaggeration to say that the quantity of intoxicating liquors now sold in the city, except by the city agent, is not one fiftieth part so great as it was seven months ago, and the salutary effects of this great improvement are apparent among the people in all parts of the city."

The dominant party up to this time had been democratic. But parties were disintegrating. The slavery issue was splitting them. All parties furnished votes for and against the prohibitory law, and this new issue began to gather a party. The "rum" element of the democratic party opposed the re-election of Gov. Hubbard and with whig sympathizers cast 21,774 votes for an "anti-Maine law" candidate. Wm. G. Crosby, whig, was elected governor by the Legislature, there

---

* Where liquors are sold by appointment of law for medical and mechanical purposes and the arts only.

being no choice by the people. The next year, 1853, "the anti-Maine law" wing of the democracy controlled the democratic State convention and nominated Pilsbury, (anti-prohibitionist) for Governor. The temperance Democrats bolted and nominated Anson P. Morrill, In the election Pillsbury had 36, 386 votes, Morrill 11,027, Crosby (whig) 27,061, and Holmes (free soil) 8,996. The Legislature elected Crosby again. In 1854 the temperance democrats, whigs and free-soilers united, formed the nucleus of the Republican party, which declared for prohibition and free soil and gave Morrill 44,565 votes. The democratic candidate had 28,462, the whig 14,001, scattering 3,478. There being no choice by the people the Republican Legislature elected Morrill. In 1855 the various elements which had enacted the Maine Law in 1851 and had elected Morrill the year before, met as the Republican party, declared for prohibition and free soil and renominated Morrill. The Democrats nominated Wells, declared against prohibition and made this their most prominent issue in the campaign. The vote stood, Morrill 51,441, Wells 48,341, Reed (whig) 14,001. The Democratic Legislature elected Wells governor, repealed the prohibitory law, and enacted a license law. In the election of 1856 the Republicans won. In accordance with the judgment of many prohibitionists who thought their cause could stand better if the people could have a chance to see the full working of license, no action was taken on the subject till after the election of 1857. At the session of the Legislature in 1858 the Republicans repealed the license law and re-enacted the prohibitory law, submitting the law for the popular verdict. It was ratified by the people with a majority of 22,952. Thus early was the timidity and time-serving of politicians apparent, and the loyalty of the masses to prohibition demonstrated.

Since 1858 no attempt has been made to repeal the Prohibitory Law. The politicians have had no love for it, but like some of old "they feared the people" too much to attempt its repeal. But policy of non-enforcement was open to them, to some extent; and in the cities and larger towns into which the vicious elements of society are more apt to drift, great laxity has existed.

"From that day to this, with occasional revivals, the principle of prohibition has been gradually moved towards the rear by the political managers, while the *policy* of prohibition has been retained, as a convenient instrumentality for retaining temperance votes, and securing liquor votes.

The rightful order has been thus reversed, and instead of putting temperance into politics, (which is so much needed,) they have put *politics into temperance.*"

It is to this that is to be attributed the persistent continuance of an illicit traffic to some extent.

The legislature of 1882 by a vote of 91 to 30 in the House and 22 to 2 in the Senate submitted a Prohibitory Constitutional Amendment, which was voted on at the general election Sept. 8th, 1884, and it was ratified by a majority of 46,972.

The law has recently been amended and to show the nature and probable effects of the amendment, I quote the following from the *Globe Democrat* of recent date:

GETTING ALARMED.

The new Maine liquor law which went into effect yesterday is causing great alarm among vendors of liquors who have gloried in the fact that prohibition has not hitherto prohibited. Under the new law the payment of special taxes, or an indication or sign that liquor is sold or given away, is to be held as "prima facie evidence" that the parties are "common sellers of intoxicating liquors and the premises so kept by them common nuisances." When it is remembered that 1180 persons in Maine hold United States liquor licenses, it will be understood that just 1180 persons are trying to make up their minds whether they had better quit selling or go on as before and trust to apathy in the enforcement of the new law.

And here is one from the Governor:

AUGUSTA, Maine, March 23.—The finances of the State were never more prosperous. Drink habit is fatal to prosperity in any community. Prohibition promotes morality everywhere. Nearly all crimes can be traced to rum, either directly or indirectly. The law is well enforced in the country towns. In some of the cities it is not quite so effective. It is hoped the new law will aid the enforcement there.

JOSEPH R. BODWELL.

IOWA.

STATE PROHIBITION SINCE JULY 4, 1884.

This new State has a brief but instructive prohibition history. It was admitted as a State Dec. 25, 1846. The fruits of the agitation which produced prohibitory and anti-license in almost all the northern states between 1845 and 1856, produced in 1855, a prohibitory law in Iowa, passed by the whig and republican legislature, and approved by Gov. Grimes.

"Its vitality was dependent upon adoption by the people at the ballot box. The people adopted it. The next legislature but one practically annulled it, without asking the people whether they would sanction this summary setting aside of their verdict as given at the polls. Every means was employed to secure re-enactment of the law, or else the re-submission of the subject to the people, but without avail. It was finally decided by some leading minds to ask Prohibitionists to withhold their suffrages from the various parties, and endeavor by show of strength to demonstrate the necessity of their vote to any party which desired to remain in power in the State.

To this end, and as a guaranty of good faith in their profession of desire to co-operate with the republicans as the dominant party whenever the temperance issue should be properly recognised, the temperance party steadily refused to nominate more than one candidate in any campaign, one name being sufficient to rally and show the strength of the movement, and to show the importance or unimportance of the prohibition vote,

The temperance party was organized in 1875, and J. H. Lozier nominated as its first candidate for governor. He received but 1,397 votes, while Kirkwood, the Republican candidate, was elected by a majority of 30,179 votes. This looked somewhat like a failure, and the Republican party did not feel compelled to give to prohibition the demanded recognition. In 1877 the Republicans again ignored the issue, and nominated J. H. Gear, while Col. Jessup became the candidate for the prohibitory vote. He received 10,639 votes, being almost eight times as many as were cast for Lozier only two years before. Mr. Gear ran behind his ticket and was a minority governor, lacking 674 of a majority. All other names on the ticket were given strong majorities. This change was a very suggestive one, and Jessup's vote was not the occasion of so much hilarity among politician as was that of Lozier. One more such stride, or even a six-fold increase, would depose the Republican and put some other party in power, the position of the prohibitionists still being : Recognice our cause, and we will merge our force with yours. The Republican convention of 1879 came on. It was desired to renominate J. H. Gear, and to elect him this time by a majority vote. The prohibitionists were on hand, and so far as those present could speak for the convention to assemble five days later, guaranties were given that no candidate would be nominated, provided the standing prayers of the prohibitory element were granted. There were just then no such important reconstruction problems unadjusted to specially hold Republican voters, as had been the case in each preceeding campaign, and the most sagacious politicians feared the result if they nominated Gear, an avowed opponent of the principle, and also failed to give favorable recognition of the issue in the action of the convention. As the result of the conference, the Republican convention did adopt a resolution which was referred to in the platform of two years later as making "provisions for submission of the so-called prohibitory amendment of the constitution of Iowa to a vote of the people." Was the "temperance party" dead, a failure, or abandoned as yet? It was tolerable active for a defunct body, as the largest convention in its history met the week after the Republican convention and held a vigorous session. Under the circumstances referred to, however, it was determined to put no candidate in the field, save that a small portion of the convention who would not vote for Gear under any circumstances, withdrew from the convention and nominated D. R. Dungan, who, as an independent, received 3,258 votes. The result of this union was that Gear, though running considerably behind his ticket, was elected by a majority of 23,828."

In accordance with the pledges made, the republican legislature of 1880-81 prepared a prohibitory amendment and passed it. By the provisions of the constitution it laid over for action by the legislature of 1881-82, thus giving the people an opportunity to elect a new legislature in full view of the pending amendment. The second and final legislative vote adopted the amendment by a vote of 65 to 24 in the house, and 35 to 11 in the senate. On the 27th of June, 1882, at a special election, there were cast for the amendment, 155,436 votes, and against it 125,677; majority, 29,759. This was hailed as a great and decisive victory, and it sufficiently proved the great underlying fact—the *people want prohibition.*

But the resources of the alcoholists were not exhausted. A test case was made, and upon its reaching the supreme court the amendment was declared invalid, owing to some alleged technicalities. A rehearing of the case resulted in a similar decision.

Great confusion resulted. As usual, the politicians only yielded a reluctant consent to the demand of the people. The opponents of prohibition were vigorous, and did their best to secure at the election Oct. 9, 1883, a legislature which would enact a license law. The democratic party espoused this side and openly advocated it. The republicans, in a rather vague and uncertain way, depending an the sentiment of the locality, advocated prohibition, if they said anything about it, some condemning, others strongly defending the principle. The party was in the dilemma a party must always be, in attempting to take on an issue not originally embraced in its creed. Still, the general result was favorable. The republicans carried the State, electing a majority which said: "The people want prohibition, and they shall have it." A strong and carefully prepared prohibitory statute was enacted, which went into effect July 4, 1884, and the Iowa Prohibitionists were at the end of their trouble—the first end.

In reply to a letter written by the Secretary of the central committee of the prohibition campaign of this State in regards to the workings of prohibition in Iowa the Governor says:

> In eighty out of the ninety-nine counties of the state prohibition is enforced, and in the remaining nineteen counties it it is partly enforced ; that no property has been depreciated by its enforcement, as saloons make room for better and more legitimate business; that the enforcement of the law has had no noticeable effect upon the population beyond causing the removal from the State of some incurable consumers. The effects of prohibition upon the general welfare and habits of the people, he says, are decidedly wholsome. The prohibi-

tion sentiment is on the increase, and there is no doubt that prohibition is an established power in Iowa.

We also append the following telegram from the commissioner of labor statistics:

DES MOINES, IOWA, March 23.
Governor and attorney-general both say prohibition has constantly improved the moral, social and financial condition of Iowa, and is successfully enforced in eighty-five of the ninety-nine counties, also growing rapidly in the remainder.
E. R. HUTCHINS.

On February 3, 1887, Governor Larrabee also said:

"I find in the cities and counties where the prohibitory law is well enforced, crime and police expenses fall off wonderfully. Not a saloon is open in this, the largest city in the state. The sheriff of this county told me a few days since that he had spoiled his business by enforcing the law. He also stated that he was glad of it. Several of the judges have recently told me that there was a marked falling off in criminal business in their courts in consequence of the enforcement of the law. There are several judicial districts without a single open saloon. If our courts and sheriffs and constables would do their duty properly, the saloons would soon be completely driven out.

KANSAS.

STATE PROHIBITION.*

As an example of the utter inefficiency of prohibitory liquor laws of any kind in the suppression of drunkenness and its concomitant vices, the opponents of such laws often refer

---

*Communication published by the author in *Greenville Herald*, October, 1886, pending local option contest.

to the failure of constitutional, or State prohibition in Kansas. It is a very easy thing for them to assert that prohibition in Kansas is a failure, and there are many of our people who are doubtlessly misled by the reckless assertion. But few will take the trouble to procure the statistics from which the actual results of the law are unmistakably shown. It is nothing uncommon to hear men who are interested in the liquor business (and nothing else could be reasonably expected of them) that more whisky is sold and consumed in sections where prohibitory laws obtain than in other places where the traffic is legalized by the government. And strange to say that the wholesale dealers refuse to encourage the adoption or enactment of such laws, which must necessarily, according to their own theory increase their business, however destructive it may be to the saloons and doggeries of the country. Such disinterestedness is only met with among the noble-hearted, generous, and self-sacrificing liquor dealers of the land. The writer has taken the trouble to procure the official statistics relating to the enforcement and practical operation of the Kansas prohibitory laws, obtained from unquestionably reliable authority. In 1879 a prohibitory amendment to the Constitution was submitted to a vote of the people, which in 1881 became a part of the organic law of the State.

In May of the same year the legislature of Kansas enacted such penal statutes under said amendment as were thought necessary to carry prohibition into practical operation. In some respects the laws passed by the legislature were similar to those of our own local option system, but decidedly more rigid. The penalty for violation of these various provisions were more severe and extended not only to the unlawful seller, but to the buyer who resorted to any kind of a subterfuge in order to obtain the forbidden article. While the purchase and sale of intoxicating liquors for medical and mechanical purposes were permitted, under severe restrictions, it was made extremely dangerous for both buyer and seller to attempt an evasion of the spirit of the law through the medium of the exceptions. When the law went into effect quite a number of the saloon-keepers of the State determined to resist its enforcment. Among other grounds they claimed that the law was sumptuary, unconstitutional, and subversive of personal liberty. They were convicted, and appealed to the Supreme Court, which promptly affirmed the judgment, overruling all objections urged against the law on the ground of unconstitutionality or otherwife. In the course of a few months it became evident that the law had come to stay, and so the saloon-keepers concluded that it would be safer and healthier to yield to the inevitable. Those who refused to obey the law were vigorously prosecuted, especially in the rural counties, and, if the records do not lie, it would seem that a large majority of them, judging from the original number of saloons which held out against the enforcement of the law, suffered the severest penalties.

The record shows that seventy-nine per cent of all the prosecutions instituted for violations of the law resulted in convictions—a larger per cent by about one-third than were convicted in ordinary cases. Out of two hundred and ninety-five cases reported on the first of June, 1885, two hundred and thirty convictions resulted, as appears from the Attorney General's report, now before me. There were then about seventy-five of the eighty-four counties of the State which were entirely rid of saloons and their baleful and damaging influence. The special reports of the various county attorneys to the Attorney General's office show that the law was strictly enforced in all parts of the State, except in some of the larger cities, especially those on the border. This is accounted for in some instances by the fact that the city governments and their officers were in full sympathy with the liquor element, as is not unfrequently the case, even in our own State. In one of these cities the mayor was successfully impeached and disgraced on account of his connection with this class of lawbreakers. The reports show that whisky has been successfully routed from the city of Topeka after a long and apparently doubtful struggle between the two contending forces. The county attorney of Shawnee county, writing from Topeka, Kansas, says: "All the saloons were closed about February 1, 1885, since which time there has not been an open saloon in the city (Topeka). There have been several backrooms up-stairs, down-cellar, and back-alley places, but their lives were short."

The prohibitory law has been the means of reducing drinking more in this city than can be written by my pen. There is not in my mind one-tenth of the drinking there was before. The best evidence of this is the record of our city court. Many of the prosecuting officers complain that they are not supported and sustained in their efforts to enforce the law, by the people, including specially some of the most enthusiastic and vigorous advocates of the cause.

In 1885 the act of 1881 was amended and changed in many of its features. The penalties for violation of its various provisions were increased, and in addition to pecuniary fines, which were frequently paid by contributions from the opponents of the law, imprisonment of not less than thirty days was added, and some times the maximum punishment was unusually severe. The effect of the imprisonment was very perceptible, as a large number of the transgressors soon afterwards found themselves individually and personally languishing in the jails of the State. There is, as in our State, a provision authorizing druggists to sell liquors for medical and mechanical purposes, but the restrictions imposed are much more stringent than in ours, and ample provision is made for the punishment of such druggists, and such physicians as may attempt to take advantage of the law granting a special permit to them to dispense such liquors for the purposes named in the exception in their favor. Means are provided for the immediate forfeiture of their permits, which are granted by the probate judge, upon certain conditions.

It is admitted by all that there are some of these druggists who use their permits as a means of violating the spirit and intent of the law, but it is thoroughly demonstrated by the reports from all official and reliable sources that there is not one-tenth of the drinking and drunkenness that prevails under the old system. Every person holding such permit is required under severe penalties to keep a register of every sale of liquor he makes and to report the same with the purposes for which it is made, to the judge issuing the permit. From this report a fair estimate of the amount used can be obtained and furthermore it furnishes an indication of the manner in which the permit is being used by the druggist. This feature of the law is objected to by many prohibitionists of the state. As to the effect prohibition has had upon the State, I will content myself with an extract from a speech of Governor Martin delivered at Topeka on the 16th day of September last, which seems to have been taken from the statistics on file among the archives of the State.

In 1880 the population of the State was 996,096. We had been twenty-five years in attaining that population. To-day Kansas has not less than 1,500,000 inhabitants. In five years we have gained half a million. In 1880 only 55 towns and cities had a population exceeding 1,000, and six had each over 5,000. In 1885, 91 towns and cities each had over 1,000, and twelve had each over 5,000. In 1880 we had only 8,868,884 acres under cultivation; in 1885 we had 14,252,815 acres, In 1880 the farms of Kansas were valued at only $235,178,936, and the farm products for that year aggregated only $84,521,486; in 1885 the farms of the State were valued at $408,073,454, and the farm products of that year aggregated $143,557,018. In 1880 the live stock of Kansas was worth only $61,563,950; in 1885 it was worth $117,881,699. In 1880 the assessed valuation of the property of Kansas, real, personal and railroad, aggregated $160,891,689 ; in 1885 it aggregated $248,845,276. In 1880 we had only 3,104 miles of railway ; we have now 5,117 miles. In 1880 we had 5,315 school houses ; in 1885 we had 6,673. In 1880 we expended $1,818,-336 for the support of our common schools; in 1885 we expended $2,977,763. In 1880 we had only 357 newspapers and 2,514 churches ; in 1885 we had 581 newspapers and 3,976 churches."

This speech contains other valuable statistics proving to a moral certainty that prohibition does prohibit, the assertions of whisky advocates to the contrary notwithstanding, and prohibition is working out a great moral and social reform in the State of Kansas.

As an evidence of the efficacy of the law, I quote as follows from the late message of Governor Martin, delivered to the Legislature during the present year, 1887:

A great reform has certainly been accomplished in Kansas. Intemperance is steadily and surely decreasing. In thousands of homes where want and wretchedness and suffering were once familiar guests, plenty, happiness and contentment now abide. Thousands of wives and children are better clothed and fed than they were when the saloons absorbed all the earnings of husbands and fathers. The marvelous material growth of the State during the past six years has been accompanied by the equally marvelous moral progress, and it can be fairly and truthfully asserted that in no portion of the civilized world can a million and a half of people be found who are more temperate than the people of Kansas.

There is not a town, city or neighborhood in the State in which an illegal traffic in liquors can be carried on for a single week if the local officers discharge the duties plainly enjoined upon them by law with zeal and fidelity. Provide the necessary laws to compel local officers to discharge their sworn duties, and to remove them when they neglect or refuse to do so, and there will be no need to make any changes in our statutes. On the other hand, no matter what amendments are made nor what provisions are added to the present laws, they will be ineffectual so long as the municipal authorities or cities or counties can nullify or disregard them without fear of removal or punishment.

The public sentiment of Kansas is overwhelmingly against the liquor traffic. Thousands of men, who a few years ago opposed prohibition, or doubted whether it was the best method of dealing with the liquor traffic, have seen and frankly acknowledge its beneficent results and its practical success. The temptations with which the open saloon allured the youth of the land to disgrace and destruction; the appetite for liquor bred and matured within its walls by the treating custom; the vice, crime, poverty, suffering and sorrow of which it is always the fruitful source, all these evil results of the open saloon have been abolished in nearly every city and town in Kansas.

There is not an observing man in the State who does not know that a great reform has been accomplished in Kansas by prohibition. There is not a truthful man in the State who will not frankly acknowledge this fact, no matter what his opinions touching the policy of prohibition may have been; and I firmly believe that if the amendments to the law that I have suggested are made, and if authority is provided for compelling local officers to discharge the duties required of them by law, within three months there will not be an open saloon in Kansas, and the sale of intoxicating liquors as a beverage will be practically abolished."

In 1881 Governor Martin was opposed to the law because he did not think "it would work." The prohibitory laws of Kansas have recently been amended in important particulars, and it is said that it is now practically impossible to engage in the illegal sale of liquor in that State without detection and severe punishment.

OHIO.

NO LICENSE CAN BE GRANTED BUT THE STATE MAY LEGISLATE UPON EVILS RESULTING FROM THE TRAFFIC.

In Ohio as in every other State of the Union, and in every civilized country the liquor traffic has been regarded as a proper subject of legislation. Unrestrained and unregulated it has been considered a dangerous business. In a period of six hundred years there have been four hundred laws enacted on this subject in England by the British Parliament.

In all the States and Territories of the United States more legislation has been had upon this than upon all other occupations.

From the adoption of the first constitution of Ohio in 1802 down to 1852, the legislature of the State was continually trying to mitigate the evils connected with this traffic, by a judicious and well-regulated license system. Every person who proposed to engage in the business was required to prove a good moral character, and be well qualified for the work; he must keep a quiet and orderly house and procure a license, paying a stipulated sum for the privilege. He was also required to prove by persons residing in the vicinity that a grogshop was necessary in the locality. Year after year new and more stringent conditions were added. Judges of the courts were required to grant licenses to sell drinks to suitable persons in proper localities within their jurisdiction. Courts were more or less strict in the exercise of their power as they were favorable or unfavorable to the business. It created no little public excitement and comment when Judge Fishback, of Clermont, turned away all applicants for a license.

He claimed that, while the law was imperative, that he should grant licenses to persons of good moral character in suitable places, it did not define what localities were suitable, but left that to the sacred discretion of the courts, and he was clearly of the opinion that there was no suitable place for such a nefarious business in his jurisdiction, and while he occupied the bench he would not entertain any application for a license. In 1851 a convention was called to form a new constitution. The friends of temperance throughout the State petitioned to the convention to put a no-license clause in the new constitution. Fears were entertained that such a clause would result in a rejection by the people of the instrument. By strong and persistent pressure and personal appeals the convention consented to submit to the people a schedule which it adopted by a majority of the voters in a separate ballot; it should be section 18, of article 16 of the Constitution. The schedule submitted read as follows : " No license to traffic in intoxicating liquors shall hereafter be granted in the State, but the General Assembly may by law provide against the evils resulting therefrom." A most exciting canvass followed. The friends of temperance, believing that a great point in favor of their reform would be gained by taking away the legal sanction of a license, marshaled their forces to secure the insertion of the above clause in the organic law of the State. The result was its adoption by a majority of 8000, greater than was given for the Constitution itself.

From that date to the present no commission has ever been given by any court, or city, or town council to any person to make drunkards. The liquor traffic has not had any legal sanction. The caustic, but just, criticism upon the license system by the immortal Cowper has not been applicable to Ohio since the year 1852. More than one hundred years ago in his inimitable verse he said:

"The ten thousand casks, forever dribling out their base contents
Touched by the Midas finger of the State,
Bleed gold for parliament to vote away. —
Drink and be mad then, 'tis your country bids;
Gloriously obey the important call;
Her cause demands the assistance of your throats;
Ye all can swallow, and she asks no more."

"To provide against the evils resulting from the traffic" as authorized by the new constitution, the General Assembly in 1854 passed a law which in some rural districts was attended with beneficial results, and which, if it had been enforced throughout the State, would have been as effective as any prohibitory law anywhere. Among its provisions were the following, briefly stated: No liquor should be sold to be drunk on the premises where sold. None should be sold to minors or persons intoxicated or who were in the habit of getting intoxicated. All places where sold contrary to the provisions of the law were declared to be nuisances, which should be shut up and abated and the keeper fined and imprisoned. In 1859 amendments were made providing for the punishment of the drunkard, and additional penalties against selling liquor to drunkards.

In 1870 the law was still further amended by authorizing a wife or child, or other person injured in person or property, or means of support, to sue and recover exemplary damages from any person who sold liquor to any one in the habit of becoming intoxicated. This law—called the Adair law—authorized a wife or minor child to sue in their own name. Judgments were made lien upon the premises where the liquor was obtained.

As a general and almost universal rule the courts were not inclined to enforce the law. Occasionally heavy exemplary damages were recovered by a wife or child, but the criminal provisions of the law were a dead letter. It was generally held that the constitution protected the traffic, and only allowed attacks to be made against the *evils resulting from it.* When the constitution was adopted, temperance men supposed that full power was given to the legislature to prohibit the traffic, as that was the only way possible to provide against the evils; in other words, that the evils were incident to, and always and everywhere concented with, the existence of the traffic.

In 1870 the General Assembly gave to cities and incorporated villages the power to regulate, restrain, and prohibit ale, beer, and porter houses, and places of notorious and habitual resort for tippling or intemperance.

In pursuance of this authority the town council of McConnellsville, in Morgan county, passed a stringent prohibitory ordinance against tippling shops. Prosecutions were had under it, and appeals were taken to the Supreme Court. To the surprise of every body and the mortification of the liquor-sellers, the constitutionality and legality of the ordinance were affirmed. This McConnellsville ordinance became a pattern or model for other incorporated villages. The later rulings of the Supreme Court gave to the General Assembly the constitutional authority to entirely prohibit the traffic and does not limit its power to the evils resulting from it.

In 1881 a law was passed called "The Stubbs Bill," prohibiting the sale of spiritous liquors on Sunday; the penalty for a violation was a fine of $50. This is substantially a dead letter, as Sunday is a principal day for carousals, especially in the large cities.

In 1883 the "Scott Law" was enacted. It's object was to get a revenue from the traffic. It imposed an annual tax for the privilege of selling beer and wine, and $200 for the sale of whisky. The tax was made a lien upon the premises when sold. This tax was to be collected, like other taxes, by the

County Treasurer, one-fourth to go into the poor fund, and the balance distributed to the cities and villages where the traffic was carried on. It also prohibited selling on Sunday, and gave to municipal corporations the power to regulate and control the sale of beer and native wine on Sunday. Selling to minors or intoxicated persons or to persons in the habit of becoming intoxicated, was prohibited under the penalty of a fine from $25 to $100 and imprisonment from five to thirty days.

Hundreds of thousands of dollars were paid into the county treasuries by the liquor-sellers in obedience to the requirements of this law. The constitutionality of this law was questioned, and, to test it, cases were taken to the Supreme Court. The court held that the tax was virtually a license, and therefore unconstitutional.

In 1866 "The Dow Law" was enacted. It was substantialy a re-enactment of "The Scott Law." Of course its constitutionality was questioned, and cases were taken to the Supreme Court. The political composition of the court had been changed from a majority of Democrats to a majority of Republicans, and, as the Republican party had committed itself fully in favor of the measure, the Republican judges sustained the law. Now, in Ohio, everybody is permitted to engage in the traffic upon the payment of the tax. The amount is the same in city and country, whether the sales are large or small. The beer tax is $100 and the whisky tax is $200 per annum, and is a lien upon the premises where sold. The manifest object of the "no license" clause in the constitution was, to outlaw the liquor traffic and prevent getting a revenue from it. By this tax law a large revenue is secured, which quite reconciles a large number of tax payers. It is in effect a universal license to everybody, without regard to qualifications, who can pay the tax. The large brewers, for the sake of furnishing their beer, pay the tax of the saloon keeper.

The constitutionality of the McConnellsville ordinance having been sustained, incorporated villages may, by their councils, prohibit the liquor traffic within their jurisdictions.

In many villages the councils are submitting the question to the electors and are being governed by the decision. There is no local option for those living outside of a municipality.

The General Assembly of the State may, according to the decision of the Supreme Court, entirely prohibit the liquor traffic without any amendment to the Constitution. As the State can now derive a large revenue from the traffic, the sentiment is strong to keep things as they are.

The struggle for prohibition in Ohio will be a protracted one. Her native population is largely in favor of entire prohibition. The distilling and brewing interests are very great. There is a very large foreign population, and all political parties court their patronage. The large revenue derived from taxation of the traffic goes very far to quiet and reconcile the people with the saloons. In 1883 two propositions were submitted to a vote of the electors, namely: "License," or "Prohibition." A vote for a restoration of the "License System" was very small; of those who voted on the question "Prohibition" had a large majority. As it required a majority of all the votes given for the highest candidates on the tickets cast at the election, it failed by a very small majority. By a fair construction of the law and an honest count, prohibition carried by more than thirty thousand majority.

INDIANA.

LICENSE SYSTEM.

The first law passed by the legislature of Indiana for the regulation of the liquor traffic was enacted in 1807, which provided that no person should "keep any public inn or tavern, ale house, or public house of entertainment at any place within the territory unless such person shall first obtain permission or license from the Court of Common Pleas, etc," and providing the length of time such permission should continue with appropriate penalties for its violation, including forfeiture in some cases. It also contained a provision that the Governor should issue a proclamation prohibiting the sale of intoxicating liquors to the Indians within thirty miles of any council, treaty, or conference. In 1813 the law was amended so as to require clerks to furnish lists of taverns to the grand juries, and allowing them to grant temporary permits during the vacation of their courts. A bond was also required conditioned for the good behavior of those holding permits or licenses to deal in intoxicating liquors. In 1817 a law was passed prohibiting the sale of liquors on Sunday, (except to travelers). In 1818 the selling of liquor to be drank on the premises where sold was prohibited under appropriate penalties. Also, prohibiting gaming, rioting, or disorderly conduct about such premises. The act further prohibited the sale of intoxicating liquors to minors, apprentices, or servants, or to persons in a state of intoxication, and provided further that no debt contracted for liquor above five dollars should be collectable by law.

In 1820 an act was passed requiring tavern keepers to set up for one whole day, "the bill of prices," and punishing severely any person charging more than was allowed by law.

In 1824 it was provided that any person applying for license should produce the certificate of twelve respectable freeholders that the applicant was of good moral character. In 1825 the number of respectable free holders signing the applicant's certificate of "good moral character" was increased to twenty-four. In 1828 the license was permitted to be issued to others than tavern keepers, which marked the beginning of the era of saloons and "tippling houses" in Indiana. The law was amended in 1831 providing for the collection of taxes from the keepers of "tippling house" or saloons by the municipal authorities in incorporated towns or cities. The license act was so amended in 1832 as to require the certificate by twenty-four freeholders, not only of good moral character of the applicant therefor (if a tavern-keeper), but an assurance that it would be for the benefit and convenience of travelers and conducive to the public good. The act required the applicant to show that he owned or rented a good house of at least three rooms with four good stalls, two beds and bedding more than are used by the family. The license was not transferable.

One section of the act provided for license to other persons than tavern-keepers, similar to previous acts. From 1834 to 1873 a number of special acts were passed allowing towns and cities to issue licenses to retailers of spirituous liquors.

By act of 1837, the board of county commissioners were required to levy a tax upon liquor dealers of not less than fifteen nor more than one hundred dollars. In 1838 an act was passed making it unlawful to keep a tippling house within the bounds of any incorporated town without a town license for a sum at the discretion of the corporation authorities not less than twenty-five dollars for the benefit of a public school fund for such town. In 1839 it was provided in the act for levying taxes that the commissioner should issue on each license to retail spirituous liquors not less than twenty-five nor more than one hundred dollars. In 1841 a law was passed declaring "all tippling houses or places wherein spirituous or intoxicating liquors were sold without license and drank about the same, if kept in a disorderly manner," to be common public nuisances, providing adequate penalties therefor, and means for their abatement. The county taxes were also increased to a maximum of two hundred dollars, and it was provided that a majority of the citizens, householders, might remonstrate against the issuance of such license, which latter provision authorizing a remonstrance was repealed in 1843. The act of 1843 provided for the payment of a tax to the incorporated town in which liquors were sold not less than ten dollars nor more than two hundred dollars, for the benefit of the free schools of such incorporated town. In 1847 the first local option law was passed, which provided that a majority of the voters of the several townships of the several counties with some exceptions, should determine at the ballot box whether or not any license should be granted.

In the same year a number of towns and cities were specially authorized to restrain and prohibit the sale of spiritous liquors, unless those proposing to engage in the traffic should be licensed by such cities and towns prescribed, the general laws and their ordinances imposing taxes and restrictions. From 1849 to 1851 a number of special prohibitory laws were enacted for different counties of the State, and proper penalties imposed for their violation. In 1852 a fine was imposed upon any person selling intoxicating liquors, cider, beer, or other drinks within two miles of any collection of inhabitants met together for worship. In 1853 a general law was enacted prohibiting the sale of spiritous liquors in any quantities less than one gallon except for sacramental, medicinal, chemical or culinary purposes without the consent of a majority of the legal voters and people of the township, nor without filing with the auditor a bond conditioned for the payment of all fines, penalties, and damages that may be incurred under such act. In 1855 a stringent State prohibitory law was enacted of which the following are the main features: First, it was provided that no person should sell by himself or agent any spirituous or intoxicating liquors, except as thereinafter provided.

Second, ale, porter, malt beer, lager beer, cider, and all wines, and fermented liquor which will produce intoxication, and all mixed liquors of which a part is spirituous or intoxicating liquors are included in the terms "intoxicating liquors" and within the meaning of the act.

Third, the county commissioners could give authority to manufacture at such places as they should designate, and to sell the same at such places only in any quantities to the duly authorized agents of the several counties for not more than one year, the authority being subject to revocation at any time.

Fourth, the commissioners could appoint suitable persons or agents of the county they represented for the purchase and sale of spirituous liquors for medicinal, chemical, and mechanical purposes only, and wine for sacramental use.

Fifth, the manner of dispensing such liquors by the agent of counties was rigidly prescribed so as to prevent the abuse of the authority conferred upon them.

Sixth, adequate penalties including fines and forfeitures were provided for by the prohibitory statute.

A mode of procedure for the condemnation and destruction of the liquors kept for unlawful sale was provided, and, taking it altogether, it appears to have been a very tight paper on the traffic of that State. In 1858 the law of 1855 was repealed. In 1859 a license system was adopted similar to the one existing upon the enactment of the general prohibitory law in 1855. In 1861 the law was slightly amended, and in 1865 a severe penalty was imposed upon persons selling spirituous liquors on Sunday, or election day, etc. In 1873 the license law was amended making it more stringent and effective in some important particulars. In 1875 a law was passed punishing drunkenness in office, and the general law again amended, but the changes were not such as materially affected the general features of the system. In 1877 a severe penalty, including imprisonment, was prescribed for selling spirituous liquors, even by druggists, except on written prescription on Sunday, Fourth of July, New Years, or Christmas, Thanksgiving, or election day.

In the same year incorporated towns were authorized to license the sale of liquors at a tax not exceeding the prices charged by the State. This last provision was re-enacted in 1879. In 1881 the Legislature proposed to submit to the vote of the State the following amendment to the constitution:

Section 1. The manufacture, sale, or keeping for sale, in said State, spirituous, vinous, malt liquors, or any other intoxicating liquor, except for medical, scientific, mechanical, and wines for sacramental purposes, shall be, and is hereby forever forbid.

Section 2. The General Assembly of the State of Indiana shall provide by law in what manner, by whom, and at what places such liquors shall be manufactured or sold for medical, scientific, mechanical, and sacramental purposes.

During the same session of the Legislature another act was passed defining and punishing drunkenness in office. Also providing for the punishment of drunkenness generally, and amending the law prescribing the manner, times, etc., of selling liquors by persons licensed by the State. Under the Indiana constitution it requires that a proposed amendment shall be agreed to by two Legislatures before submission to the people. No amendment has yet been submitted. The lower house of the last Legislature passed a stringent local option law which failed in the senate. As to the practical workings of the various license systems which have prevailed in Indiana it is unnecessary to speak. They are generally known and understood by the people who have been able to discern for themselves the results in their own States.

Upon the history of the prohibitory legislation in Indiana I quote from the very excellent little book by Rev. T. A. Goodwin, entitled "Seventy-six years Tussle with the Traffic":

" A study of the legislation for the first thirty years will interest the reader and show why I call this contest a tussle — now one on top, now the other. At first a man, to be qualified to sell liquor, had to be of "good behavior." But so many behaved badly that eleven years later in 1818 he had to prove that he was a man of "good moral character" by twelve respectable householders. But seven years later, in 1825, it took twenty-four witnesses and they all had to be free holders. But this proving inconvenient, three years later, 1828, the traffic was on top, and twelve were enough; but as they all had to live in the town or township, it was not much of a victory, especially since, if a majority of the freeholders remonstrated, there should be no license at all! Four years later the traffic was again on top, for though it again required twenty-four free holders to prove the necessary facts, they could go anywhere in and out of the town to get them, though still a remonstrance of a majority of freeholders could exclude taverns altogether. And this tussle has continued to this day, with the traffic most frequently on to."

Referring to the period of local legislation, the same author says :

A glance at the liquor legislation of this period is interesting. It was within these five years that those numerous attempts to obtain local prohibition were—now a town, now a township, and now a county—until, by one sweep in 1847, a general law was passed that if a majority of all the votes of any township should vote no license, then there should be none for that year in that township. It was something of a concession to the temperance sentiment, but still recognizing the right to keep a tippling-house as a natural one ; but it was more than neutralized by the insignificant penalties for selling without licenses.

It is an interesting fact, which may as well be mentioned here as elsewhere in this history, that from the first to the very last, every temperance organization has started out to ignore politics and save the world wholly by moral suasion, and that they have always found friends and advisers in that large class of "good temperance men," who never attend temperance meetings, or contribute to the cause anything more substantial than good advice. The Sons of Temperance were no exception to this. They assured every candidate before entering the room that the ceremonies and duties of the order should not interfere with his political views, be they what they may ; hence, when at the Grand Division held at South Bend in July, 1848, it was proposed to memorialize the next Legislature to so amend the liquor law that no votes should be counted for license unless expressly so cast, the proposition was voted down by a large majority. "Our mission is to save the fallen," was the pious purpose of the order, as then interpreted. But the "Sons of Temperance," like every other temperance organization, before and since, got bravely over such nambi-pambyism.

Nine months later, at Evansville, the Grand Division resolved unanimously to take steps looking towards prohibition, and from that day until the prohibitory law of 1855 was enacted it never faltered.

MORE STRINGENT LAW DEMANDED.

Higher and still higher the sentiment in favor of more stringent legislation arose. It will be seen by studying the law of 1853 that it was a Mosaic, composed of gems from the several local laws which had been tried in many townships and counties of the State, and if it could have been sustained by the courts, it would no doubt have done much good for humanity. It worked admirably while it was permitted to work, but it fell. It is too late now to criticise the reasoning of the court which first robbed it of its local option feature, and then, little by little, dismembered its license features and finally declared it null and void.

THE CAMPAIGN OF 1854.

What followed is a history worth studying. It was midsummer when the hastily prepared and hastily decided case of Maze vs. the State struck the fatal blow. It was soon followed by a series of crusades by women—not crusades of prayers and songs, such as was the fashion twenty years later, but crusades of hatchets and axes. Fifty women, headed by a resolute girl, went fort at Winchester and destroyed several saloons, and similar appeals were made in behalf of sobriety at Cambridge City, Centerville, and elsewhere.

The Grand Division met soon afterwards in its annual session. It was composed of many of the leading men of the State. Dr. Ryland T Brown, then in the vigor of mature manhood, was elected Grand Worthy Patriarch, and was requested to devote as much time as possible to a canvass of the State for prohibition after a model of the Maine law, and prohibition became the watchword everywhere. It was preached from the pulpits and declared from the platforms, so that early in the following January the temperance people held a meeting in Masonic Hall and raised twelve thousand dollars in a short time for a thorough organization of the State on the issue which the liquor interest of the State had thrust upon them. They appointed an effective State central committee, opened an office in Indianapolis, and proceeded to organize for the campaign, with the legend, "Search, seizure, confiscation, and destruction," flying from their penants. Every county was organized, and allegiance to all political parties was distinctly renounced, so that by the first of May the temperance element of the State was well in hand.

WORKINGS OF THE LAW.

On the workings of the law, the same author quotes from the leading papers of the State as follows:

* * * * * * * * * *

Such is a history of the passage of the law. It was to take effect on the twelfth of June, and it took EFFECT. On the morning of the thirteenth every saloon in Indiana was closed, and crape was hung upon many of the doors in token of the bereavement; and not a single saloon was open for public business from that day till the eighth day of the following November.

Speaking of the workings of the law in Indianapolis, the Indianapolis *Sentinel* of the fifteenth of June said: The temperance law so far has been universally and faithfully observed. We hear of no disposition to violate its provisions." And the local editor, the same day, said: "The new liquor law has knocked police items into a cocked hat. Not a single item is to be obtained now on account of John Barlecorn." Recurring to the subject again on the twentieth it said : "That the people of Indiana desire and will have a reasonable and constitutional law for the suppression of the evils of intemperance, none are blind enough to deny." Recurring again to the same subject, on the 28th of June it said: "During the past fifteen days there has not been a single commitment to the county jail for the violation of city ordinances, and in the way of arrests by the city police, there is little or nothing doing"

The Indianapolis *Locomotive*, of the 23rd of June, said : "There has not been a single arrest or commitment to prison since June 12th. The mayor sits quietly in his official chair, and the night-watch doses on the store boxes." Such was the peace and order which followed, that on the twelfth of July, just one month after the taking effect of the law, the Indianapolis Conncil reduced the night watch one-half. Referring to this fact, the *Locomotive*, of the 21st of July, said: 'The temperance law has nearly abolished rioting, drunkenness, and rowdying, and the taxpayers are reducing their expenses." The *Journal* referring to this reduction in its issue of July 24th, said: 'The reduction of the night watch was on account of the diminution of disturbance and drunkeness from the enforcement of the prohibitory law.'

The Indianapolis *Evening Republican*, of the 29th of June, said : " Rummeys no longer perambulate the streets, making night hideous: and the watchmen have little to do. The *Journal* of August 20th said : " The law diminished crime, reduced drunkenness, saved money, and emptied jails until the Supreme Court took hold of it." It was the same everywhere. The *Sentinel's* New Albany correspondent, of June 24th, said : "The liquor law is generally and faithfully observed in this section of the State." And the New Albany *Tribune* of the 27th said : "The sixty or seventy saloons of this city have been closed for two weeks." The Lafayette *Journal* of July said : "Since June 12th the mayor's court of this city has been almost deserted. Our jail is now clear of all corporation prisoners, and the good effects of the law have been felt at many firesides." The Madison correspondent of the Indianapolis *Republican* July 3rd, said : "The liquor law works like a charm. Sorrow and sighing have fled away. Liquor can not be purchased illegally in this city."

The Lafayette *Courier* of July 2, said- "What words can express the heartfelt gratitude of those whose happiness has been promoted by the enforcement of the prohibitory law?" And the Bloomington *Times* of July 3, said: "We have not seen a drunken man in town, or heard of a single fight or quarrel since July 12." Such was the testimony everywhere. The law worked like a charm everywhere; sorrow and sighing were diminished everywhere. Men came to town and returned sober who had not done so for years, and no class of men hailed it with more delight than that class whose appetites had such mastery over them that they could not resist the temptation when liquor was within easy reach. They had pleaded for the law, and they greatly rejoiced in the protection which it afforded. Drunken men were never seen in the smaller towns, and but few in the larger, and it is to this day the boast of several counties that not a single case of drunkenness was known during the hundred and forty-eight days of its continuance. Though one Beebe had procured himself to be nominally imprisoned for the purpose of making a case before the courts, yet not even he had dared to sell openly. That he and others did sell clandestinely, none denied. But the law had placed the keeping of tippling houses on the same footing of other crimes, and sought to suppress, not to license and protect it, and it succeeded as well as the law against adultery, and gambling, and larceny, and murder ever did. It was the fact that it was enforcable and was enforced, that arrayed against it the mighty powers of traffic.

THE ANNULMENT OF THE LAW.

There is some history about the annulment of this law that deserves to be rescued from oblivion before those who know whereof they speak pass away. Even before the bill had passed, some preliminary steps to annul the law by the courts had been taken, and the echo of the cannon which was fired on the final passage—for everybody knew that it would pass that afternoon, and men by the hundreds, who could not get into the hall, had congregated in the open grounds north of the old state house with cannon, to give expression to their joy, and they fired round after round—the echo of that cannon had hardly died away before the most eminent legal talent in the State had been employed to destroy, by the courts, what the people had so emphatically demanded at the ballot-box, and they at once began to prepare the case, and to prepare arguments for the courts ; so that when on the 12th of June it went into effect, their plans were already perfected and their arguments in readiness.

In pursuance of the programme, on the 2nd day of July, one Rhoderick Beebe, the tony saloon-keeper of Indianapolis, openly manufactured and sold beer. He was forthwith arrested and taken before the mayor, and fined fifty dollars. Refusing to pay, he was hypothetically committed to jail, whereupon he sued out a writ of habeas corpus before the Marion court of Common Pleas. The court sustained the law. An appeal was taken to the Supreme Court to try the validity of the law. It was midsummer, and the court had taken a recess for its summer vacation, but swift messengers were dispatched, and the court was brought together in less than a week. On the 8th all were in the city, and early on the 9th of July they were listening to the arguments which had been five months preparing on the part of the traffic, while the counsel for the state had to take hold of the case with but a few day's notice.

The final result of the case is history. The attorneys for the State asked time to prepare their arguments and the court adjourned till the November term. But the traffic grew impatient. The law was everywhere manufacturing public sentiment in its behalf by its happy results, and the liquor sellers demanded an immediate action. Meanwhile Judge Perkins had repeatedly foreshadowed his opinion. As early as the 12th of March he had written to the Richmond *Jeffersonian* and published over his well-known initial "P", a tirade first, against Gov. Wright for signing the bill, then again at the law itself. The tone of the letter may be inferred from this one sentence: "It may be enforced here, but it could not be in any despotism in Europe without producing revolution", and his conversations on the streets and everywhere abounded in such choice illustrations as this: 'Why the State might as well appoint a commission to do all the begetting of children and make eunuchs of the rest of us, as to appoint a commission to do all the liquor-selling'. In order to bring an influence to bear upon the subject, a meeting of the leading Democrats of the State was called for the 27th of August. On the preceding Friday, Judge Perkins called his colleagues to meet in chambers on the 23rd and to decide the case. Judges Gookins and Stuart refused to come, as Judge Perkins had no right to make such a call. The Democratic meeting was held on the 27th, and a series of resolutions was adopted denunciatory of the law, and one urging the court to hurry up the decision in view of the demoralization of business as the law stood. About the first of November Judges Gookins and Stuart signified a desire to have certain points re-argued when the court should convene in November.

This alarmed the traffic. It might mean a devided court, it might mean many additional months of deliberation. Something must be done, and that at once. In this emergency a parley was held at the Bates House saloon on the night of the seventh of November. Whether Judge Perkins was present or not was never known outside of that little coterie; but the conclusions of that consultation were soon made public. Early on the morning of the eighth, a boy of the saloon by the name of Herman, openly violated the law. By those in waiting he was at once hustled before the mayor, where he was fined, and on refusing to pay the fine he was sent to jail. He was hardly in before he was out on a writ of habeas corpus, issued by Judge Perkins who sat in his judicial chair before two o'clock ready to try (?) the case.

The attorneys for the liquor-sellers proposed to submit the case on the argument in the Beebe case, and the attorneys for the State, comprehending the situation at a glance, consented. The Judge repeated a few of his arguments against the law that had appeared months before in the Richmond *Jeffersonian* and had been often expressed on the streets, and concluded by saying : " The law is void, let the prisoner be discharged."

THE CONSEQUENCES.

The news of this decision was telegraphed to "the boys" at once and reached every town then on the line of the telegraph before four o'clock, and one universal carouse followed, making the night hideous, and resulting in a murder before midnight at Columbus. More drunken men were seen in Indiana within five hours after the decision was rendered, than had been seen in five months of the existence of the law, and there has not been a day since, Sundays not excepted, in which more drunkenness has not disgraced the state than during the entire period of one hundred and forty-eight days. For twenty-seven of those days the Marion county jail had not a single prisoner, and for seventeen other days, but one, and he was committed for an offense not connected with liquor—a state of affairs never known before or since.

But the younger men will ask, was there no whisky sold and drank during those months? Of course there was. No one ever expected any thing else. Those who could, in anticipation of the coming drought, had plentifully stocked their cellars, but those who did not do this and were skilled in the methods, still found means to get it. Cincinnati, Chicago and Louisville were connected by rail with Indiana, and there was no prohibition in those cities, hence by one device or another liquor was obtained from those outside places as well as legally at home. Many of these devices were curious enough. John L. Robinson, of Rushville, then the United States Marshall, and the managing editor of The *Jacksonian*, and for many years the Democratic Congressman from that district, ordered a keg from Cincinnati for his private use, and it evaded the search, seizure and confiscation clause by being marked 'Lard Oil', and the poor man was ever afterwards known as John Lardoil Robinson.

But men of less money and even less cunning found means of getting liquor. Why should they not? With all our bolts and bars and burglar proof appliances there are men who break into our houses and rob us. They make the business a study, but the millions do not get in, however much they may desire to. Everybody knows that men will go to extremes for whisky that are unknown in almost everything else. Men will swear falsely for whisky and in the interest of the whisky seller, who would not to save the life of a wife or child. Men will rob their families of food, take even their wife's shawl or shoes and pawn them for whisky, so utterly overpowering are their depraved appetites. Does any sane man imagine that such men can not find whisky under any law? More than that, prohibitory laws, when analyzed and properly understood, aim only at suppressing these schools of vice known as dramshops. If, in accomplishing this it becomes necessary to make more difficult the procurement of liquors for the less harmful use of them, the fault lies more in the stubbornness of the traffic than in the purpose of the law. Prohibition is simply a general name applied to that class of temperance legislation which contemplates the absolute suppression of public tippling by whatever measures may be necessary. If, therefore, it shall become necessary to wholly forbid the manufacture and sale that this may be accomplished, then, all that, and more, may be expected; and, as slavery defied all modifications, and required utter abolition, so, probably will the liquor traffic.

There were several cases of "search, seizure, confiscation and destruction" under the law. The lower courts, nearly all, or quite all, enforced the law. Notably among these was the Common Pleas Court of Tippecanoe county, presided over by Hon. John Pettit, one of the best lawyers Indiana ever had, and afterwards a member of the Supreme Court, elected by the Democratic party. The number of appeals from his court, which will be observed in the decisions of that period which follows, is thus accounted for. The Legislature of 1859 which repealed the law, provided for reimbursing all who had suffered in its enforcement.

ILLINOIS.

LICENSE SYSTEM.

Illinois was admitted as a state in 1818. The first temperance law was passed in February, 1819, during the session of the first State legislature, and provided for a license fee to be fixed by the commissioners, not to exceed twelve dollars per annum. The penalty for selling liquor or keeping a public house of entertainment without such license was one dollar per day. License to be granted for one year only. License to be revoked, if drunkenness, disorder or gaming were allowed. Good entertainment for man and horse were to be provided, under penalty of five dollars for failure. Bond to be given, with security if required, not to exceed $200, that licensee should be of good behavior at all times and obey all laws in force relating to the business. The sale to be drank on or adjacent to the premises; or to companies of slaves, servants or others, or in quantities less than one quart of spirituous or two gallons of malt liquors, was prohibited under penalty of twelve dollars. The law also forbade the sale to minors or the harboring of minors or bond-servants, and provided that the commissioners should fix a table of "rates" which should be posted conspicuously, and fixed a fine of $20 for violation of such rates. To prevent devices for evading the law nearly all kinds of liquors known were specified and the term "strong water" was added, and to cover every possible locality the terms "shelters," "places" and "woods" were included among the localities coming under the inhibition of the law. This law passed by a Legislature democratic in both houses, and was approved by Governor Shadrack Bond, a Democrat.

The second law was passed February 14th, 1823, legislature overwhelmingly democratic, Governor, Edmund Coles, anti-slavery democrat. It was entitled "An Act *to prevent*," etc. It prohibited sales to Indians, made all accounts for liquors greater than fifty cents void, and prohibited the courts from taking jurisdiction in such cases. It also prohibited the licensing of any "tippling shop, commonly called a grocery," and required applicants for license to sell liquor to give security that they would also keep "meat and lodging for at least four persons over and above his common family, and stabling for their horses." This act prevented the keeping of saloons as they are now kept, the inn, or tavern idea only being recognized.

In 1833 an act was passed making the sale of cider in less quantity than two gallons unlawful. Legislature Democratic. Governor, John Reynolds, democrat.

In 1835 a mild high license measure was passed, making the license not more than $50 taking into consideration "the stand where the '*tavern*' was located." The dram-shop idea was not recognized. Legislature democratic; Governor, Joseph Duncan, democrat.

In 1837 the cider law of 1833 was repealed and all "*citizens of the State*" were authorized to sell cider and beer in any quantity. Legislature democratic ; Governor Duncan, democrat. The Governor and his council of revision, the Supreme Judges, refused to approve the bill, but it became a law through the neglect to return it with the Governor's objections within the ten days prescribed by law.

In addition to these statutes, specifically aimed against the traffic, the criminal code, revised 1833, made it unlawful to sell in quantities less than one quart, without first having obtained license, and inflict a fine of $10 for each offense. A like fine for selling to a slave or servant without the master's consent ; and sale to Indians absolutely prohibited.

March 3rd, 1845, Legislature democratic, Governor Thomas Ford, democrat, a law was passed making the license fee not less than $25 nor more than $300 and requiring bond in $500 to keep orderly house and not permit gaming or riotous conduct. The principle of local option was introduced by conferring upon the president and trustees of incorporated towns exclusive authority to grant or withhold license, but requiring the license money to be paid into the county treasury. The law still held to the "grocery" idea, but defined a grocery to be "a place where spiritous or vinous liquors are retailed in less quantities than one quart." The penalty was a fine of ten dollars for each offense, and the law prohibited the sale to negroes or Indians under penalty of $10 and $20 respectively, and if a sale was made to a minor or servant the seller was fined $3 and forfeited the price of the liquor sold for the first and second offenses and for the third offense a fine of $12, forfeiture of license and the seller forever rendered incapable of keeping a grocery in the State.

THE PROHIBITORY LAW OF 1851.

February 1st, 1851, the Democratic Legislature passed an act prohibiting the sale of vinous, spirituous or mixed liquors in quantities less than one quart, or in any quantity to be drank on the premises, and fixing the penalty at $25 for each offense. The giving away of liquors was declared a sale within the meaning of the act. All license laws were repealed. The sale to a person under 18 years of age in any quantity was punishable by fine not less than $30 nor more than $100. The penalties might be enforced by indictment or action for debt, the latter provision being intended to do away with the delay of an indictment and render the enforcement of the law more speedy and certain. The judge was required to furnish the act to every grand jury, and the law was made to include incorporated towns and cities, anything in their charters to the contrary notwithstanding. The law was approved by Augustus C. French, democrat, governor. This law was in force two years and six days, during which time there was no legal sale of liquor in Illinois.

Feb. 7th, 1853, the legislature, largely democratic, Joel A. Matteson, of Will county, governor, repealed this law, and on Feb. 12th restored all laws pertaining to license which were in force at the time the prohibitory law was passed. This was a long step backward, but some allowance must be made for the legislature of 1853. It was composed of the barbarians who passed the black laws of Illinois, and marks the blackest era in the State. The law restoring the license laws provided that the fee should not be less than $50 nor more than $300.

Feb. 22nd, 1861, the legislature passed the law prohibiting the sale of intoxicants or keeping open of bar rooms on any election day. There have also been several minor acts passed at different times, prohibiting the sales on Sunday, or at Fairs or within two miles of same, at elections, at camp meetings or within one mile of the same. The latter law is a part of the criminal code. The law relating to the organization of cities and villages, found in paragraph 46, revised statutes of

1874, authorizes city councils in cities and the president and board of trustees in villages to license, regulate or prohibit the sale of intoxicating drinks, to determine the amount of the license fee, and limits the term of the license to the municipal year. This law is subject to any general state law concerning license which may be in force. There have also been special charters granted to certain cities conferring similar powers.

THE ACT OF 1872.

The year 1872 marks a decided advance in temperance legislation, as it was in that year that the law sometimes mistakenly termed the "Reddick" law was passed. The law was prepared under the direction of Hon. H. W. Austin, member of the house of representatives from the third district of Chicago. It was drafted by O. H. Horton, Esq., of Chicago, at Mr. Austin's request, and embraces the principal features of the Adair law of Ohio. Mr. Austin introduced this bill in the select committee on temperance in March, 1871. The measure met with favor in the committee, and in order to secure its more certain and speedy passage, it was thought best to have it pass the Senate first. A printed copy of the bill was taken by Hon. Wm. Reddick, senator from LaSalle, from the House, and presented by him to the body of which he was a member. This was the only connection Mr. Reddick had with the bill, except to vote in favor of its passage, and he never claimed to be the author of the law or that it should bear his name. To Mr. Austin the state is indebted for the law and whatever of excellence it contains.

As before stated, Mr. Austin introduced the bill in the committee in March, 1871. It was presented in the house by the chairman of the committee, March 3, read a first time and printed. It remained in committee of the whole until the adjourned session in November, and on the 27th of that month was introduced in the senate, which body it passed, with very slight amendment, December 19, 1871, by a vote of 40 in favor to 5 against it. In the house it was debated for three days, when it passed January 11, 1872, by a vote of 114 to 48. Both houses were strongly Republican, but the bill passed by a decidedly non-partisan vote, Democrats and Republicans supporting it. On the 13th of January it was approved by the Republican Governor, John M. Palmer, and went into effect the first of July following. The main provisions of the law are as follows:

SEC. 1, Makes selling without license unlawful; requires bond in $3,000 for all damages that may result to person, property, or means of support by reason of sale under license, and provides that such bond may be sued and recovered upon.

SEC. 2. Forbids sale to minors, intoxicated persons or habitual drunkards.

SEC. 3. Makes all places where liquors are sold contrary to the provisions of the act, public nuisances, and orders their abatement as such.

SEC. 4. Provides that any person may take charge of an intoxicated person, and makes the one who caused such intoxication liable in action for debt for reasonable compensation for such care, and two dollars per day in addition for every day such person shall be kept on account of such intoxication.

SEC. 5. Makes seller of liquor and owner of property where sold liable for damages, and gives right of action to all persons damaged, including married women who are given *femme sole* right to bring suit. Also, provides that suit may be brought by any appropriate action in any court having competent jurisdiction.

SEC. 6. Makes penalty for violation of first or second sections fine not less than $20 nor more than $100, and imprisonment in county jail not less than ten nor more than thirty days, with costs of prosecution, and for violation of third section, fine not less than $50 nor more than $100, with costs, and imprisonment not less than twenty nor more than fifty days. It also orders places in the latter case to be abated and shut up by order of the court until convicted person gives bond and security in $1000 not to sell contrary to law, and to pay all fines, costs and damages assessed. It also provides that fines may be enforced separate from imprisonment before justices of the peace.

SEC. 7. Makes giving away, or any other device to evade the same, as selling.

SEC. 8. Provides that all real estate and personal property of the seller not exempt under the homestead laws of the State, or from levy under judgment and execution, shall be liable for fines, costs at the rate of $500 for one year for the privilege of keeping a dramshop ,provided, that in all cases where the license is for the sale of malt liquors only, the fee shall not be less than $150 per year. The penalty, bonds, petitions, etc., do not materially differ from those provided in the laws of 1873 and 1874.

The opinion is somewhat general that Illinois has a local option law, but a careful perusal of this abstract will show that such is not the case. The license laws simply say that the proper authorities *may* (not shall) issue licenses. It is thus left optional with them, and the sale of liquors may be prevented by electing boards and councils themselves opposed to license.

MASSACHUSETTS.

CLASSIFIED LICENSES.

Efforts to "regulate" alcoholism began with the early settlers in Massachusetts. Men were fined heavily, imprisoned and "whipt" for being "drunck" in 1629. In 1637 it was an offense to remain in a licensed drinking house "longer than necessary occations" and to be punished with a fine of "20 shillings." In 1639 there was a law forbidding "the drinking of healths," because "it was an occation of much wast of the good creatures," etc. In 1645 inkeepers were fined "five shillings for suffering any to be drunck in their houses, or to drink excessively, or to continue tippling above the space of half an hour." It was "excessive drinking when above half a pint was allowed at one time to one person to drink."

These and many other "regulations," seeking to secure men of standing and good judgment to deal out the liquors so as to avoid excess, fencing with restrictive laws proceeded upon the conviction that alcoholic liquors were a potent remedy for human ills. This was not questioned by anybody. Excess was a crime in the stricter days of the long period up to 1836 or a fault which however was condoned by its universality during most of these years. In spite of all regulation drunkenness increased until it became almost universal. Few adult persons did not drink, and occasionally to excess, and this included ministers and women. In spite of the most stringent license regulations the quantity of distilled liquors drank in the years 1790 to 1830 inclusive probably averaged seven gallons to every man, woman and child, besides enormous quantities of cider, beer and wine. And all these years as earnest and honest men as history has any account of, did their best to suppress "intemperance." Their uniform defeat arose from one cause. They did not recognize alcohol as in its own nature a destructive poison.

It would be monotonous to recite the "regulations" attempted during two hundred years, all of which were efforts to retain a cause and prevent the effects, a style of "reform" still in favor with many people. But gradually it began to dawn upon the leaders that the trouble was the alcohol, and whether in "rum" or in "cider" made little matter. The result of this conviction was the total abstinence action of 1836 at Saratoga. As early as 1823 Henry Ware had said : "There is no man or body of men who can strike at the root but the legislature of a nation." As the truth began to permeate the better classes, the demand for prohibitive legislation grew. The county commissioners up to 1835 had been appointed officers and they had entire control of the licenses. This year the office was made elective, and the question of license entered into the election. In many towns the "no-license party" triumphed, and thus the question assumed much the shape it has now : 'total abstinence for the individual and Prohibition for the State".

On the Fourth of July, 1838, the fifteen gallon law went into effect. No person except licensed apothecaries and physicians might sell less than fifteen gallons of spirituous liquors, "all of which was to be carried away at one time." The law was violently opposed by the dealers and their sympathizers, and remained in force only a year and a half. But the people rallied, elected no license commissioners, and it is affirmed that from 1841 to 1852 no licenses were issued in Boston, and very few in the State. It was a period when the license system had fallen under general condemnation. In almost every State where opportunity was afforded to vote there were heavy majorities against the license system, and Ohio and Michigan incorporated their condemnation in their constitutions. In New York, at a general election, April, 1846, more than five-sixths of the towns and cities gave large majorities against license. This was the prevailing sentiment from 1845 to 1856, when the whole question was over-slaughed by the "anti-slavery agitation."

PROHIBITORY LAWS,

BY REV. A. A. MINER, D. D. L. L.D.

The first prohibitory statute in Massachusetts was enacted in 1852 by a Democratic, Whig, and Free Soil Legislature, George S. Boutwell, (democrat) governor. Having been pronounced unconstitutional in some details, it was repealed in 1853. Thereupon, General Benjamin F. Butler was employed by friends of temperance to draft a bill which was enacted into law in 1855 by a legislature representing the American party; Henry J. Gardner, Governor.

The law was attacked at every point, withstood every legal assault upon it, was sustained in the highest court, and was retained upon the statute books till 1868. In 1867, Judge Sawyer, then District Attorney of Suffolk county, pronounced it the strongest law that can be made, and declared that it was executed—600 of the strongest dealers, within the space of four weeks, having pledged themselves to leave the business.

During all those twelve years, the Republican party, as a party, trembled before it like an aspen leaf—lacking equally the courage to repeal it and the manliness to execute. The government of Boston, then in the hands of the Republicans, was specially open to censure. By measures studied and treacherous, it continuously and persistently nullified the law. Several members of the Board of Aldermen took the utmost care to select liquor sellers exclusively for the list of names whence jurors were to be drawn, and when assailed therefor by citizens, justified themselves on the ground that they could not say that they were not "free from all legal disabilities." They thus passed by citizens about whom none would raise a question, and selected those who at the next turn of the wheel might themselves become the victims of the law. By such means there were sure to be some liquor dealers, all violators of the law, on every panel—a procedure as flagrant and indecent as would be the selection of counterfeiters to try counterfeiters, forgers to try forgers, or thieves to try thieves.

Sometimes the Mayor would make a most ostentatious effort to execute the law, and on its failure would declare its execution impracticable. The Hon. Alexander W. Rice furnished a conspicuous example of this. We put hundreds of cases into court, very few of which were ever tried, and those before jurors selected to prevent conviction. Of course, these efforts were futile, as they were intended to be—proved by the utter neglect of the seizure clause of the law, in the use of which the heaviest dealer in the city could have been broken down in a week. His honor has made several efforts since his administrations as mayor of the city and governor of the Commonwealth to repair his temperance record, but with very indifferent success.

After years of vain endeavor to secure an honest and patriotic execution of the law on the part of the city authorities, the temperance people appealed to the State to create a metropolitan police, and thus itself attend to the execution of its own laws. After repeated effort it became probable such a bill would be enacted, whereupon His excellency, John A. Andrew, then Governor of the Commonwealth, and one of the most renowned governors we have ever had, consulted with his friends in the legislature, warned them of the political dangers attending their proposed action, presented them a bill for a State constabulary force which he would prefer to a metropolitan force, and which was enacted into law.

The constabulary force thus created, which should have been aided by the ordinary police of the city, as the law required, was opposed and obstructed by it, and for some time accomplished very little in the chief centers of population; while in all the rural regions of the State the traffic was substantially at an end.

The friends of temperance did not sleep. They pushed the constable to handle his State force with more vigor and precision. These efforts were not in vain. In the latter part of 1865 and through 1866, much good work was done, though the authorities of both State and city exerted quite other than a helpful influence. In proportion as the State force showed itself efficient, it was the subject of the most malignant attacks. Its action was severely felt by many dealers in the city. Their liquors were seized, condemned by the courts, and poured into the streets. Many thousands of dollars worth were thus destroyed, many dealers utterly crushed, and the whole fraternity were in the utmost consternation.

At length the plan was devised by the liquor dealers' committee of getting the merchants of Boston to petition for a repeal of the prohibitory law and the enactment of a license law, professedly for the greater restraint of the traffic, but really to remove the restraint already crippling the traffic.

This plan was acted upon in 1867. A large body of professedly most Christian merchants, with the Hon. Alpheus Hardy at their head, sent their petition to the Legislature. It was referred to a joint special committee of thirteen, who occupied the representatives' hall six weeks in hearings on the subject. The then ex-Gov. John A. Andrew and the Hon. Linus Child were counsel for the petitioners. They were faithful to their clients. Nominally employed by the merchants, they were really in the employ of the liquor dealers, who paid Mr. Andrew fifteen thousand dollars, and Mr. Child five thousand dollars, respectively, for their services. The Hon. William B. Spooner and the Rev. A. A. Miner, D. D., then president of Tuft's College conducted the case for the remonstrants, without fear or reward. They summoned witnesses to prove the facts above stated, and those witnesses were some of the liquor dealers who subscribed the money, and the refusal to let them testify was a confession of the truth of the facts alleged. The petitioners summoned a hundred and twenty-five ex-officials, dignitaries, and clergymen, almost every one of whom confessed that he used wines or liquors as beverages, and almost all of whom chafed more or less at being questioned. The remonstrants called about seventy-five, all of whom where total abstainers. The committee submitted three reports, and the Legislature retained the law by a very large majority, ninety men in the house and senate, uncommitted at the opening of the hearing, voting against a change. Thus prohibition triumphed, and the foes of good order were discomfitted.

In the autumn of 1867 the Personal Liberty League, a dark lantern association, was organized in all the cities and principal towns, controlled the caucuses, packed the Legislature, republican still, and in 1868 repealed the prohibitory law and enacted a license law. This repeal by a Legislature largely republican, Hon. Alexander H. Bullock, governor, was a surprise. It was not believed that the party dare repeal it. A year of free liquor ensued. In the autumn of 1868, the people rallied, nominated Hon. William Claflin, republican, a total abstainer and prohibitionist, for governor, and triumphantly elected him, with a senate and house to correspond.

There was great satisfaction among temperance men. Everybody looked for the restoration of the law of 1855, repealed the year before. In name it *was* restored ; in fact, it was destroyed. The governor had no sooner taken the oath of office than he proceeded to one of the most treacherous acts from which the cause of prohibition in our State has ever suffered. He recommended the restoration of the prohibitory law, but counselled that cider be exempted from its operations. He thus broke the principle of the law, furnished a cover for the sale of all sorts of liquors, and made detection in the highest degree difficult.

One of the leading Republican papers of the State, *The Daily Evening Traveller*, of Boston, up to that time entirely sound on prohibition, took ground with the governor in a series of articles written by a leading member of the State central Republican committee. The Republican Legislature of that year, 1869, followed the counsel of the governor, and began the work of debauching the prohibitory sentiment of the State. The next year, all fermented liquors were exempted from the operation of the law, the constabulary force found its work increasingly difficult, and ceased to be handled with either integrity or efficiency. After various unimportant changes, the law was made prohibitory again, but left unexecuted, and was replaced in 1875 by our present local option law. All this was done by a studied, stealthy, persistent effort to place the question of prohibition in such an attitude that, whatever else it might do, it could not be made an issue in the politics of the State. The deadening influence of this condition of things is apparent. The State is disintegrated.

The rural districts, by their "No-license" vote, drive the traffickers from their midst, who fly to the city where license, at a moderate cost, can be had for the asking, and where, if they prefer, they can with impunity sell without a license, since the law which it was assumed public opinion would sustain and execute, is substantially prostrate.

Some statistics of arrests and prosecutions for the license years 1875—77 were presented by Governor Alexander H. Rice in contrast with those of the last year of nominal prohibition, to the disadvantage of the latter; but Col. Carroll D. Wright, by whom the statistics were gathered at the command of the governor, refused to be held responsible for any such inference. He knew that the authorities executed the laws far better in the license than in the prohibitory period, and that during 1875—77 many men out of employment had no means to procure liquor. Besides, it was ascertained that the number of arrests for drunkenness, during those years, was very exactly in the inverse ratio to the activity of the Reform Clubs in the various cities and towns of the State.

In surveying the history of the republican party in Massachusetts, I have no hesitation in saying that, as a party, it is entitled to little else than condemnation in its conduct towards the temperence cause. It found the strongest law possible when it came into power. It has wrestled with a good voting prohibitory majority in the State and overthrown it. When it has not been treacherous it has been timid, not only leaving the law unexecuted, but handling the police of the city in ways to prevent its execution. It is, and ever has been, in full complicity with the opulant lawbreakers of the State.

THE PRESENT LAW.

The present law of Massachusetts may be termed a very stringent license law. It provides for licenses of six different classes as follows :

First Class : To sell liquors of any kind to be drunk on the premises.

Second Class : To sell malt liquors and cider and light

wines, containing not more than 15 per cent of alcohol, to be drunk on the premises.

Third Class : To sell malt liquors and cider to be drunk on the premises.

Fourth Class : To sell liquors of any kind, not to be drunk on the premises.

Fifth Class : To sell malt liquors, cider and light wines, containing not more than 15 per cent of alcohol, not to be drunk on the premises.

Sixth Class : To druggists and apothecaries to sell liquor of any kind for medicinal, mechanical and chemical purposes only and to such persons only as may certify in writing for what use they want it.

The fees for licenses are : for the first class not less than $100, nor more than $1000 ; second or third class, not less than $50, nor more than $250 ; fourth class, not less than $50, nor more than $500, *provided*, that a distiller who distils not over fifty barrels per year, shall pay $50 and one who distils over fifty not less than $300 nor more than $500. For a license of the fifth class, not less than $50 nor more than $500, *provided*, that a brewer shall pay not less than $200 nor more than $400. For a license of the sixth class, one dollar.

Makers of cider and native wines may sell the same without license, not to be drunk on the premises. Druggists may sell pure alcohol. Every druggist must register date, person, kind, quantity and price at every sale, and the purpose for which purchased; register always to be open to inspection by proper officers. Importers may sell in original casks, or in casks not less than required of importers under U. S. laws without license. License can only issue in towns and cities which so vote at the annual municipal election or town meeting, and run only until the first of the next May. Notice of application for license must be published, or posted ten days before the licensing board can act thereon. In case the owner of adjacent real estate files an objection before the ten days expire, no license can issue.

The mayor and aldermen may refuse to issue license to parties they deem unfit. Every license forbids the sale on the Lord's Day, (except inn-holders to guests) also, between the hours of twelve at night and six in the morning on week days; forbids the sale of any but liquors of good, standard quality free from adulteration; to a drunkard, intoxicated person, or one known to have been intoxicated within six months preceding; or to a minor, either for his own use, the use of his parent, or any other person. All disorder, indecency and gaming is forbidden either on the licensed premises or premises connected therewith by interior communication. Licenses of the second, third or fifth class forbid that other liquors than those specified be kept on the premises. Licenses of the first, second and third classes are subject to the condition that the licensee shall not keep a public bar, and shall hold license only as an inn-holder, and the room in which liquors are to be sold shall be specified. Licenses must be displayed where they can be easily read. The violation of any of these conditions works forfeiture of the license.

The board granting the license may require the permanent closing of all entrances except from the public street. No blinds, screens, or other obstructions are allowed, and any obstruction which interferes with a clear view of the interior makes the license void. Bond is required in the sum of $1000, to be signed by surety worth $2000, property to be designated and statement kept on file with the bond.

One fourth of the license money must be paid to the State by the treasurer of the city or town. Any authorized officer may enter premises at any time to see how the business is conducted and may take samples of liquors for analysis, the town or city to pay for said samples if found of good quality and unadulterated. Mayors and aldermen of a city and selectmen of a town may declare a license forfeited after due notice, and if so declared the holder is disqualified to receive license for one year, and if he own the premises no license to be exercised on said premises can issue for the balance of the term.

Any person taking liquors to sell, or to be sold into a town in which licenses are not issued, forfeits the liquors to the State.

Whoever violates any provision of his license or of this law is liable to a fine not less than $50 nor more than $500, or to jail not less than one or more than six months, or both, and the licensee also forfeits his license and becomes disqualified to hold license for one year, and no license can be issued for the premises, if he be the owner, for the rest of the term.

Any person injured in person, property or means of support by an intoxicated person, has right of action against any person, who, in whole or in part caused such intoxication, and against the owner of the premises unless the occupant holds a license. Persons selling to minors or allowing minors to loiter on premises are liable in the sum of $100 for each offense, to the parent or guardian of such minor.

The husband, wife, parent, child, guardian or employer of any person having the habit of drinking to excess, may notify any person in writing not to sell to person having such habit, and if persons so notified sell to such person within twelve months, the person giving the notice may recover in any sum not less than $100, nor more than $500, *provided*, that an employer giving such notice shall not recover unless injured in person or property.

Any liquor containing more than three per cent of alcohol is declared intoxicating liquor.

Other sections of the law provide for the inspection of liquors and against their adulteration. The law is very strong and explicit on this point. The seizure of concealed liquors is also provided for, and such liquors may be forfeited to the State.

A mayor, alderman, selectman, sheriff, or deputy, chief of police or deputy, city marshal or deputy, police officer or constable may arrest violators of the law without warrant and seize liquors, vessels and implements in their possession, and it is made the duty of these officers to enforce penalties against offenders. If they neglect so to do for two weeks after being notified in writing that the law is being violated and the names of witnesses are given them, any person who makes complaint thereafter is entitled to all fines collected for such violation.

All liquors kept for sale and the implements and vessels used in selling contrary to law are declared common nuisances ; also all club rooms used for the purpose of selling or dispensing liquors to member or others, and those who keep or maintain such rooms are liable to a fine not less than $50 nor more than $100, or imprisonment in the house of correction not less than three months nor more than twelve.

Amendments provide that no license shall be granted for sale within four hundred feet of any public school ; provide for the inspection and seizure of liquors ; forbid tampering with samples taken, and require common victualers having license to close their places from midnight until five in the morning.

Other amendments add to the stringency of the Sunday and gaming laws ; the restrictions upon licensed victualers provide against giving credit for drink, food or livery hire to students in educational institutions, and against selling liquor or beer without license at any show or exhibition.

There is also a law in Massachusetts against drunkenness. Any person getting intoxicated by the voluntary use of liquor, may, for the first offense, be fined not more than one dollar and costs, and be imprisoned until such fine and costs are paid, not exceeding ten days. A male person for the second offense may be fined not more than five dollars and costs or imprisoned not more than two months. If he has been convicted twice in the twelve months preceding, he may be fined not more than ten dollars or imprisoned not more than one year.

If a woman has been convicted twice within twelve months she may be fined not exceeding ten dollars, or imprisoned in the reformatory prison for women not less than one or more than two years, or, in any place provided by law for common drunkards, not more than one year.

It would seem from a perusal of these laws, that if there were any virtue at all in license laws and other so-called restrictive and regulative measures, it should be manifest in Massachusetts, yet we find that according to the Census and Revenue reports of 1880 that State had one saloon to every sixty-four voters, a proportion equalled by only fifteen other States, while the adjoining State of Vermont, with a prohibitory law moderately well enforced had but one saloon to 201 voters, and South Carolina with such Prohibition as she could secure through local option had but one saloon to each 246 voters. These figures speak volumes.

CONNECTICUT.

LICENSE WITH LOCAL OPTION FEATURES APPLYING TO TOWNS.

"An interesting incident," says Doctor Dorchester, "shows the state of public sentiment in this colony at a very early date. A vessel, touching at Norwalk, prepared to land a barrel of rum. The civil authorities and principal inhabitants gathered and forbade its landing. They said to the captain of the vessel, 'You shall never land it on our shores. What! a whole barrel of rum! It will corrupt our morals and be our undoing." In 1650 a heavy duty was laid on all imported liquors and an execise tax on home manufacture. Drunkenness was fined five shillings for first and ten for second offense. Sellers were fined if they allowed men to get drunk in their houses.

According to Rev. Geo. A. Calhoun D. D., as early as 1800 there was extreme poverty, caused by drink. He says, in North Coventry, an average town for that period (1800 to 1820). "Only four floors had carpets on them, but four houses painted white, and not more than ten four-wheeled vehicles in the town. Even whitewash on the wall was rare. Real poverty was the cause. The gains of the people were consumed in intoxicating drink. *At least one man of every score became a drunkard*, and not a few women were given to the habits of intemperance."

A prohibitory law was passed in 1854, the legislature at the time being democratic and anti-Neb. The present law is a mixture of local option and license, and is only enforced on the surface, even in no-license towns. It is considered an obstacle in the way of prohibition, deluding many honest men with "the mirage" or non-partisan local option work.

License was granted upon application signed by applicant and endorsed by five electors and tax-payers of the town within the limits of which the business carried on under such license is to be transacted. A bond of $300 required. License for not less than $100, nor more than $500.

Sec. 7 of the law in force is as follows:

"No spirituous and intoxicating liquors shall be sold, exchanged, or given away in any building belonging to or under the control of the State, or of any county or town in the State; nor shall any license be granted for the sale of spirituous and intoxicating liquors in any building, except a hotel, when said building is also used as a dwelling-house, unless access from the portion of said building used as a dwelling to the portion appropriated to the sale of spirituous and intoxicating liquors is effectually closed, and if any way of access from the other portions of said building to the portion used for the sale of such liquors shall be opened after said license is granted, such license shall thereupon be revoked by the county commissioners. No license for the sale of spirituous and intoxicating liquors shall be granted to any sheriff, deputy-sheriff, constable, grand juror, justice of the peace, prosecuting agent, or to any female who is not known to the county commissioners to be a woman of good repute; or to any female who is a member of the household of any person to whom a license has been refused, or by whom a license has been forfeited, or to any person keeping a house of ill-fame, or a house reputed to be a house of ill-fame, or to any person keeping any gambling place of any description."

Severe penalties are prescribed for the violation of any of the provisions of the law.

From a recent report of an important commitee of the Conference of the Congregational Church, of Connecticut, I take the following, which may seem to indicate the condition of affairs in that State with reference to the liquor traffic:

3. The statistics of crime in the State since the dram-shop was legalized, justify the demand for its suppression. In the first year of the operation of the law of 1872, commitments for crime in the State went up from 2,986 to 4,481, and for drunkenness, from 1,470 to 2,125. The commitments of the last criminal year, as reported to the present General Assembly, were, for all crimes, 6,416; and for drunkenness, including "common drunkards," 2,905. Comparing these figures with those of the year before the legalization of the dram-shop, viz: total commitments 2,905, and drunkenness 1,290, we have an in

crease of all crimes of 125 per cent,, in a period of fifteen years. And the dram-shop is the chief fountain and minister of crime. Ought it not to be suppressed?

RHODE ISLAND.

A prohibitory law was passed by a democratic legislature in 1852, declared unconstitutional in 1853, re-enacted in 1855 and ratified by the people. It has since been repealed and the state is now under license law. It is opitional with the authorities to grant or withhold license, as they see fit, and thus far the law posesses a local option feature. The license fee is from $150 to $300. In most places where license is refused it is difficult to obtain liquor. In others the law is entirely ignored.

I append here an extract taken from the annual address of Hon. George P. Wetmore, governor of Rhode Island 1887:

"All things considered, I think it may be said that as good results have been obtained in its enforcement as could have reasonably been anticipated, and as evidence of this I may cite the official records of the police departments of the cities of Providence and Newport, whose statements, which I assume to be correct, indicate a large reduction of drunkenness, and of that class of disorder and misery which intoxicants provoke and stimulate."

In the same connection I append two telegrams sent out during the recent Michigan campaign:

PROVIDENEE, R. I., March 23. — Increase of arrests for drunkenness and revelry in Providence last six months license, over 18 per cent. Decrease in first six months prohibition, over 42 per cent. Common drunkeness in same time decreased in Newport, 100 per cent; Pawtucket, 50 per cent; last two months, 75 per cent. Official figures.

H. W. CONANT.

PROVIDENCE, R. I., March 24.—The statistics from the city of Providence, the largest city in the State, show an increase of drunkenness during the last six months of the license law of 183 per cent. While during the first six months of prohibition, as compared with the corresponding period under license, drunkenness decreased more than 42 per cent. The commitments to the State workhouse, whose inmates are largely victims to the intemperate use of intoxicating liquors, for the first six months of prohibition, as compared with the corresponding period under license, show a falling off of more than one-half, and resulting in the large saving to the State, of more than $1,800,000 per annum in the item of board alone. The "growler," or tin kettle trade has almost entirely disappeared from the streets, and children are not now seen frequenting liquor saloons for supplies of liquor, as before prohibition went into effect. Many families that never saw a penny of the weekly earnings of its head, now receive the full benefit of its labor. The legislature now in session has indefinitely postponed, by an almost unanimous vote, a proposition to submit the repeal of the prohibition amendment to the people, and will at this session make the prohibition law more effective.

C. R. BRAYTON,
Chief of State Police.

VERMONT.

The prohibitory law passed by a whig legislature in 1852 is still the law of the State. Towns appoint agents to sell liquors for medicinal and mechanical purposes. A number of laws to aid in enforcement have been passed, and prohibition is the settled policy of the State. An effort was made to submit a constitutional amendment in 1884, but owing to defects upon the cider question it was not favored by the Prohibitionists and failed to pass. The present law is fairly executed and liquor is only sold clandestinely.

NEW HAMPSHIRE.

New Hampsire has a prohibitory law, under which the traffic in alcoholic liquors is illegal, excepting by duly appointed but not licensed agents. Neither the State nor any of its municipalities derive revenue from the sale of liquors. Efforts for a State constabulary force for the better enforcement of the prohibitory law have been unsuccessful.

NEW JERSEY.

This State has a license local option law. The license fee is from $10 to $100 per annum. The local option feature is by petition and special enactment. The laws reported not a success where no license is voted, owing to difficulty in its enforcement.

PENNSYLVANIA.

Mr. Peter Findley, of Bradford, writes to the *Voice* as follows :

"The General Liquor Law of 1875 under which the traffic is now carried on in Pennsylvania, seems to have been intended chiefly to govern the courts in their treatment of violators of the law ; but, as a rule, the courts seem to be afraid to administer liquor laws as they do others, although there are a few noble exceptions. It is difficult to say in a word how the law, such as it is, is enforced. Here in McKean county no violations are furnished by the sworn officers, except when driven to it by the Law and Order Society and similar agencies. During the last four years, the good citizens have spent much time and money in trying to have the law enforced, but have received for their trouble only odium and abuse. These things are not much minded by most of us, and we have set our faces against the great curse of our race, its friends and abettors. The simple truth about the liquor traffic is that it is a lawless traffic, and it cannot be regulated like a legitimate business."

The law is a license law. From Hon. James Black we learn that 272 laws have been passed at different times. The license fee is very light, only $58 per annum in Philadelphia, and in many places much less, and not always collected. Several counties and towns have prohibition by special enactment.

NEW YORK.

LICENSE SYSTEM.

In 1851 the Prohibition law was passed by the Legislature of Maine, and Prohibition at once became a question in the politics of the state of New York. It was at first confined to the legislative districts, but here it gained such a hold that, largely through the influence of that issue, the Legislature of this State, which in 1853 was constituted as follows : Senate : Whigs, 16 ; Democrats, 16 ; Assembly : Whigs, 42 ; Democrats 86, was in the following year composed as follows, Senate : Whigs, 23 ; Democrats, 9 ; Assembly : Whigs, 78 ; Democrats 50. It was this Legislature which passed the Prohibitory Bill which Gov. Seymour vetoed.

The Senate, led by Myron H. Clark, attempted to pass the bill over the Governor's veto, but failed to secure the requisite two-thirds vote, though the bill receiving 14 votes, while only 13 were cast against it. In the Assembly it met a similar fate, and the question was thus returned to the people.

The New York *Herald*, in an aditorial on the veto, on Saturday, April 1st, 1853, said :

"The people of the State will turn aside from all the other political questions of the day. The various national questions now agitating Congress, such as the Kansas-Nebraska Bill, may float about during the approaching agitation ; but the principal issue, and the great contest will spring out of the bill just vetoed by Governor Seymour ; and there can be no doubt that the organization of the old parties, and the various factions of them, will be smashed, and there will be, to a greater or less extent, a new division of parties on this issue.

"Hitherto, the history of the contest upon the temperance question has been a story of dodging on one side and skulking on the other, by the politicians of the old parties. They have temporized and traded between the radical men on both sides, and whether the temperance men trusted to the Whigs or Democrats the word of promise was kept to the ear but broken to the hope.

"A common dodge, and it has been tried in other States as well as New York, has been to make 'a good strong law,' and thus intrust its execution to officials who depend upon rum for their posts."

Mr. Seymour was renominated by the Democrats on his anti-Prohibitory sentiments, and the veto was circulated as a campaign document, it being reprinted in full in the New York *Herald* of October 21. In that veto, Mr. Seymour not only gave his constitutional objections to the bill, but he added his opinion against Prohibition itself.

Mr. Bronson was the candidate of the hard-shell Democrats, and in a letter during the campaign declared his opposition to Prohibition, and favored the license system.

Mr. Ullman was nominated by the Know-Nothings, whose platform was silent on the question, but he was opposed to Prohibitory legislation.

Myron H. Clark was nominated by the Whigs, and subsequently at Auburn, on September 26, by a State Temperance Convention, and by the Free Democrats, and still later, by the first Republican Convention held in the State, at Angelica, on October 14. The Free Democrats in their platform declared in favor of Prohibitory legislation. The State Temperance Convention passed strong resolutions on this question, from which the following extracts are made:

"We advocate, and will labor for the enactment of a law prohibiting the traffic in intoxicating beverages.... We regard the enactment of such a law as the greatest and most vital issue in State politics, and we cannot subordinate this question to any other, nor defer its settlement to any more convenient season.... We ask a Legislature that will enact such a law, a Governor who will approve, and magistrates and other officers who will enforce it."

Myron H. Clark was nominated for Governor by acclamation, and Henry J. Raymond, editor of the New York *Times*, was nominated for Lieutenant-Governor on that platform, and both having accepted the nomination, were subsequently nominated by the Angelica Republican convention.

The vote in the State was as follows: Clark, 156,804, Seymour, 156,495; Ullman, 122,282; Bronson, 35,850; Clark's plurality, 309. Thus, the State was carried for Prohibition when the Governor received only 17 more than one-third of the total votes cast. The same issues prevailed in the election of the Legislature, which was composed as follows: Senate: Whigs, 22; Democrats, 10. Assembly: Whigs, 82; Democrats, 41; Main Law Independents, 3.

The bill vetoed by Governor Seymor was repassed April 9th, 1855, and was made to take effect July 4th of that year.

The court held that the act violated the Constitution, which provides that no person shall be deprived of his property without due process of law. As the act applied to liquors owned or possessed at the time it took effect, it virtually deprived the owners of their property. The section which provided for the trial of accused persons before a Court of Special Sessions was also held invalid, as it deprived them of the right of the trial by jury.

Under this decision, all that was requisite to bring the law under the Constitution was to grant trial by jury, and make it apply only to liquors made or purchased after it took effect; but, instead of doing this, the Legislature elected in the following November passed a license law.

That Legislature was constituted as follows; Senate: Republicans, 16; Americans, 11; Democrats, 4; Temperance, 1. Assembly: Republicans, 81; Americans, 8; Democrats, 31; Americans and Democrats, 8. Thus, we find that, whereas the State two years before had been carried for prohibition, the Republican party having elected its candidate for Governor, John A. King, by a plurality of 65,424, and having a majority in the Senate, with the one Temperance Senator, of two votes, and in the Assembly a majority of 37 votes, we find that, instead of maintaining what had been gained by making prohibition a leading question, that Republican Legislature, the first in this State, restored the licence policy to the State, and thus adopted license as the Republican plan of dealing with the liquor traffic. From 1854 until the organization of the prohibition party in 1869, no reference was made in any State platform in this State to the question of prohibition. Since that time, that party, in its annual conventions, has virtually adopted the platform on which Mr. Clark was elected, "a legislature to enact, a governor to sign, and officers to enforce prohibitory legislation." Three years later, in 1872, the sixteenth resolution of the Republican national platform was declared by its author to have been adopted with the understanding that its object was to condemn prohibitory and Sunday legislation. This resolution was endorsed by the Republican convention of this State. In 1876, four years after the Republicans in their national platform had committed their party to oppose prohibition, the Democratic National Convention adopted a resolution opposing all sumptuary laws, and that position has been reaffirmed in all subsequent National Conventions. The party, in its several State Conventions in this State has endorsed this action.

In no State convention of any party, in this State, except the Prohibition, has there been, since 1854, any resolution adopted condemning the license policy.

In the Richfield Springs Republican State Convention of 1883, the following resolution was adopted:

"We believe in the wisdom of the people in deciding all questions pertaining to the public welfare, and would accede to the desire of a large body of our citizens to submit to the voters of the State, Constitutional Amendment in regard to the manufacture and sale of intoxicating liquors."

This resolution in no way defined the policy of the party on the question, further than to declare a willingness to allow the people an opportunity to decide by a vote on "a Constitutional Amendment in regard to the manufacture and sale of intoxicating drinks," what the subsequent legislative policy of the State should be, no matter what party should be intrusted with this legislation.

From a letter dated Little Valley, N. Y., October 2, 1884,

and signed Charles Z. Lincoln, the following extracts are made:

"I had the honor to represent the Second District of Cattaraugus county in the Republican State Convention of 1883, held at Richfield Springs. One object I had in attending that Convention was to see what could be done toward committing the party, in some degree at least, to the cause of Prohibition; not that I expected the party could be unqualifiedly committed to prohibition as a principle of immediate party action, as that was too much to hope at the outset. * * * * At the election the preceding year the Prohibitionists polled about 26,000 votes. This showed such a growth of the prohibition sentiment throughout the State as to demand some attention. * * * * After conversing with delegates from different parts of the State, representing various shades of opinion on this question, I prepared and introduced a resolution favoring the submission to the people of a Prohibitory Constitutional Amendment. The substance of it was embodied in a plank of the platform, and the party became thereby pledged to give the people an opportunity, at the polls, to express their opinion on the subject of Constitutional Prohibition.

Under this pledge the Republicans elected 70 members of the Assembly, and the Democrats 53. Mr. Olin, of Broome, was elected by the joint votes of the Republicans and Prohibitionists, and became the champion of the Constitutional Amendment, which was defeated by the following vote: 61 ayes, 63 nays, 9 Democrats voting for the Amendment and 17 Republicans against it; among the latter being Mr. Roosevelt, the recognized leader of the Republican majority. Thus, with 9 Democrats voting against this party platform for submission, the Republicans, with 17 majority in the Assembly, failed to redeem their party pledge to allow the people to decide what the future policy of the State should be on this question. Thus closes the last chapter of the history of prohibition in this State, which shows the Democratic party unalterably opposed to prohibition, the Republican party responsible for the present license policy of the State, and guilty of breaking a party pledge in order to deny the people the privilege of changing that policy and restoring prohibition, which was made the State policy by being made a party issue in 1854, so that the prohibition party was left the only party in the State which favors prohibition either as a party or State policy.

In a letter dated December 27th, 1884, written by ex-Governor Myron H. Clark, to the writer of this article, he says:

"Prohibition was one of the leading questions which led to my election as Governor."

That election was, as already stated, secured by 156,804 votes in a total of 469,432 votes, which would require about 400,000 votes in this State at the present time to have prohibition as strong, relatively, as it was when Mr. Clark was elected Governor on that distinctive issue, and we leave it for the people to decide how soon, under the policy of non-partisan action, which has restored license and has maintained it, prohibition can be secured in this State?

MARYLAND.

LICENSE GRANTED WITHOUT REGARD TO QUALIFICATIONS OR CHARACTER ON PAYMENT OF TAX REQUIRED BY LAW.

HON. WM. DANIEL.

The act of 1780, chapter 24, empowered the County Courts in session, to grant licenses to keep ordinaries to such persons as they shall think fit, being persons of good repute, to keep ordinaries in such, and as many places, within their respective counties, for the ease and convenience of the inhabitants, travelers and strangers, as to them may seem proper.

2. Power was given the courts to suspend them if disorderly.

3. They were required with two sufficient sureties, "to keep good rules and order, and not suffer loose, idle or dissolute persons, to tipple, game, or commit any disorder, or other irregularity in said ordinary."

They were prohibited from selling to apprentices or slaves.

And, by the 11th section, all persons were prohibited from selling, except merchants, but what they sold could not be drank in the stores.

Nor could the keeper of the ordinary, at a horse race, sell after sunset.

Now it is manifest from the legislation, that the license system was established solely for the purpose of regulating the sale of liquors, and for confining the right to sell to such number of persons, who kept inns, as would, in the judgment of the Court, be sufficient for the accommodation of the public.

1. The Courts were to grant the licenses.
2. The persons, to whom this privilege was granted, were to be persons of "good repute.
3. They were required to enter into recognizance, "to keep good rules and order, and not suffer loose, idle or disorderly persons to tipple, game, or commit disorder."

In the year 1825 the legislature removed the restriction imposed by the original laws, which only granted licenses to persons of good repute, and in such numbers as were required for the public, and under the other restrictions named.

By the act of 1826, the power of the judges to grant licenses was taken uway, and the county clerks were directed to grant licenses to ordinary keepers, upon their entering into recognizance before justice of the peace that they would comply with the provisions of the several laws of this State, relative to ordinary keepers.

Now even this restriction as much diminished as it was, as compared with the old law, was still some restriction, as it requires them to keep orderly houses.

It removes, however, all supervision as to the character of the men to whom license was given ; and as to the numbers to whom given.

Then came the act of 1827, chapter 117, which required the clerks to grant licenses to sell liquors in such quantities, less than a pint to all keepers of ordinaries, grog-shop, victualing and oyster houses, who pay the licenses, the only exception being, that the grand jury should signify to the court, their opinion that a license ought not to be granted to any individuals, named in the list of applicants therefor, required to be laid before them ; the clerk could not grant the same without the special direction of the court.

Next came the act of 1858, chapter 414, which was intended as a revenue measure alone, the only requirements for the granting of licenses being that in the case of ordinaries (such as hotels, &c.) and liquor saloons, beer shops, &c., where spirituous or fermented liquors are sold in quantities less than a pint, the applicant for license should be recommended by *"two respectable freeholders of his immediate vicinity."* Truly by no means a difficult condition to comply with. And even this last, nugatory restriction, if restriction indeed it could be called, so far as it relates to grog-shops, oyster houses, &c., was swept away by the act of 1862, chapter 119.

Thus was fully completed by these last two acts, and especially by the act of 1858, the entire change in the prior policy of the State, and which was inaugurated by the before mentioned act of 1827.

And it is these last two acts that are now the law of the State as codified in our present code. Licenses by our present laws are classed under three heads: 1st, those called "retailers' licenses," and where the sales are in quantities greater than a pint, the amount to be paid for, the same being according to the quantity of the stock kept on hand at the principal season of sale; 2nd, license to ordinaries, (hotels, &c.), the amount being regulated by the rental; and thirdly, those to beer shops, liquor saloons, victualing houses, &c., the amount being $50 in every case, and in both of the latter cases the sales being allowed in quantities less than a pint.

The old laws looked alone to the good of the community, and were restraining laws; designed to limit the right to sell liquors to a few selected men of good character, who kept taverns, and imposing upon them several wholesome and salutary restrictions to that end.

These more recent laws looked only to the revenue to the treasury.

1. License to sell liquors must be granted to any one who applies, regardless of character.
2. No discretion is given to the officers issuing them.
3. No restriction as to tippling; he may sell to any man, no matter how drunk he may be.
4. Though in violation of law, they do sell to minors every day.
5. Many of them permit gambling in their houses, in violation of law.

The only general laws, that are at all exceptional to these very loose license laws, (believed to be as bad or worse than those of any other State), is the law against selling liquor to minors, (and which is rarely enforced) ; that against selling on election days, and that against selling on the Sabbath day, the last named of which, the liquor fraternity have made strenuous efforts, within the last eight or ten years past, to get repealed.

In addition to this general legislation, local option laws have been passed authorizing many counties and localities to decide by ballot whether liquors should be sold. These laws are so similar in their nature that it is unnecessary to specify them in detail. They define the method and time of voting, make it illegal to sell in opposition to the vote, prescribe penalties, usually a fine not less than $50 nor more than $300, or imprisonment for thirty days. They also forbid sale by druggists except upon physician's prescription, and prescribe penalty for any person actually sick and in need of liquor as a medicine ; also penalty for any person who shall procure such prescription by deceit. The penalty in the last two cases is fine of from $50 to $200, for the first offense and not less than $200 nor more than $500 for each subsequent offense. One half the fine goes to the informer and one half to the county school fund.

The net result of the agitation for Prohibition in this State, by the method of local option, more especially, has been the adoption of prohibition in the whole of Anne Arundel, Calvert, Caroline, Cecil, Hartford, Howard, Kent and Montgomery counties; and in twelve of the fourteen election districts in Dorchester county ; in nine out of about twenty districts in Frederick county ; in five out of eleven districts in Garrett county; in six out of the seven districts in Queen Anne's county; in eight out of the nine districts in Sommerset county ; in four out of the five districts in Talbot county; in about seven localities in Baltimore county, and one in Allegany county.

The political complexion of the above counties is as follows: Anne Arundel, Cecil, Dorchester, Garrett, Harford, Howard, Kent, Montgomery, Queen Anne and Talbot are Democratic, a number of them being the very strongholds of

Democracy in this State. Frederick is Republican; while Caroline and Sommerset are doubtful.

In the counties where Prohibition has been wholly defeated, as hereinbefore stated, Allegany, Charles and St. Marys are Republican; Carroll, Wicomico and Worcester, are Democratic, and Prince Georges is doubtful.

All the legislatures of Maryland, from 1868 to the present have been Democratic in both Houses, and for nearly the whole time about three-fourths Democratic on joint ballot.

From 1872 to 1874 Wm. Pinckney Whyte, (who was elected to the U. S. Senate in 1874) was governor, from 1874 to 1875, Jas. Black Groome, who filled the unexpired term of Whyte, was Governor. From 1875-79, Jno. Lee Carroll, from 1879-83, Wm. T. Hamilton, and in 1883, Robt. M. McLane, who is still Governor. All the above named are democrats, as was also Oden Bowie, who was Governor from 1867-71.

The prohibitory laws in these counties, have been generally well enforced, the counties of Prince Georges and and Calvert being the exceptions. The lack of enforcement in the former, was one of the principal reasons of its recent repeal.

WISCONSIN.

TOWN BOARDS, VILLAGE BOARDS AND COMMON COUNCILS HAVE AUTHORITY TO GRANT LICENSES AT THEIR DISCRETION.

This article is not intended to be exhaustive. Nothing more will be attempted than to give some account of the more important and interesting action in this direction.

The Territory of Wisconsin was organized in 1836. In the legislation of the year 1836 authority was given to license "groceries, victualing houses and ordinaries with permission to sell spirituous liquors and wine." The license fee was $108. The penalty for violating the law was a fine not less than $10 and not to exceed $50.

In 1839 a volume of territorial laws was published in which the laws on this subject were given as they existed at that date.

Licenses were authorized to be granted "to keepers of inns and taverns to sell strong and spirituous liquors and wine to be drunk in or out of their houses respectively." The license fee had been greatly reduced since 1836. It was now not less than $5, and not over $25. Grocery licenses for liquors to be drunk on the premises, $100.

No licenses to be granted to inn holders or tavern keepers unless the applicant was of GOOD MORAL CHARACTER, that he had sufficient ability to keep a tavern, and had the necessary accommodations to entertain travelers, and that a tavern is necessary for the accommodation of travelers where the applicant proposed to keep the same, all of which had to be especially stated in the licenses.

A bond was required of every tavern keeper, inn holder or grocer, in such sum as the commissioner may require, conditioned that the applicant will not suffer his house or grocery to become disorderly or allow gaming with cards, dice or other implements used in gaming in his tavern or grocery or any out house or yard appertaining thereto. The accomodations that tavern keepers were to have, are set forth in the law: Two beds with sufficient covering, sufficient stabling, hay, feed, grain etc., and pasturage in summer.

Penalty for selling without license, $25 fine. They were not allowed to sell to minors under 18 years of age without consent of parents or guardians.

Penalty $20 fine, with liability to have license revoked, and if revoked it could not be renewed for three years.

Licenses for selling in larger quantities than one quart were from $20 to $75. Penalty for selling without licenses, from $10 to $75.

In 1840 a law was passed forbidding the sale of liquors to Indians—penalty $50. If the sale was made by a licensed person his license was forfeited and could not be renewed for the space of one year.

No particular further changes seem to have been made in the license laws while Wisconsin remained a territory.

The State was admitted into the Union in 1848. At the session of the Legislature that met in January, 1849, most extraordinary action was had.

A law was passed at this session known at that time as the WISCONSIN BOND LAW. In its main features it was almost exactly like what have since been denominated *civil damage laws*. The question suggests itself whether this Wisconsin "bond law" was not really the first civil damage law passed in the United States.

The first section of this law provided that "in addition to all other requirements a penal bond of $1,000 with three or more sufficient sureties" should be given "conditioned to pay all damages to support all paupers, widows and orphans, pay the expenses of all civil and criminal prosecutions made, growing out of or justly attributable to such traffic, that community or individuals may sustain by reason of such traffic."

Married women were authorized to institute and maintain in their own names suits on any such bond for all damages sustained by themselves or their children.

"No suit for liquor bills shall be entertained by any court in the State."

"When in any suit or promissory note, it was made to appear that it was given in whole or in part for liquor bills the court must dismiss suit at once at cost of plaintiff."

It was only necessary to prove on trial, to sustain the action, that the principal in the bond sold or gave liquor to the person intoxicated or in liquor on that day previous to the commission of the offense.

When a person became a pauper by reason of intemperance, a suit could be instituted by the proper authorities on the bond of the person who had been in the habit of selling or giving liquor to the person who had become a public charge.

A person against whom judgment was obtained could sue all others engaged in the traffic in the place, who had been in the habit of selling to the person, to compel contribution towards paying the judgment.

Penalty for selling without first giving the required bond was not less than $50 nor more than $500, and imprisonment not less than 10 days nor more than six months, and also liability to the public and to individuals the same as though the bond had been given.

The passage of this law was hailed all over the land, by the friends of temperance as the most advanced step ever taken in legislation touching the liquor traffic.

The legislature was largely democratic, with about a dozen

each of whigs and free soilers. Among these free soilers was Hon. J. F. Willard, the father of Miss Frances Willard, as a member from Rock county.

But the passage of this law was by no means all that was done by this legislature touching the liquor traffic.

A LARGE NUMBER OF PETITIONS were presented asking for the repeal of all laws providing for the sale of intoxicating liquors.

A bill was introduced to repeal all such laws. This bill and all petitions upon the matter were referred to a select committee of which Samuel D. Hastings, a member of the essembly from Walworth county was the acting chairman.

The committee consisted of two democrats, two free soilers and one whig.

Mr. Hastings, a free soiler, presented the report on behalf of the committee, and as showing the views held at that time on the question of license the report is given in full. It was signed by all the members of the committee:

"The committee to whom were referred No. 68 A." A bill repealing all laws providing for licensing the sale of spiritous liquors together with sundry petitions praying for action on the subject would respectfully REPORT.

That in entering upon the consideration of the various matters referred to them, they have felt deeply sensible of their importance and of the propriety of giving them a candid examination.

The whole question of licensing the sale of spiritous liquors is one that has been the occasion of much discussion in the several states of the Union, and one upon which there is a wide diversity of opinon among the wise and good of the land.

Your committee have felt diffident of their ability to throw much additional light on a subject that has been so ably and so fully discussed by those who have given it much thought and patient investigation ; still endeavoring to profit by the facts and arguments of others, and guided by the lamp of experience, they would present to the assembly some of the considerations which have led them to the conclusions they have reached.

The license laws of our State authorize the sale of spirituous liquors as a common beverage, with certain conditions therein specified.

Your committee would call attention to the following facts:

FIRST. It is established by uncontrovertible testimony that the intoxicating principle of these liquors is *poison*, and that their habitual use as a beverage is not conducive to the well being of mankind.

SECOND. It is an equally well established fact that their general use operates injuriously upon the best interests of a community in various ways, among which may be mentioned the following, viz : (*a*) It destroys the prosperity, the health, the happiness, and the lives of thousands of those who use them. It is estimated that not less than thirty thousand drunkards die annually in the United States. (*b*) As an inevitable result it operates injuriously upon the families and connections of its more immediate victims. It destroys their prosperity and happiness, and in many cases reduces them to pauperism. (*c*) It has been proved by reference to official documents that the use of spirituous liquors as a beverage is the cause of at least three-fourths of the pauperism of the country. (*d*) It is estimated that at the present time there are not less than two hundred thousand individuals in the various alms-houses of the United States, who have been brought there entirely through the influence of the use of such liquors by the individuals themselves or by those upon whom they were dependent. (*e*) Their use is a fruitful source of crime. The larger amount of the more heinous crimes committed in the country are committed under the exciting influence of these drinks. There are at the present time, probably not less than fifty thousand criminals in confinements as a penalty for crimes committed under the influence of intoxication produced by the use of spirituous liquors. (*f*) It can be shown by reference to data that cannot be controverted that the cost to the United States in consequence of the use of these liquors, is not less than one hundred million dollars annually.

This amount is made up in part by the following items, viz:

1. The cost of the liquor consumed, paid by those who are in no sense benefitted by it. 2. The loss of time which its use occasions. 3. The diminished productions of land, labor and capital. 4. The loss of health and reason and all the expenditures occasioned thereby. 5. The cost of the support of paupers and of the prosecution, trial and support

of criminals occasioned by it. 6. The property lost in consequence of its use, by casualties on the land and on the waters. 7. The shortening of human life and the consequent loss of human labor.

We have laws upon our statute books which license men to traffic in an article, the use of which produces all the evil results we have noticed.

The business is thus made legal and respectable. The man who is engaged in it in one sense may be said to stand on a higher ground than the man who is engaged in any other business, for he acts under an express license granted by the authority of the State.

Your committee are unanimous in the opinion, that all laws on our statute book, which license the sale of spirituous liquors and thus give the high sanction of the State to this traffic ought to be immediately repealed for the following, among other reasons:

FIRST. Because all such laws are ANTI-DEMOCRATIC. They give special privileges to a few, that are not enjoyed by the many. One man is authorized to pursue a business, which perhaps, his next neighbor is not allowed to pursue.

If the business is right and proper in itself, all should be allowed to pursue it without restraint. If it is wrong no one should be legally authorized.

SECOND. Because it is going beyond the legitimate scope of legislative authority to pass such laws. It is authorizing a man, by law, to pursue a business that is injurious to the best interest of the community,

The facts already presented prove conclusively, that the use of spiritous liquors, while they do no good to any human being are productive of evils of the greatest magnitude.

While license laws are in force all these evil results follow under the sanction of law.

The law should give its sanction only to that which is right in itself, and just and equal in its result. It should authorize and sanction the right and condemn the wrong. In all its requirements and sanctions it should be in strict accordance with natural justice, and should consult the best good of all its subjects. We are told by high authority that "all laws derive their force from the law of justice, and those who do not are accounted no laws." — *Fortescue, Jac, Law Dict.*

"The law of nature is that which God, at man's creation, infused into him, for his preservation and direction, and this is an eternal law and may not be changed"—*2 Shap. Abr. 356 Jac. Law Dict.* "Jurisprudence is the science of what is just and right."—*Justinian.*

These extracts could be multiplied to almost any extent but enough we think have been adduced for the purpose of the present argument. It is not competent for legislative authority to authorize wrong—to authorize a man to injure his neighbor or to injure the community in whose midst he may reside, or to authorize him to pursue a business which would produce these results. The traffic in spirituous liquors does produce these results. To sanction and protect it by law is wrong. It is transcending the rightful authority of the law making power. It is a violation of those great principles which lie at the foundation of all just legislation, and its influence upon the well-being of the community is injurious in the highest degree. So long as the traffic is shielded by the fostering and protecting arm of the law, so long will the business be regarded as an honest and respectable calling — and so long will the ten thousand times ten thousand evils which follow in its train continue to curse the land.

Withdraw from the business the sanction of the State and fix upon it the frown of a correct and indignant public opinion and if it does not sink away into obscurity the people will then be prepared to call for such remedies as the nature of the case may demand.

It may be objected to the view taken by your committee that the license laws are prohibitory in their character and design. THE ORIGINAL DESIGN, without doubt, of the passage of license laws was to create a revenue to the government. They had their origin in England at a time when expedients of all kinds were resorted to for this purpose. The first license law passed in this country, that your committee have any record of, was passed in Massachusetts, in 1646. This, doubtless, had the double object in view of raising a revenue and regulating the business. License laws have been in existence from that period to the present, and almost if not quite every State in the Union has passed such laws, and still, in the face of them all, the use of intoxicating drinks has increased, and the evils of intemperance have spread and enlarged until their magnitude and extent have become almost beyond endurance. Whatever, then, may have been the design of the license laws, their operation has not been prohibitory. Under their influence intemperance has increased and our country has been cursed with a curse of the most awful character.

A few moments examination, we doubt not, will satisfy anyone that these laws could not be prohibitory in their operation, for any good practical purpose. The law merely prescribes who shall sell and how the seller shall procure his authority to carry on the traffic. *It places no limit to the quantity to be sold. The supply is always equal to the demand.* In a community where spirituous liquors are sold by anyone who has the means and desires to procure them can do so just as effectually as though they were sold in every house. Were it not for the sanction of the law, public sentiment might long since have rendered the business disreputable and driven from it all who regard their standing among their fellow men. While the law protects it, it will be impossible to fix upon it that odium which should justly attach to it. WHAT IS THE LAW? By what authority does the liquor seller pursue his business?

The law is the expression of the will of the whole people placed upon the statute book, by their chosen representatives. The man who pursues this business does it by the authority of the whole people. What right have they to complain of him for the course he is pursuing? What right have they to charge upon him the entire responsibility of the evil results which flow from the sale of his poisonous liquors? He is doing no more than the people in their collected wisdom have authorized him to do, and in doing which he is protected by the strong arm of the law. The responsibility rests upon the people who have made and who now sustain the law.

The effect then of our license laws not *prohibitory:* They furnish a supply equal to the demand, and place it within the reach of all, and then stand as a guardian angel to shield the traffic from the effects of that virtuous indignation of an outraged community which might otherwise compel the hydra-headed monster to hide itself in the caves and dens of the earth. These laws are anomalies in legislation. They are based upon wrong principles. To license wrong is not the way to prohibit and restrain it. To license is to declare that if practiced legally it is right, and hence it is almost impossible to produce upon the minds of a large portion of the community the conviction that it is wrong.

In view of the foregoing considerations, your committee are unanimous in reporting back to the assembly "No. 68." A bill repealing all laws providing for the licensing of the sale of spirituous liquors, without amendment, and recommending its passage."

The bill passed the assembly by a vote of 41 in its favor to 8 against—five to one.

When sent to the senate it was referred to the "committee on expiration and re-enactment of laws," who reported it back with an amendment, with the recommendation that when amended it be passed.

The amendment was the addition of the following proviso: "Provided that nothing herein contained, shall be so construed, as in any manner to interfere with any of the provisions of 'an act relating to the sale of spirituous liquors,' passed at the present session of the legislature.

The act referred to was the "Bond law" already spoken of. The bill passed the senate by a vote of 8 to 5, but was reconsidered before it went to the governor for his signature, and was then defeated by a vote of 9 to 7, and here the matter rested.

In 1850 an effort was made to REPEAL the BOND LAW which only resulted in some amendments which added to its efficiency.

The amendment passed the senate by a vote of 11 to 8, and the assembly by a vote of 36 to 24.

In 1851 the "Bond law" was repealed and a license law put in its place.

Under the provisions of this law the supervisors of towns, aldermen of cities and trustees of villages, were authorized to grant license "to grocers, saloon keepers or places of any name whatever," to retail to as many as they see proper. License fee for retailers $100, for wholesalers $50. A bond of $500 was required, conditioned that the applicant would keep an orderly and well regulated house, permit no gambling, and obey all legal requirements of the authorities, granting the license. Penalty for violating the law, a fine of $100 and costs or 60 days imprisonment.

It was made the duty of supervisors, aldermen, trustees of villages, justices of the peace, marshals, deputy marshals, and constables to make complaint when they knew or where creditably informed that the law had been violated, and if they neglected to do so they were liable to a fine of $25.

The officers granting licenses were authorized to forbid the sale of liquor to excessive drinkers, spendthrifts, or persons liable to become public charges. Licenses could be revoked if the law were not obeyed.

The law repealing the "Bond law" and enacting the license law passed the assembly by a vote of 30 to 24 and the senate by a vote of 9 to 8.

In 1852 no changes were made in the license law, other than to reduce the fee for retailing to not less than $10 nor more than $100; for wholesaling not less than $10 nor more than $40. Penalty not less than $10 nor more than $40.

In 1853, a large number of petitions were presented to the legislature asking for a prohibitory law. A bill for a prohibitory law was introduced, and for a while seemed likely to pass, but finally the matter was compromised by submitting the question to a POPULAR VOTE. A law was passed providing that "At the general election to be held on the Tuesday succeeding the first Monday in November, A. D. 1853, at the usual place of holding elections in the state for the election of all officers required by law, then to be elected, it shall be lawful for the qualified electors of this state to vote for or against a prohibitory liquor law, such vote shall be by ballot * * * and shall contain the words 'prohibitory liquor law, No,' or 'prohibitory liquor law, Yes,' and the ballots so cast shall be canvassed and returned in the same manner as the votes cast for state officers are required to be canvassed and returned.' The secretary of state was required to publish the result and communicate the same to the next legislature.

This law passed the assembly by a vote of 40 to 12, and the senate by a vote of 15 to 7—a more than two-thirds vote in both houses.

In 1854 the governor in his message to the legislature said: "At the June session of the last legislature an act submitting to the electors of the State the question of a prohibitory liquor law, was passed.

"The Secretary of State in pursuance of a requirement of that law, reports the whole vote cast at the late election upon that question to be 51,632, and that 27,519 votes were for, and 24,109 against the law.

"The expression of public opinion comtemplated by the act referred to, submitting the question to the popular vote, is now before you, and it remains for you in your wisdom to determine what will best satisfy the sentiments of the whole people in relation to the subject, subserve there true interests and be best adapted to the actual condition of things in the State at large."

This portion of the message was referred to a special committee consisting of James H. Knowlton. John W. Davis, Harlow S. Orton and C. C. Remington.

This committee reported A STRINGENT PROHIBITORY LAW and recommended its passage.

The bill passed the assembly by a vote of 43 to 28. It went to the senate, where it was amended, providing that it should be submitted to a popular vote before going into effect, and as thus amended passed by a vote of 16 to 6. The assembley refused to accept this amendment, claiming that the people had just voted upon the question and given a decided expression of their views in favor of such a law. Committees of conference were appointed but neither house would yield, and thus the law failed.

In 1855 a bill for a prohibitory law was again introduced and passed the assembly by a vote of 42 to 23, and the senate by a vote of 13 to 7, nearly a two-thirds vote.

Thus it will be seen that the Wisconsin legislature has twice been at a point where it passed a prohibitory law by large majorities in both houses.

Up to 1854 the State had always been democratic. In 1855 the assembly was republican while the senate and the executive still remained democratic.

The prohibitory law passed this year was VETOED BY GOV. WM. A. BARSTOW.

The vote in the assembly upon passing the bill over the veto was 39 to 30, thus failing to secure its passage.

There does not appear to have been any special legislation

on the liquor question until 1859, when a law was passed forbidding the sale of liquor on Sunday at the annual town meetings, and at the fall elections.

In 1861 a law was passed forbidding the sale of liquors within two miles of a camp-meeting or religious assembly without the consent of those having charge of the meeting, unless by persons previously licensed.

In 1862 slight changes were made in the price charged for licenses and in the penalty for violation of the law.

No further special legislature on the subject seems to have been held until 1866, when a law was passed forbidding the sale of liquor to minors, and forbidding their playing billiards in saloons.

In 1867 a law was passed forbidding the sale of liquor within one mile of the State Hospital for the Insane.

In 1872 the civil damage law generally known as THE "GRAHAM LAW" was passed.

This law was substantially the "Bond law" of 1849 with some of its best features omitted.

In 1873 a strong effort was made to repeal this law, but it failed. The effort to repeal was repeated in 1874, and succeeded, when a license law was again put on the statute books.

The law of 1874 is essentially the law now in force, and has many excellent provisions for a license law.

Town boards, village boards and common councils have authority to grant as many licenses to retail or wholesale liquors as "they may deem proper."

It is at the discretion of these boards to grant or to refuse to grant licenses, and hence it will be seen that the law is really a "local option law," as the voters can prevent the licensing of the traffic by electing a board that will refuse to grant licenses.

Every applicant has to give a bond of $500, with satisfactory sureties, "conditioned that the applicant, during the continuance of his license, will keep and maintain an orderly and well-regulated house, that he will permit no gambling with cards, dice, or any device or implement for that purpose, within his premises, or any outhouse, yard or shed appertaining thereto; that he will not sell or give away any intoxicating liquor to any minor, unless upon the written order of the parent or guardian of such minor, or to persons intoxicated or bordering upon intoxication, or to habitual drunkards, and that he will pay all damages that may be recovered by any person pursuant to section 1560, and that he will observe and obey all orders of such supervisors, trustees or aldermen, or any of them, made pursuant to law."

The law MAKES IT THE DUTY of "every supervisor, trustee, alderman, justice of the peace, police officer, marshall, deputy marshall and constable, * * who shall know or be credibly informed that any offense has been committed against the provisions of this chapter to make complaint against the person so offending, * * to a proper justice of the peace, and for every neglect or refusal to do so, every such officer shall forfeit $25."

The law provides that "When any person shall, by excessive drinking of intoxicating liquors, misspend, waste or lessen his estate so as to expose himself or family to want, or the town, city or village to which he belongs to liability for the support of himself or family, or so as thereby to injure his health, endanger the loss thereof, or to endanger the personal safety and comfort of his family, or any member thereof, the wife of such person, such supervisor, alderman, trustee, or any member thereof, shall, in writing signed by her, him or them, forbid all persons licensed by this chapter, to sell or give away to him any ardent, spirituous, or intoxicating liquors or drinks, for the space of one year."

This authority is extended so that these officers can forbid the sale in any other town, city, or village to which the spendthrift may resort for the same. This prohibition to sell can be renewed from year to year.

The law provides (Section 1560.) that any person or persons who shall be injured in person or property or means of support by or in consequence of the intoxication of any minor or habitual drunkard, shall have the right of action severally or jointly, in his, her or their names, against any person or persons who have been notified or requested in writing by the authorities designated in Section 1554, or by the husband, wife, parents, relatives, guardians or persons having the care or custody of such minor or habitual drunkard, not to part with liquor or other intoxicating drinks to them, and who notwithstanding such notice and request, shall knowingly sell or give away intoxicating drinks, thereby causing the intoxication of such minor or drunkard, and shall be liable for all damage resulting therefrom.

Married women have the same right to sue as others.

"All places of whatever description in which intoxicating liquors are sold in violation of law shall be held and are declared public nuisances, and shall, upon conviction of the keeper thereof, be shut up and abated."

THE SALE OF LIQUOR ON SUNDAY, on the day of the annual town meeting and the day of the fall election is forbidden.

"The giving away of intoxicating liquors, or other shift or device to evade the provision of this chapter shall be deemed and held to be an unlawful selling within its provisions.

The sale of liquor to Indians is forbidden.

In 1882, a law was passed providing that in case a person to whom liquor had been forbidden to be sold was found intoxicated, he could be arrested and made to tell where he had procured his liquor, and in the event he refused to do so he was liable to imprisonment. It was also provided that any person who procured, in any way, liquor, for a person to whom it had been forbidden to be sold, should be liable to punishment.

In 1878 petitions were first presented to the Legislature asking for the submission to the people of an AMENDMENT TO THE CONSTITUTION of the State, prohibiting the manufacture and sale of intoxicating beverages.

The matter was before the Senate only.

A joint resolution was introduced, providing for such submission. Ths result of the first vote upon the question was thirteen in its favor, seven against, and thirteen not voting.

The final vote was thirteen in favor, fourteen against, and six not voting. About 15,000 names were signed to the petition presented this year.

In 1879 petitions were again presented asking for the submission of a prohibitory amendment.

This year there were about 40,000 names to the petitions; and memorials were presented representing about 100,000 of the citizens of the State. The matter was before both houses.

In the Senate the measure was defeated, the vote being eleven in favor, twenty against and two not voting.

In the Assembly the matter was indefinitely postponed. The vote not given.

In 1880, the matter was again before both houses of the Legislature.

In the Assembly the life was taken out of the joint resolution of submission by putting off the operations of the amendment until 1890, and by excepting from its operation beer, and possibly wine.

It barely passed the Assembly, in this diluted form, and was sent to the Senate where it was defeated by a vote of twelve in its favor, fourteen against, and seven not voting.

The result of the several votes in the assembly were as follows. On a motion to indefinately postpone, the motion was lost — 38 in favor, 47 against and 15 not voting.

It was ordered to a third reading by the following vote : 50 for, 37 against, 13 not voting.

On the question of its final passage, it was defeated by the following vote : 44 in favor, 33 against, and 23 not voting. It requires a majority of all the members elect—51—to pass a resolution submitting an amendment to the constitution.

The last named vote was reconsidered and the resolution adopted by the following vote ; 53 for, 44 against and 3 not voting.

In 1881, the matter was again before the assembly and was lost by the following vote : 40 in favor, 48 against and 12 not voting.

This vote was reconsidered, and the final vote was 39 in favor, 51 against, and 10 not voting.

The question was not before the senate this year.

In 1882 it was again before the assembly.

On the question of ordering to a third reading, the vote was 43 for, 49 against and 8 not voting.

It was reconsidered the next day, and then immediately laid on the table without a count.

It will be noticed that the show for carrying the resolution for submission through the senate was better the first time it was presented in 1878 then it has ever been since.

In the assembly the first recorded vote in favor of the measure was 50 in its favor in 1880, while the last vote in its favor, in 1882, was but 43.

The republican party was largely in the majority in the Legislature when these votes were taken.

What hope of the measure being carried by this party in

view of these facts? The policy of the friends of the measure since has been to labor to make prohibition sentiment among the people, and to organize the sentiment when made, rather than to spend time in asking the Legislature to grant what it is well known they would refuse.

The law was slightly amended by the last Legislature (1887.)

VIRGINIA.

LICENSE SYSTEM.

The laws of Virginia up to 1860 were in the nature of mild license laws. In the code of 1860, page 224, we find a somewhat more rigid law, making it illegal to either sell liquor or rectify or distil ardent spirits without license. Those who manufactured cider, or distilled from fruit or grain raised by themselves, were exempt from the law, provided their distilleries did not run more than four months in the year. The penalty for distilling, brewing or rectifying without license was from $30 to $200, and for selling without license, $60. These sections did not apply to those who sold from products of their own raising, at the place where manufactured, if not sold to be drunk on the premises. Any person selling to a slave without written consent, forfeited to the master of such slave four times the value of the liquor sold, and was liable to a fine of $20. In addition, the violator of the last two provisions was liable to have his license revoked. A person who gave a written permit to a slave to purchase liquor for him, with intent to sell the same, forfeited $20, and must give security for good behavior for one year.

In 1873 the sale from sunset the day before until sunrise the day after any election was made illegal, the violator being deemed guilty of a misdemeanor and liable to fine of not more than $100 and imprisonment not to exceed one year.

At the session of 1883-4, the legislature passed an act providing for three kinds of licenses, viz: wholesale dealers, retail merchants and bar-room keepers. The first could not sell in quantities less than five gallons; the second could sell in quantities less than five gallons, not to be drunk on the premises; the third in quantities less than five gallons, to be drunk on the premises only. Any person desiring to sell in any two or more of these methods must take out license for both. Wholesalers of malt liquors might sell in bottles or jugs in quantities not less than one dozen. The law applied to clubs and corporations as well as to individuals. Violators were subject to fine, not less than $100 nor more than $500, and to imprisonment not exceeding twelve months in the discretion of the court. Persons who felt aggrieved by the issuance of license could contest the application for the same, and after hearing the evidence on both sides, the court could refuse the license, or, if he thought person and place proper and suitable, might grant the same. In the latter case the applicant must give bond in not less than $250 nor more than $500 for faithful compliance with the law. Appeal could be taken to the circuit court by either party. The decision of the circuit court, or of a circuit judge in vacation was final and no farther appeal or writ of error allowed.

Druggists must take out license as retail dealers, and were subject to the same penalties.

In addition to these general laws, special laws for localities, and charters for towns and cities, authorize the voters to decide by ballot whether licenses shall be granted, and it is provided that the State law shall in no way interfere with these local option laws. Under these laws a number of localities prohibit the sale. There is also a law prohibiting the sale on Sunday, or to minors.

The law of 1860 was passed by a democratic legislature and approved by Governor Letcher, democrat. That of 1873 was also passed by the democrats, who assumed at that time the name "true republicans," and was approved by Governor Gilbert C. Walker. The act of 1883—4 was passed by a legislature largely democratic, and was approved by Governor Cameron, republican, elected upon a re-adjuster platform.

WEST VIRGINIA.

LICENSE SYSTEM AND RESTRICTIONS WHICH ARE NOT ENFORCED.

Frank Burt.

The laws regulating the sale of spirituous and malt liquors when this State was formed are found in the Code of Virginia, 1860.

No free negro could be granted license to sell ardent spirits. A license to a white man to keep tavern, gave also the right to retail liquors. A merchant could get license to retail liquors by paying an additional fee (he could not be a merchant without procuring a license), provided the county court would certify that he was a person of good character. Distiller's license also gave privilege to retail liquors on the premises; but the party buying must not drink it there. The only restriction imposed on one having license to sell liquors, was that he should not sell to slaves.

In the year 1863, the Legislature of this State enacted, that if boards of supervisors of any county could give to person applying for license to sell liquors, a certificate of good moral character and demeanor, and not of intemperate habits, they might issue license after taking bond in the penalty of not less than $500 nor more than $1000; conditioned, that person to be licensed would not permit any one to drink to intoxication on the premises, and not to sell to any person intoxicated or one known to have the habit of intoxication, nor to any person under 21 years of age, or on Sunday.

In 1865: enacted that places where liquor is sold must close on the day of an election and the night succeeding, if within two miles.

In 1866: enacted that *all* places where liquor is sold must be closed on the day preceeding, as well as on the day of an election, and made it unlawful to sell it or to permit it to be drank at such places on election days. Also unlawful for a person to be drunk at a place of holding an election.

In 1873 a law was enacted very similar to the Adair civil damage law of Ohio, or the Austin law of Illinois, both of which are given elsewhere, but with the additional provisions that any person elected to any office shall forfeit same if it be proven that on the day of his election he offered to sell or give, or did so sell or give or distribute any intoxicating drink to any voter; and if *any* person did so offer or sell or distribute to any voter on election day, he forfeits $20 to $100. Engineers and railroad conductors intoxicated on duty, guilty of misdemeanor and liable to fine not exceeding $500.

In 1877 a still more stringent law was enacted, which is still in force. Bond $3500, conditioned that any restriction violated by either selling or giving, shall render liable to prosecution. Unlawful to permit any person to drink to intoxication on the premises, to sell or give to any person intoxicated, or to one in the habit of becoming so, or one of unsound mind, or under 21 years of age, or to sell or give to any one on Sunday. Any husband, wife, child, parent, or guardian may serve notice (written) on any person engaged in the sale of intoxicating liquors, not to sell to the husband, wife, child, parent or ward, and thereafter the seller is liable for any damage to person, property or in means of support, and for exemplary damages, by reason of the intoxication of the person to whom sale was made in violation of such notice. The owner of place where liquor law is violated may be indicted for maintaining a public nuisance, and the place closed up. An officer with a warrant may break open any place where liquors are sold clandestinely, when necessary for the arrest or indentification of the person selling. County court cannot grant license in corporated towns without consent of Town Council.

For the past ten years drug stores have multiplied in some parts of the State, and in many instances become vile doggeries. The law governing them in the sale of liquor has therefore been getting more strict. The following, passed in 1883, now governs: Druggists can only sell alcoholic liquors for medicinal, mechanical or scientific purposes, and no sale to be made except upon written prescription of a practicing physician in good standing in his profession, and not of intemperate habits, specifying name of person and quantity to be furnished him, but no druggist who is himself a practicing physician can sell upon his own prescription. Upon two convictions the druggist loses license.

The Constitution of this State gives the legislature power to prohibit the sale of intoxicating drinks within the State.

After 1860, and prior to 1872, this State was governed by the Republicans, and all Legislation was done by legislatures having Republican majorities. Since 1872 the legislation has been done by legislatures having Democratic mojorities, and the executives have been Democratic also.

With reference to the workings of the present and such liquor laws as we have heretofore had, would say: that the restrictions imposed under the license system seem to be worthless. When a person obtains a license to sell, he generally sells without molestation. The restrictions seem to contemplate that no sales are to be made to intoxicate, but reverse results prevail from the nature of the business. The liquor law has no tendency to decrease the evils of alcoholic drink, except in counties and towns where the temperance element is strong enough to withhold license. In fact, nearly all the prosecutions are for selling without license in places where the sale is prohibited by withholding license. Prosecutions by indictment and jury trial do not effect any good; delays are too great and perjury is too common. When the municipal authorities under their charter and ordinance take it in hand, illegal retailing can be in the main suppressed. Often, however, these authorities are in sympathy with the liquor interest and do not act, or acting it is done so irregularly as to render the proceedings defective.

The temperence people of this State have endeavored for the past five years to get the legislature to submit to a vote of the people, an amendment to the constitution forever prohibiting the manufacture and sale of intoxicating liquors to be used as a beverage. The petitions to the legislature for this purpose have been numerous and signed by the best men of the State. It requires a two-thirds vote in each branch of the legislature to submit this question. It passed the lower House in 1883, but was defeated in the Senate by two votes. The people have elected men enough to the legislature to have accomplished their desire, but have been frequently betrayed through the influence brought to bear by the liquor interest. The minority party (the republicans) have generally supported the measure. It is the general feeling that if the people get an opportunity to vote, they will adopt prohibition, and for this reason the liquor interest, while desiring to be rid of the question, yet dare not let it come to a vote. The democratic party during the present session of legislature exerted their influence against the measure. The republicans during the last campaign would have nothing to do with it. Had the legislature therefore, submitted it to vote and the people had declared for it, we should have had a law which neither party would have respected. There are thousands of voters in this State ready to join any party with the leading principle of prohibition engrafted in their platform. In more than two thirds of the counties, men are elected to the county court who will not grant license. Voters in this State are coming to believe more and more every day that there is no effectual way to be rid of the evil, except to banish the cause.

KENTUCKY.

SPECIAL LEGISLATION.—LOCAL OPTION.

In this State "special legislation" prevails. There is a general "local option law," passed in 1874, under which a certain number of voters may present a petition to the judge of the county court, who thereupon issues an order for an election in the "county, city, town or district" described in the petition, to determine whether "spirituous, vinous or malt liquors" may be sold at retail in the locality indicated. It does not apply to manufacturers, wholesale dealers and druggists, simply to "saloonkeepers," or as known in Kentucky "coffee-house keepers." This vote may be taken every two years and not oftener. It is not used generally. The difficulties in the way of "local option" when applied to a small extent of territory are too many and too great to justify its use except in extremity. If a man has nothing better than a hot iron with which to bore a hole through a board it is wise to use the iron. But an auger is better. When the question of the dram-shop is liable to be fought out every two years in a popular election, it is not surprising that earnest men hesitate to enter the fight. Especially is this true in the South where the colored vote, which is notoriously unreliable on this question, is so large a factor. It serves a good purpose in affording opportunity for agitation, and in some instances an actual victory over the saloon is accomplished in the use of its provisions.

For several years, and especially in 1873, and subsequently, the Kentucky legislature has been familiar with bills whose title reads as follows, viz : "An act to prohibit the sale of ardent, vinous, malt, spirituous or intoxicating liquors, or the mixture thereof, in the County of Breathett," Jan. 31, 1873. Twenty-nine bills of similar import became laws in 1873, besides other laws authorizing a vote in certain localities. Some of these laws embraced a county, others a town or a precinct, or "near Harmony Church, in Garrard county." In the years 1878, 1882, and 1884, especially the latter, the number of these bills was increased, amounting to 86 in 1884. Among these are a few acts to repeal, indicating the presence of opposition forces. This fact and the kindred fact that a locality which is "no license" this year may be "license" the next if the tenure by which they hold prohibition is the general local option law of 1874, makes it very difficult to give reliable statistics of the prohibition territory of the State. This is true almost everywhere in the south, and must be as long as the local option method prevails. For it is an ever beginning, never ending battle until it is established in the public mind that it is a crime to assist in maintaining the system of alcoholism, and liquor selling and stealing stand in the same relation before the law. No one would think of putting to a popular vote the question of licensing a person to steal.

The present condition of the State as set forth by a committee of gentleman in Louisville in November, 1884, is as follows, viz:

"The following counties have adopted local option: Bullitt, Breckenridge, Hardin, Clay, Letcher, Bell, Cumberland, Ballard, Laurel, Martin, Pike, Wayne, Lewis, Perry, Owen, Hopkins, Breathett, Washington, Rock Castle, Jackson, Owsly, Knox, Whitly, Robertson, Magoffin, Harlan, Leslie, Bracken, Union. Outside of these counties 150 odd magisterial districts in other counties and 50 odd towns in other counties, have adopted local option, thus bringing under local option influences nearly three-fourths of the voting population of the State. Four districts in this county adopted it at the last August election."

As an evidence of the practical working and effect of local option on the material prosperity and morals of the counties in which it has been adopted, we make this extract from a letter from the Elizabethtown *News*, August 1, 1884, in which the writer compares Hardin and Bullitt counties:

"About eleven years ago that county voted for local option law, and here is how she stands in comparison to Hardin county, according to the Auditor's report for the year 1883: Total property listed for taxation, $1,797,158; amount of revenue paid into the treasury, $8,750.27; amount drawn out of the treasury, $6,718.83; leaving in the treasury, $2,034.44. Total property for Hardin county listed for taxation, $3,238,271 amount paid into the treasury, $15,642; amount drawn out of the treasury, $20,911.76, making a deficit of $5,269.76. Bullitt county, without her whisky, pays into the treasury $2,034.44 more than she draws out, while Hardin county, with her whisky, annually draws out $5,269.76 more than she pays in. Since the local option law took effect in Bullitt county, its wealth has increased and expenses diminished. In the year 1883 the prosecutions in Bullitt county cost the State $417.83, while the prosecutions in Hardin county for the same year cost the State $3,748.83, nearly nine times that of Bullitt county. The population of Hardin county is about double that of Bullitt county. Then, on that basis, the prosecutions in this county should have cost double that of Bullitt, which is $835.76. Now take that from the actual cost, $3,748.83, and we have $2,913.07, which whisky annually adds to the cost of our criminal court. The State receives $1,075 for license in Hardin county, and pays out $2,613.09 to collect it according to the above statistics. In the last ten years Hardin county with her whisky has had thirteen cases of homicide before her courts, while Bullitt county without her whisky has had but one, and that was sent there from Hardin on a change of venue."

Hardin county adopted local option by a large majority at the August election 1885.

TENNESSEE.

NO LIQUOR TO BE SOLD WITHIN FOUR MILES OF AN INSTITUTION OF LEARNING.

Tennessee was admitted into the Union in 1796. From that time until the "Four Mile Law" was enacted, if there was any special temperance legislation, we are ignorant of what it was. For the following interesting account of the Four Mile Law and its workings, we are indebted to Mr. R. L. Hayes, of Nashville:

"This law was passed March 19, 1877, by a democratic legislature, John C. Brown, Governor, and reads as follows: "Be it enacted by the General Assembly of the state of Tennessee, that it shall not hereafter be lawful for any person to sell or tipple any intoxicating beverages within four miles of any institution of learning in the State, and any one violating the provisions of this act shall be guilty of misdemeanor, and upon conviction, shall be punished by a fine of not less than one hundred dollars, nor more than two hundred and fifty dollars, and imprisonment for a period of not less than one, nor more than six months.

"SEC. 2. Be it further enacted that this act shall not apply to the sale of such liquors within the limits of any incorporated town, nor to sales made by persons having licenses to make the same, at the date of this act, during the time for which such licenses were granted, nor sales by manufacturers of such liquors in wholesale packages or quantities.

"SEC. 3. Be it further enacted that this act take effect from and after its passage, the public wellfare requiring it."

An amendment making the law apply to towns and taxing districts of less inhabitants than five thousand was enacted by the democratic legislature of 1882, but has since been declared unconstitutional by the Supreme Court of the State.

Over one hundred towns in the State have abolished their corporation charters, in order to come under the provisions of the law, and it is safe to say that two-thirds of the State is now under its operation. In Judge N. W. McConnell's judicial district (eight counties) there is not a single legalized dram-shop. Where the law has been enforced, crime and pauperism have decreased over sixty per cent. Judge Robert Cantrell, and Judge N. W. McConnell deserve great credit for the manner in which they have enforced the law in their districts. The law, where it has been enforced, has proven such a blessing that no political party dare attempt its repeal. It was rather by accident, than otherwise, that the law was secured.

Gen. Johnson, who has a school up in the mauntain district of the State, was tormented by several saloons, in vicinity; so much so, that he was compelled to get clear of the saloons, or remove his school. He came to Nashville and asked the legislature to give him the "Four Mile Law." This was on the eve of adjournment of the legislature, and it was hurried through without a dissenting vote; it was not passed as a temperance measure, but for the protection of Gen. Johnson's school. For two years the people of the State were ignorant of the fact that they had a law on the statute books equal, almost, to the best prohibitory law in the nation. An advertisement giving this as one of the advantages possessed by Gen. Johnson's school, was the first thing that attracted the attention of the public. About this time a convention of Good Templars was held at Goodlettsville, a proposition to petition the legislature for a local option law was under consideration, and it was then suggested that as all laws enacted in Tennessee, must be, to be in harmony with the constitution, of a general character, that is, apply to the whole State, and if such was the fact we had a better law than local option, because, with local option it would require a majority of all the voters in the district, whereas, with the "Four Mile Law" and five citizens could charter a school. A resolution was introduced calling for a committee to investigate the matter, which was agreed to by the convention, and the following parties appointed by the chairman: R. L. Hayes, Jas. A. Herman, and J. M. Shivers Esq. This committee, it is needless to say, found the law to be all that their hopes expected; sub-committees were appointed throughout the State, blank charters printed and distributed, and in less than one year half of the the State was under the operation of one of the best laws ever enacted for the protection of the home."

The last Legislature (1887) submitted a Constitutional Prohibitory Amendment to be voted on in September next, and the good people of Tennessee are now fighting valiantly against the great enemy and destroyer of their homes and happiness, with fair prospects of winning the victory.

Following is the constitutional amendment to be voted on by the people of Tennessee on the the 29th, Sept. next :

Section 18. No person shall manufacture for sale, or sell, or keep for sale as a beverage, any intoxicating liquors whatever, including wine, ale and beer. The General Assembly shall, by law, prescribe regulations for the enforcement of the prohibition herein contained, and shall thereby provide suitable penalties for the violation of the provisions hereof.

NORTH CAROLINA.

The following is the gist of temperance laws in North Carolina :

1. Has a minor law, which forbids selling to minors. 2. Has a Sunday law. 3. Has an election law, which is a constitutional provision. 4. Has a local option law, which authorizes townships to vote upon the question of selling liquor. 5. And the act which authorized the people of the State to vote upon the question of prohibition in 1881. 6. In addition to all which, has hundreds of acts of incorporation prohibiting the sale of liquor within certain distances of churches, schools, etc.

SOUTH CAROLINA.

NO LICENSE GRANTED OUTSIDE OF THE INCORPORATED CITIES, TOWNS AND VILLAGES.

Prior to 1880, South Carolina was under general license laws. Intoxicants were sold at almost every crossroads grocery as well as elsewhere. In 1880, when Hon. Johnson Hagood (democrat) was governor, the legislature enacted a bill of which the following is a part: "No license for the sale of spirituous or intoxicating liquors shall be granted in South Carolina outside of the incorporated cities, towns and villages of this State; and it shall be unlawful for any person or persons to sell such liquors without a license so to do." The bill provided that when applications for license in incorporations were made, the party applying was required to pay into the treasury of the county, in which said corporation was located, the sum $100 for county purposes, the $100 to be in addition to the license fee charged by the town. He must also be recommended by six respectable tax-payers of his neighborhood, and give a bond of $1000, with three good sureties, freeholders, owning property to the value of $500 each, over and above all liabilities "for the keeping of an orderly house, and for the due observance of all laws relating to the retailing of spirituous liquors."

The sales of all wines, fruits prepared with spirituous liquors, bitters and other beverages of which spirituous liquors formed an ingredient, were subject to the conditions above set forth.

The penalty for not observing requirements of the act is not less than $200 or six months imprisonment, or both fine and imprisonment in the discretion of the judge presiding. One half of the fine to go to the detective. The county commissioners are charged specially with the duty of obtaining information as to violations of the law, and are to institute prosecutions therefor.

The act further requires: "Willfully furnishing any intoxicating drink, by sale, gift or otherwise, to any person of known intemperate habits, or to any person when drunk or intoxicated, or to a minor, or to any insane person for use as a beverage, shall be held and deemed a misdemeanor," subject to a fine of from $10 to $100, or imprisonment for from 10 to 60 days.

Wives, parents or guardians notifying saloonkeepers not to furnish by sale, or gift liquors to members of the family, such notification would continue in force for three months, subject to severe penalties.

Sunday sales prohibited: "It shall not be lawful for any person to sell trade, or barter, any spirituous or malt liquors, cider or wine on Sunday." Penalty $10 to $200, or imprisonment 10 to 60 days.

DRUGGISTS: "It shall not be lawful for any apothecary or druggist, except upon the prescription of a regular physician for a patient upon whom he is in attendence, or other person, to sell, trade, or barter any bitters of which spirituous or malt liquors are an ingredient, or any other medicated liquor, by the bottle or by the drink, to any person, unless such apothecary, druggist, or other person, shall obtain a license to sell such liquors as provided in this chapter." Penalties same as for selling without license.

It is also provided that licenses must be exposed to public view; sales must be in rooms on public streets, without screens, curtains or other devices for preventing the passing public from fully viewing what may be transpiring within.

Upon conviction for selling on Sunday, or without a license, besides the fines imposed, two years must elapse before license can be granted again. Should any be granted within that time they would be utterly without effect and afford no protection.

In 1882, Hon. Hugh Thompson, governor, democrat, the Legislature passed what is known as "A LOCAL OPTION LAW." * * * * This law is the basis of the present temperance struggle in the State. It applies to incorporated cities, towns and villages only, and does not interfere with the prohibitory law in places outside of such municipalities. The law provides that a special election for license or no license shall be ordered whenever a number of citizens equal to one third the votes cast at the preceding election shall so petition, and the status of the matter shall remain as decided at such election for two years hereafter. License shall expire at the close of the year in which granted. The act does not apply to any place in which the sale of liquor is or shall be prohibited by special legislative enactment. Druggists may not sell except upon certificate of a practicing physician, in actual attendance upon a patient, nor may a physician give such certificate except when in bona fide attendance upon a patient. Penalty, fine not less than $200, or imprisonment not less than three months, or both. The law covers "bitters" and "fruits prepared with liquors as well as liquors themselves."

In a number of municipalities in the State the sale of liquor is prohibited by special legislation.

Under this act many towns to-day are under prohibition, while many have tried at the ballot box to overthrow the saloon power, but have been defeated. The Legislature of 1883 amended the local option laws, so that elections could be held every two years instead of annually. Hence a town voting say December 1, 1884, and "no license" prevails, the election must stand for two years.

What good has it all done? Well there are numerous sections in this State where there is not a dram shop, and liquors cannot be had for love or money. I am reliably informed by the Presiding Elder of the Marion District covering large sections of Marlboro, Marion and Henry counties, that there is not a place where liquors are legally sold throughout the bounds of his district. To my knowledge there is not a licensed barroom in Marlboro, Marion, Henry, Spartanburg, Pickens, Laurens, Barnwell, and Union counties. Only one place has bar rooms in Sumpter, Clarendon, Kershaw, Chesterfild, Greenville, Edgefield, Williamsburg, Pickens, Oconee counties. There are but two places in Colleton, Hampton, Georgetown, Beaufort, and Anderson counties, where there are licensed bar rooms. There may be other counties which might be added to the list, but of them I am not informed. Aiken county at a late election voted whisky out of its bounds, but there is a hitch somewhere which the advocates of the law are now trying to overcome. If successful, bar rooms must go. The change is so marked where county seats are without barooms that grand juries are recommending that the people hold on to no license. Wherever the law is enforced peace, good order, etc., reigns. As there are but thirty-four counties in the State, the efficiency of the law is apparent.

How does the law work? Like a charm when the officers do their duty. The law never has been a failure—all failures are to be attributed to the inefficiency of liquor committed councils.

To what extent is the law enforced? In some places to the letter. But be it said to our sorrow in many sections the officers in charge of the law are whisky pets, and consequently clandestine sales are passed by. The desire for office is so strong—even if it is for the little office of county commissioner—that such officers are afraid to act for fear of becoming unpopular. I have seen some such officers hanging around questionable places. Party before principles is the watchword in many instances. But the battle is growing rapidly, and the notes of the bugle calling the good, law-abiding people to the front are sounding. Prohibition in South Carolina is in the near future.

LOUISIANA.

CLASSIFIED LICENSE AND LOCAL OPTION.

In Louisiana the tax imposed upon the sale of intoxicating liquors ("anything to be drunk or eaten on the premises") is proportioned to the annual gross receipts of the business, as follows : There shall be one extra class ; Class A, $50,000 or more, $750 per annum; First, $37,000, $500 ; Second, $25,000, $400; Third, $20,000, $300; Fourth, $15,000, $250; Fifth, $10,000, $200; Sixth, $7,500, $150; Seventh, $5,000 to $7,500, $100; Eighth, $2,000 to $5,000, 75; Ninth, less than $2,000, $50. Provided no license shall be charged for selling refreshments for charitable or religious purposes; provided that no establishment selling or giving away or otherwise disposing of any spirits, wines, alcoholic or malt liquors in less quantities than one pint shall pay less than $50. The State has a stringent Sunday law, requiring all stores, shops, groceries, saloons, and all places of public business which are or may be conducted under any law of the State of Louisiana or under any parochial or municipal ordinance, except those herein exempted, to be closed on Sundays and forbidding all giving, trading, bartering and selling on Sundays by the proprietor or employes of such establishment, and declaring it a misdemeanor to violate the provisions of this act, and to fix penalty for all violations of same, and to repeal all laws or parts of laws contrary or inconsistent therewith.

Section 1, takes effect from and after the 31st of December, 1886, and requires houses to close at 12 o'clock Saturday nights, and to remain closed for twenty-four hours. Sect. 2. Violators pay a fine not less than $25 and not more than $250, or imprisonment not less than ten nor more than thirty days, or both at the discretion of the court, except news-dealers, keepers of soda fountains, places of resort for recreation and health, watering places and public parks for the sale of ice, newspaper offices, printing offices, book-stores, drug-stores, apothecary shops, undertakers shops, public and private markets, bakeries, dairies, livery stables, railroads–steam or horse, hotels, round-houses, steam-boats and other vessels, warehouses, restaurants, telegraph offices, and theatres, or any place of amusement, provided no intoxicating liquors are sold on the premises, except when actually administered or prescribed by a practicing physician in the discharge of his professional duties in case of sickness, physicians administering liquors may charge therefor. The law was for two or three Sundays fought, but the Supreme Court has passed upon it, and all the violators have been fined $25 each, and now the law is rigidly enforced and obeyed. Local option prevails in some fourteen parishes, and others are likely to fall into line soon. Prohibition conventions have been held and largely attended in the State, and the cause is gaining strength every day.*

---

*The anti-prohibitionists are quite fond of the assertion that State prohibition is worse than a failure in Maine, Iowa and Kansas, and that as a fact more whisky is sold in those States and with more damaging results to society than in other States, while no revenue is derived from the traffic. Is it not strange that the good people of those States should be so long deceived about this matter, or that, realizing the fact that prohibitory laws are not only ineffectual but actually detrimental to the best interests of society,

DELAWARE.

A prohibitory law was passed by a whig legislature in 1847, which was declared unconstitutional in 1848. In 1853 the whigs passed a local option law and in 1855 an American party legislature re-enacted prohibition. Both these laws were repealed by the same party, which is still in force. Licenses cost but $100 a year, and little attention is paid to the law.

GEORGIA.

Local option, high license, and prohibition by special legislation. Over 100 counties out of 137 are under prohibition. The laws are generally enforced. Licenses where granted are very high, and many towns prohibit the sale by this method. In Gordonsville, for example, the fee for license is $100,000. The State will soon be free from the liquor traffic. All temperance legislation has come through the democratic party.

---

they do not rise up in their majesty and demand the instantaneous repeal of such laws?

If there is any thing in the way of their repeal and abrogation I am not aware of it. What is to hinder the people of Kansas, who have been suffering so long from the evil effects of prohition, from abolishing the obnoxious constitutional amendment and returning to the old system or of adopting a different one for the *regulation of the evil*? Will Governor Ross and others of his opinion answer this practical question and tell us why it is that those people of Maine who have been suffering so terribly from the evils of prohibition do not take prompt and vigorous steps to rid themselves of the crime breeding policy which has prevailed in that State for about forty years? Will they pretend to say that those people know less about their own business than the immaculate, infallible representatives of the True Blues of Texas? There are a few men in the State of Maine, who may be credited with ordinary common sense and political foresight.

ALABAMA.

This State has a law providing for the granting of local option upon petition to the legislature, and also a large number of special prohibitory laws covering localities, counties and territory within specified distances of churches, school, etc. The laws are generally well enforced. The sentiment of the State in favor of prohibition is growing, and Alabama may be safely counted among the promising States. A general prohibition bill passed one house in 1883. Legislation has been by democratic assemblies.

ARKANSAS.

The question of license or no license must be voted upon every two years. The license fee is about $700. More than one-fourth the State refuses to grant license, and the sale of liquor is prohibited within three miles of churches and school houses. The law was passed by a Democratic legislature in 1881.

MISSISSIPPI.

A general license law is in force in Mississippi, which requires a petition signed by a majority of men over twenty-one years of age. Prior to 1876 the consent of a mojority of the women over eighteen was also required. The fee cannot be less than $200 nor more than $1000. More than one-half of the State is under prohibition through special enactment. The legislature of 1884 passed over one hundred local prohibitory laws. The laws are well enforced. The State is and always has been Democratic.

FLORIDA.

LICENSE WITH LOCAL OPTION FEATURE.

Florida was admitted into the Union March 3rd, 1845, and from that time until 1883 the tendency of temperance legislation was in the direction of rather liberal laws.

Early in 1885 the General Assembly enacted a stringent license law, with a local option feature. It prohibits the issue of license except upon petition of a majority of the registered voters of the precinct or election district in· which the dram-shop is to be located. Each signature to such petition must be attested by two responsible witnesses and published for two weeks before the application is made to the county board. Dealers have sought by every species of fraud to evade the law. Twice or three times legal questions have been raised against the constitutionality, and other features of the statute, before the Supreme Court, and have been decided in favor of the law.

Much good has been accomplished, even under the disadvantages of an experiment. The saloons have been reduced in number and entirely suppressed within six counties. The Legislature was democratic, but all parties joined in passing the law.

Hon. W. D. Bloscham, a democrat, was the governor who approved the law.

MICHIGAN.

DRAM SHOP TAX OF $300.—LOCAL OPTION MAY BE ADOPTED IN VILLAGES OF A CERTAIN CLASS.

In Michigan, a clause prohibitory of license was made a part of the state constitution in 1850, prepared by a convention largely democratic. It read as follows: "The legislature shall not pass any act authorizing the grant of license for the sale of spirituous or other liquors." This, it will be seen, was one year earlier than the enactment of the celebrated "Maine Law", and under this constitutional provision Michigan had no legalized liquor traffic for twenty-five years. The first prohibitory statute, however, was not enacted until the month of Feb., 1853. Robert McClelland, democrat, was Governor. The legislature was also democratic. This law was declared unconstitutional in 1854; and was, in substance, re-enacted by the first republican legislature, in 1855. It was several times amended, usually to its disadvantage, and finally repealed by a republican legislature, in 1875. In 1875, the present tax law was enacted, and the above cited constitutional provision was submitted to be striken out; both were strictly republican measures. In 1881, and again in 1883, the temperance people petitioned largely to have a prohibitory amendment of the constitution submitted to a popular vote, but were both times refused, the legislature being each time strongly republican.

Under the present law the dram shop tax where all kinds of intoxicating liquors are sold is $300. The sale of liquors to minors and on Sundays and election days is forbidden. The saloons may also be closen after a designated hour at night, and on legal holidays, but these provisions of the law are not very thoroughly enforced.

In 1883, by a gross blunder which passed without observation until too late, an act was passed which extends the privilege of local option to villages of a certain class, embracing about one-half the villages of the State. The law grants power to the authorities to regulate, restrict or *prohibit* the sale of liquors. The word "prohibit" was not noticed by the opponents of prohibition in the legislature until too late to reconsider the measure, as its friends had hastened to Governor Begole and secured his approval as soon as it was passed. Comparatively few of the villages have availed themselves of the protection the measure affords.

A bill to submit the question of a constitutional amendment to a vote of the people was again introduced in the legislature in 1885, but again failed to receive the requisite two-thirds and was defeated.

The Proposed Constitutional Amendment was recently (1887) voted on and defeated by a small majority. The returns of that election show that the county vote was largely in favor of the Constitutional Amendment, but the city of Detroit giving an overwhelming majority against it, it was defeated.

CALIFORNIA.

There are no local option or prohibitory laws in California. The constitution of the State gives the supervision of the saloons to the Boards of Supervisors of the counties. In a few of these the supervisors have attempted to exercise their police powers by imposing high licenses, but in every case have been defeated. 'The League of Freedom,' so-called, an organization of distillers, brewers, wholesale dealers and saloon-keepers, covering the entire State, controls both political parties, and elect the judges and prosecuting attorneys, so that while high license ordinances are admitted to be constitutional, practically their enforcement is impossible.

In 1882 the democratic state convention adopted a sounding resolution against "sumptuary laws." As there were no sumptuary laws on the statute books of the State, the resolution was understood by everyone to mean the repeal of the laws preventing the sale of intoxicating liquors on Sunday. The resolution was satisfactory to the league. The republican convention met several weeks afterward, and the temperence people made strenuous efforts to obtain from it a clear and emphatic declaration in favor of the Sunday statutes with proper provisions for their vigorous enforcement. The convention was also asked to declare in favor of local option. In answer, the temperence people obtained the aggressive (?) declaration, that the republican party of California was in favor of maintaining Sunday as a day of "rest and recreation" —which to the German republicans meant beer-gardens, dance-halls, etc., etc. As neither party promised anything for sobriety and decency on any day of the week, a convention of temperance people in favor of separate political action was called to meet later on in San Francisco. The convention which assembled in answer to this call was in every respect a grand one. A clear, strong prohibitory platform was adopted, and Dr. R. H. McDonald was nominated for Governor.

The democrats carried the State, and elected a legislature overwhelmingly democratic. Their first act was to repeal the Sunday laws. The dram-shops, dance-halls, beer-dives, dagodens, and all other places of vile and criminal resort are now kept open on Sunday, as they had previously been, except in some few places. The fact is, that the whisky and beer business in California is sheltering itself behind the grape culture, and as long as the idea prevails there that the use of pure wines is conducive to health and promotive of temperance, no effective legislation can be had against the saloons.

Several years ago a local option law was passed, but as neither the democrats nor republicans claim the honor of it, it is not worth while to go back to the record of it. It was declared unconstitutional, but no lawyer believes it was so.

The present legislature is largely republican. The State prohibition committee, and the executive officers of the Good Templars, have sent out two petitions to be signed by the people, one of these covering the idea of local option, and the other providing for the submission of a constitutional amendment. These petitions will test the pretended friendship of the republican party to the cause of temperance, and the right of the people to vote whisky out of the community or State. Finally, there has never been any really sensible and effective legislation upon the temperance question in Cal-

ifornia. The good Templars have had a corps of able and
earnest lecturers in the field for several years, and they have
been doing good work for Prohibition. The outlook for the
State is encouraging, and it is confidently said that California
will not be the last State to write PROHIBITION upon her shield.

COLORADO.

John Hipp.

The following are the main features of our liquor laws.
They were all passed by a republican legislature and gover-
vor. Our State being overwhelmingly republican. Our present Legislature consists of 54 Republicans and 21 Democrats.

(1.) In the country districts the county commissioners are
allowed to control sales less than one quart; above that
quantity the permit is given by the State government, and the
commissioners cannot regulate or abolish the sale.

(2.) The board of trustees or common council, of every
corporated town or city shall have exclusive authority to
license saloons, and all places where intoxicating liquors are
sold by quantities less than one quart. But saloons are open
in nearly every town seven days in the week and as many
hours as profitable. Greeley, Colorado Springs, Evans, Love-
land, Longmont, and one or two small towns have prohibition
by special legislation, or by electing prohibition aldermen.

(3.) We have a clause in the Constitution demanding that
the General Assembly shall by law prohibit the manufacture
and sale of adulterated liquors, but no attention is paid to it
whatever.

(4.) Any one suffering through a common drunkard can
give notice to all saloonkeepers not to sell to this drunkard,
and if sales can afterward be proved to have been made, exemplary damages and costs may be collected from the one
selling, and such sale also forfeits any lease on such premises,
but the damages must be collected from the *saloon-keeper alone.*
This is also a dead-letter, as few saloon-keepers have enough
property to satisfy such claim.

(5.) The Republican party in its state convention last

summer promised to submit a prohibitory amendment to the people. Petitions are being widely circulated to ask them to fulfill this promise, but there seems to be no probability of its being done.

OREGON.

The legislation in Oregon has been hardly commensurate with the enterprise of the temperance people. In few states has more or better work been done in proportion to the population, or the prohibitory sent been more active and clear cut.

Yet the Legislature has steadily refused the demand of the people for the submission of a constitutional amendment, and what legislation has been is in the direction of license. A license law was passed in 1851, of the same general character as the contemporaneous license laws of other states. An act was passed this last winter, receiving the approval of the governor Feb. 17, making the license fee $300 for spirituous and $200 for malt liquors, providing that no license shall issue for less than six months. Bond in 1,000 is required; sale to minors, drunkards and on Sundays is forbidden. A petition is required signed by majority of all voters in precinct and greater than any remonstrance from same precinct. Said petition must be published four weeks. Penalty for violation is a fine not less than $50 nor more than $200, and it is made the duty of every grand jury to make strict inquiry and return bills of indictment against all violators of the law.

NEW HAMPSHIRE.

New Hampshire has a prohibitory law, passed by a legislature principally American and Republican in 1855, Ralph Metcalf, American, Governor. Efforts have several times been made for its repeal, and a Republican Legislature, some two or three years ago, came within one vote of accomplishing its destruction. The law is reported not generally well enforced, but satisfactory in its workings when officials do their duties.

NEVADA.

Nevada is a comparatively new State, and has had little in the way of either temperence legislation or agitation, though interest in the general subject is on the increase and some efforts have been made too late to secure somewhat stringent legislation. The declared object, however, is to provide "revenue" rather than to restrict the traffic. To this end a bill was introduced by Mr. Fassett on Jan. 13th, 1885, and soon after passed the house, but up to the present writing (Feb. 13.) had not passed the senate. It raises the license fee to $50 per month in towns of five hundred or more inhabitants, and in all cases to $10 per month, except for persons selling in connection with houses of entertainment for travelers, one mile or more outside the limits of a town or city, who shall pay $15 per quarter. The proposed law prohibits the sale on any election day.

The present law is a general license law, requiring a fee of about $40 per quarter to be paid to the State, and subject to further fee according to municipal regulations where liquor is sold. It prohibits selling or giving to minors under penalty of $25 to $100, or imprisonment not to exceed fifty days, or both. The law is not generally enforced. It was passed by a republican legislature and approved by Governor L. R. Bradley a democrat.

NEBRASKA.

The law of Nebraska differs from those in other States in this, that while in many of them license is the law with Prohibition as the option, in Nebraska Prohibition is the law with high license as the option. In other words, except in cities of more than 10,000 inhabitants, Prohibition is the normal condition under the law, unless the high license option is taken advantage of. The law was adopted by a democratic legislature in 1881. The license fee can not be less than $500 nor more than $1,000. *Treating* is a misdemeanor. When a drunkard becomes a charge upon the town his keeping may be collected from the liquor sellers. For a detailed statement of the law and its workings, see Handbook of 1884, pages 56 to 65.

MINNESOTA.

A prohibitory law was passed by a democratic legislature in 1852, so far as spiritous liquors were concerned. In 1870 a local option law was passed. Until the recent session of the legislature (1887) the license was low, from $50 to $100. At that session the license was increased and the bill goes into effect on the fourth day of July, 1887. Under the amended law the license for selling "liquid damnation" in towns and cities of over 5,000 inhabitants is $1,000. Smaller towns $500. The new law in no way affects local option which remains in force and prevails in some of the towns. Not well enforced when carried by small majorities.

MISSOURI.

The democratic legislature of 1883 enacted one of the most stringent high license and local option laws possible. The written consent of the tax payers of the district must be obtained before license is granted, and the fee is from $274 to $600. Though the law is enforced with much vigor in various places, it is not satisfactory as a temperance measure, and active efforts are in progress to secure a constitutional amendment.

TEXAS.

LICENSE AND LOCAL OPTION.

The Constitution of 1845 (art. 7, sec. 27), contained the following provision: "The Legislature shall have power to lay an income tax and to tax all persons pursuing any occupation, trade, or profession; provided that, the term occupation shall not be construed to apply to pursuits, either agricultural or mechanical. Art. 8., Sec. 1, of the Constitution of 1875, contains substantially the same provision.

In 1846 an act was passed imposing a license tax upon the traffic in intoxicating liquors, and provided for its enforcement with other salutary restrictive regulations by appropriate penalties and forfeitures. In 1848 the law was amended and the "license tax" "for the use of the State" fixed at $250 upon persons selling in quantities less than a quart. Some, if not all, of the county courts under the authority supposed to have been conferred upon them by the act of March 16, 1848, organizing them and defining their powers and jurisdiction, and acting under that section which authorized them to levy county taxes upon all proper subjects of taxation enumerated by the legislature at the same session, imposed a county tax upon the sale of intoxicating liquors. In 1858 or 1859 one Baker, a saloon keeper in Panola county resisted the payment of the county tax, and after paying same under protest brought suit against the county to recover back the amount so paid on the ground that the sale of intoxicating liquors was not under the

State law a proper subject of taxation. It was contended that the license for which those engaged in the traffic had to pay $250 was not designed as a means of raising revenue for the coffers of the State, but for regulating purposes exclusively.

The Supreme Court in the same case, (Baker vs. Panola county; 30 Texas, 87), adopted the same view of the law and held that the counties had no right whatever to levy any tax on the business. In 1858 a law was enacted providing for the collection of a tax from each and every person or firm engaged in the sale of goods, wares, and merchandise, vinous or spirituous liquors when sold in quantities of a quart or more, of twenty cents on each hundred dollars value of the article purchased for sale, etc. In 1862 the tax was increased to twenty-five cents on the one hundred dollars, and a tax of $50 was imposed on every person keeping a distillery of spirituous liquors; of twenty dollars upon every brewery, and twenty-five dollars upon every person keeping a beer-shop. In 1866 the laws of the State were generally remodeled to suit the changed condition of the State with reference to the reconstruction acts of Congress. The liquor laws of the State were recast with the great mass of legislation which had taken place during the allegiance of the State to the Confederacy. During the session of the Legislature of 1866 two acts were passed each imposing a tax of $300 on retailers of intoxicating liquors. The first, passed October 27th, required the retailer to execute and deliver to the county treasurer a bond with certain specified conditions, and then to pay into the county treasury a license tax at the rate of $300 per annum. The second act, passed November 6th, 1866, provides that the retailer, who is "pursuing or about to pursue" this "occupation" of selling such liquors in quantities less than a quart, shall be assessed with a tax at the rate of $300 per annum for the benefit of the State treasury.

This double-tax was resisted by some of the saloon-keepers, and the two acts held valid by the Supreme Court in case of Napier vs. Hodges (31 Texas 287). The constitutionality of this act and similar laws imposing occupation taxes was upheld in the same case as it had been in Aulanier vs. the Governor, 1 Texas, 653; State vs. Stephens, 4 Texas, 137; State vs. Bock, 9 Texas, 369; and many other cases. The act of August 15th, 1870, superseded the law of 1866 and that of 22nd of April, 1871, expressly repealed it (see Wood vs. Stirman, 37 Texas, 584,) and since that date the State tax has been, I believe, $300. Counties have uniformly, I think, levied half that amount, and incorporated towns and cities have usually exacted the same, amounting in the aggregate to $600.* The constitution of 1875 embodied a local option provision in the usual form. On the 24th day of April, 1876, the legislature passed the law known as the local option law, in compliance with the constitutional requirement. It has

---

* Attorney General Jas. S. Hogg, in a recently published open letter attempts to palm off up on the people of Texas, a stupendous falacy in the form of statistics, showing that the occupation taxes collected from the saloon-keepers and whisky dealers of the State exceed by several hundred thousand dollars, the total amount paid out by the State in the prosecution of all offenses known to our criminal code. The Attorney General failed to enlighten the people upon a very material subject matter of inquiring in order to a proper understanding of the statistics, that is what expenses are included in the amount *paid by the State* and what sums are not so included?

Every lawyer and other person who is at all familiar with the laws of Texas, must know that the State pays no part of the costs and expenses, incurred in the prosecution or misdemeanor cases which constitute by far the greater number growing out of the liquor traffic in general and the saloon in particular. In felony cases, not capital the District Attorneys get $30 in each case resulting in conviction, nothing when the accused is acquitted. In capital cases they are allowed $50 for convictions. — Provision is also made for the payment of fees to Sheriff's and Clerks and to the attached witnesses in felony cases. The great amount of additional expenses produced by the sale and consumption of liquor is sustained by the counties, and by the people individually in being forced to attend Court or juries, witness, etc., which amount is beyond the reach of reliable statistics.

been tried in a large number of counties, in some of which it has worked well; in others it is said to have done no perceptible good on account of the failure of the officers and the people generally to do any thing towards its enforcement. Two or three amendments have been made with a view to making it more effective, but it seems that little has been done by the legislature to remedy the defects which stand in the way of its satisfactory enforcement. Mention has already been made of the amendment passed by the nineteenth legislature, that never found its way upon the statute book.

The Twentieth Legislature has recently passed a bill amending the law in many particulars, and it is believed that it is now in a condition that it may be made instrumental in the accomplishment of much good in the suppression of the evils of intemperance. In July, 1876, a law was passed making it a misdemeanor punishable by fine of not more than $100 to get drunk or be found in a state of intoxication in a public place; also, defining and punishing drunkenness in office: these laws have not been enforced and may be considered as practically inoperative. Public sentiment has generally been opposed to a rigid enforcement of the law against public drunkenness and the courts and juries are always in doubt whether a man is drunk or a natural fool when brought up for trial. On the first day of October, 1879, the "Bell Punch Law" went into effect, which was intended to regulate the amount of tax by the number of drinks that were sold. Every saloon-keeper and beer-dealer in the State was required to purchase a bell punch, and if he desired to sell both spirituous and malt liquors, he was required to provide himself with two. It was not a success. It was everywhere violated with impunity. On the fourth day of April 1881 the Bell Punch Law was repealed under suspension of the rules, and the license system readopted substantially in its present form. It is not necessary to elaborate its provisions. They are similar to those of other States where the system prevails. The State tax is $300, county may be $150, and incorporated towns and cities may levy the same amount as is levied or may be levied by the counties. The last Legislature made some salutary amendments to the law including the inhibition of the use of screens, obscene pictures, games of chance, music, etc., which have a tendency to attract the unsuspecting and curious. The Twentieth Legislature, by the requisite number of both houses submitted to the people of Texas the following constitutional amendment to be voted upon by the people of the State on the first Thursday in August, next, (1887):

"To amend Section 20, of Article 16, of the Constitution of the State of Texas.

"SECTION 1. Be it resolved by the Legislature of the State of Texas, That Section 20, of Article 16, of the Constitution be so amended as to read as follows, to-wit: "Section 20. The manufacture, sale, and exchange of intoxicating liquors except for medicinal, mechanical, sacramental and scientific purposes, is hereby prohibited in the State of Texas. The Legislature shall, at the first session held after the adoption of the Amendment, enact necessary laws to put this provision into effect.

"SECTION. 2. The foregoing Constitutional Amendment shall be submitted to a vote of the qualified electors of the State of Texas, at an election to be held for that purpose on the first Thursday in August, 1887, at which election all voters favoring said proposed Amendment shall have written or printed on their ballots, "For State Prohibition," and those voting against said Amendment shall have written or printed on their ballots, "Against State Prohibition." The Governor of the State is hereby directed to issue the necessary publication for said election under the existing election laws of the State."

It is unnecessary in this outline to speak at length upon the practical results of our legislation upon the traffice. It is unnecessary to say more than appears in the body of this book upon the subject of local option and the proposed constitutional amendment.

I would like to mention the names of those who have worked for so many years in the face of discouragement in the temperance cause, to bring about the submission of the amendment which is the subject of this important canvass, but I could not hope to do so without disparaging those whose names I would be unable to give. I shall venture, however, to give the names of Col. E. L. Dohoney, of Paris; and of Dr. J. B. Cranfill, of the Waco, (formerly Gatesville) *Advance*. They have worked faithfully and fought valiantly, but I fear, at times they have not had enough of that *suaviter in modo* so necessary in the direction of the popular mind. While they with others may have been "as wise as serpents," I am not prepared to say that they have ever been "as harmless as doves." The effort to organize a prohibition party in 1886 was, I think, a mistake. I thought so at the time, although I was in full sympathy with the principal object in view — the destruction of the liquor traffic. Especially did I, with many others, deprecate, the tone of the resolution passed by the Prohibition Convention at Dallas during the late canvass in which the gallant standard-bearer of the Democratic party was referred to in the most disrespectful terms, because his action in the local option canvass in the county of his home indicated that he did not, from some cause, favor the measure.

When I thought of the heroic deeds of his youth upon the frontier of Texas; when I thought of the many laurels he had won as the leader of a Texas brigade in the lost cause; when I was reminded of his eminent services in the senate of my beloved State; when I thought furthermore that he was the standard-bearer of the great party of the people, I was pained indeed to know that a convention of so many respectable and well-meaning citizens of Texas in their intemperate zeal for the promotion of a righteous cause, would so far forget themselves as to denounce him as "a saloon stump-speaker," because, forsooth, he had made one unfortunate, though honest, mistake. Governor Ross may cast his vote as he pleases, and it may be either for or against the Amendment, yet we must ever honor and respect him for the gallant and patriotic deeds of his life, not the least among which was his recent official action in recommending to the Legislature to give to our people a chance to vote whisky out of the State, and in signing and approving the resolution in spite of the "True Blues" and their loud and vociferous clamoring impeaching the Democracy of the measure. I am glad, however, at this time to know that the erroneous views heretofore entertained by our people upon this great subject and the violent and abusive methods which have prevailed among many of the temperance workers in our State in the past have given way to a more enlightened public sentiment, and that bitter personalities have been everywhere superseded by a united, conservative and patriotic effort to have the great question settled upon the eternal principles of truth and of public and private justice.*

One of Illinois' most gifted writers and orators, Col. Robt. G. Ingersoll, who by the way, as is well known, is not in any way connected with the "protestant priesthood" who are charged with the authorship of the heresy of prohibition has the following to say upon the subject of the traffic in whisky:

" I am aware that there is a prejudice against any man who manufactures alcohol. I believe that from the time it issues from the coiled and poisonous worm in the distillery until it empties into the jaws of death, dishonor and crime, it demoralizes everybody that touches it from its source to where it

---

* See note on page 172, was intended for this page, but by mistake inserted in connection with the review of the "True Blue" platform with which it has no connection.

ends. I do not believe that anybody can contemplate the object without being prejudiced against the liquor crime. All we have to do, gentlemen, is to think of the stream of death, of the suicides, of the ignorance, of the destitution, of the little children tugging at the faded and withered breast of weeping and despairing mothers, of wives asking for the bread of the men of genius it has wrecked, the men struggling with imaginary serpents produced by this devilish thing; and when you think of the jails, alms-houses, of the asylums, of the prisons, of the scaffolds upon either hand, I do not wonder that every thoughtful man is prejudiced against this damnable stuff called alcohol. Intemperence cuts down youth in its vigor, manhood in its strength and old age in its weakness. It breaks the father's heart, bereaves the doting mother, extinguishes natural affection, erases conjugal attachment, blasts parental hope and brings down mourning age in sorrow to the grave. It produces weakness, not strength, sickness, not health, death, not life. It makes wives widows, children orphans, fathers fiends, and all of them paupers and beggars. It feeds rheumatism, nurses gout, welcomes epidemic, invites cholera, imports pestilence and embraces consumption. It covers the land with idleness, misery and crime. It fills your jails, supplies your almshouses, and demands your asylums. It engenders controversies, fosters quarrels and cherishes riots. It crowds your penitentiaries and furnishes victims for your scaffolds. It is the life blood of the gambler, the element of the burglar, the prop of the highwayman, and the support of the midnight incendiary. It countenances the liar, respects the thief, esteems the blasphemer. It violates the obligation, reverences fraud and honors infamy. It defames benevolence, hates love, scorns virtue and slanders innocence; it incites the father to butcher his helpless offspring, helps the husband to massacre his wife and the child to grind the parricidal ax. It burns up men, consumes women, detests life, curses God, despises heaven. It suborns witnesses, nurses perjury, defiles the jury box and stains the judicial ermine. It degrades the citizen, debases the Legislature, dishonors statesmen and disarms the patriot. It brings shame, not honor ; terror, not safety . despair, not hope ; misery, not happiness, and with malevolence of a fiend calmly surveys its frightful desolation and unsatisfied havoc. It poisons felicity, kills peace, ruins morals, blights confidence, slays reputation and wipes out national honor, then curses the world and laughs at its ruin. It does all that and more. It murders the soul. It is the sum of all villainies, the father of all crimes, the mother of all abominations, the devil's best friend and God's worst enemy."*

CONSTITUTIONAL AMENDMENTS.

HOW MADE IN THE DIFFERENT STATES.

"To amend the Constitutions of Alabama, California, Colorado, Illinois, Kansas, Louisiana, Maine, Massachusetts, Michigan, Mississippi, Texas, and West Virginia the proposed amendment must be submitted by a three-fourths vote of one legislature, and then go to people for ratification. To amend the constitutions of Arkansas, Minnesota and Missouri the proposed amendment must be submitted by a majority vote of one legislature. To amend the constitutions of Indiana, Iowa, New Jersey, New York, Pennsylvania, Oregon, Rhode Island, Virginia, and Wisconsin the proposed amendment must be submitted by a majority vote of two successive legislatures, and then adopted by a majority vote of the people, except in Rhode Island, where a three-fifth vote is required to adopt. In Georgia, Florida, Nevada, and South Carolina the proposed amendment must pass two successive legislatures by a three-fourths vote before it goes to the people. In South Carolina, however, the second vote in the legislature must be after the amendment has been passed upon by the voters. In Maryland, Nebraska, North Carolina, and Ohio a three-fifths vote of one legislature can submit an amend-

---

* The above should have followed the article on Illinois, but was omitted in making up the forms, so I insert it here.—[Author.

ment, and it can then be adopted by a majority vote of the people. In Connecticut an amendment must be proposed by the house of representatives, approved by a three-fourths vote of the succeeding legislature, and then sent to the towns to be ratified. In Delaware an amendment must be proposed by a three-fourths vote of the legislature, and, after having been extensively published, ratified by a three-fourths vote of the succeeding legislature, when it becomes a part of the constitution without a vote of the people. In Tennessee it requires a majority vote of one legislature and a three-fourths vote of the succeeding one to submit an amendment, when a majority of the people adopts. In Vermont an amendment can be submitted by the Council of Censors, and then adopted by a convention called for the purpose. In New Hampshire an amendment must be submitted by a convention, and adopted by a three-fourths vote of the people. In Kentucky the constitution can only be amended by a convention called for the purpose."

CONCLUSION.

In giving a summary of the liquor laws of the several states within the limits prescribed for this Appendix, the author has been forced to condense within a very small space the laws of many of the states, but has endeavored to cull from the great mass of prohibitory and restrictive legislation, such as will best serve to illustrate the practical workings of the different systems in force. These systems are found to be very nearly similar in the various states where they prevail, and to give them in full or even in a condensed form as they appear upon the statute books, many of which are copied from other states, would be a useless and even a burdensome repetition. It is hoped that a perusal of those which are given will not be altogether unprofitable to the reader.*

---

* I fail to find anything in the history of the practical operation of the license system of the foregoing states which recommends them as effectual remedies for the evils of drunkenness and intemperance generally. Those who advocate high license as the best means of dealing with the traffic should go to work to procure reliable statistics showing by actual experience that it will work out the desired reform. While hunting up statistics to prove that prohibitory laws are total failures, and even worse than failures, they should devote at least a portion of their time and talents in gathering facts by which to establish the proposition that high license is a better remedy.

www.ingramcontent.com/pod-product-compliance
Lightning Source LLC
Chambersburg PA
CBHW030357230426
43664CB00007BB/633